"The Dragon Has Come"

"The Dragon Has Come"

Gregory Armstrong

HARPER & ROW, PUBLISHERS

NEW YORK, EVANSTON, SAN FRANCISCO, LONDON

FIRST EDITION

Designed by Sidney Feinberg

Library of Congress Cataloging in Publication Data

Armstrong, Gregory, 1931–
    The dragon has come.

    1. Jackson, George, 1941–1971.   I. Title.
E185.97.J23A89   365′.6′0924 [B]   73–14244
ISBN 0–06–010129–6

*This book is for
Nick and Mary.*

Contents

Author's Note

I met George Jackson when he was beginning his tenth year in prison and his hair was just starting to turn gray. He had spent seven and a half years of the preceding decade in solitary confinement. Once he had been locked up for a year and a half with the door of his cell welded shut. Sleeping only three hours a night. Doing a thousand fingertip push-ups each day to keep in shape and work off sexual frustration. Reading everything from Plato to Stendhal to Marx. Sometimes talking to the authors of the books he read as if they were there in the same cell with him.

Because I was his editor, I had a special place in his life. Once when I was with him inside Soledad Prison, he explained to me how a man would feel about someone who helped him to escape. "Why, there wouldn't be anything he wouldn't do for that guy for the rest of his life." For George, in at least one respect, I became that man. I gave him a simulation of something he wanted more than anything else. In the end, his book, *Soledad Brother*, was the closest he got to an existence outside prison.

After the first two days we spent together, George wrote me that we were both desperate men. He believed that we had found a kind of mutual love in our desperation. He didn't have to know much about me to pick up on my desperation. There I was, an almost middle-aged white man, struggling to express concern and respect for a black revolutionary accused of murder. What could be more desperate just on the face of it? And I wasn't the only desperate man who found his way to George. Most of the others called their desperation political, but thinking back what I remember most about them is the ill-concealed painfulness of their lives.

For me, identifying with George was like having a second self. I think that it was like this for many of the people who knew him. George's power was our power almost as a fact of ownership. If he had been outside, he would never have belonged to us in the same way, but locked away, he was ours. We possessed him and everything he was. We even felt we had the right to live through him.

And it is exactly this kind of relationship which has no basis in a shared daily life, which doesn't grow out of being together, which is so vulnerable to perversion and fantasy. Reality slips away. Promises are made. Vows. Plans. Because I was an outsider, and because I lived out in the world (George had an almost adoring sense of the power of people who didn't live in jail), he thought that there was nothing I couldn't do. His conviction of my power made me want to show him how powerful I could really be. Since there was no everyday life to restrict our fantasies during those hours we spent together in the visiting rooms of Soledad and San Quentin, no risk seemed too great. That was why he told me so many things. Because in those rooms nothing was truly real, or at least it had nothing to do with the palpable, tangible world as I knew it. Magicians, that was what we became in those visiting rooms, practicing a kind of magic that sometimes threatened to become megalomania, creators of a myth in which the final enactment was death.

The Case of the Soledad Brothers

In January 1970 in Soledad Prison in Salinas, California, three black prisoners were shot to death. The incident which caused the shooting began when fifteen prisoners, eight whites and seven blacks, were allowed out in a new exercise yard one morning. Each was stripped and searched. This was the first time they had been let out of their cells in a number of weeks. During their prolonged confinement, about their only form of diversion had been shouting racial epithets back and forth between their cells. A fight broke out between some of the whites and blacks. A guard with a reputation as a sharpshooter opened fire from a gun tower. No whistle. No warning shot. He fired three times and hit three blacks and one white. One black died instantly. Two others bled to death. It was twenty minutes before other prisoners were allowed to carry the injured men to the prison hospital, which was right next door to the yard. The white man was injured in the groin.

The prison was immediately locked down. A grand jury investigation was started. Three days after the killings, the local DA announced on TV that on the basis of the evidence, the grand jury would be forced to find that the killings had been justifiable homicide. The broadcast was carried into the prison. Less than half an hour later, a white guard in another wing of the prison was found beaten to death, presumably in retaliation for the deaths of the blacks. That night the prison arrested three men. Supposedly there was no physical evidence to connect these particular prisoners to the crime. No prisoners had yet volunteered themselves as eyewitnesses. The three men were arrested, according to their lawyers, simply because they were regarded as black militants and so-called troublemakers. One of the men had been found with a poster of Malcolm X on the wall of his cell. Another wore a prominent Afro and was a suspected Black Muslim. The third was George Jackson. In the words of the warden, he was arrested because "no one else could have done it."

On the last day of his life,
gun in hand, George Jackson
announced to the inmates and guards
of the San Quentin Adjustment Center:
"The Dragon has come!"

Soledad Prison
The First Day
June 18, 1970

"Everything is so immaculate and beautiful, the lawn is so green
and the flowers are so colorful. Everybody is so nice and everything,
and you would think that everybody who said all those awful things
about the place were exaggerating. But that isn't where your child
is. He's back there in a hole being humiliated, degraded and being
made to feel less than a human being."

—The mother of a
Soledad inmate

The highway seems to extend in an almost straight line from
San Jose to Salinas. As we drive, dark clouds hang low over the
mountains just past the fields of fig trees and artichokes and
lettuce.

The prison is just as nondescript and featureless as its official
name—SOLEDAD CENTRAL TRAINING FACILITY FOR MEN—would suggest. No high looming walls. No heavy iron gates. The gun towers
are like industrial cranes. From a distance as we turn off the road,
it could be a factory making battery parts or telephones. I almost
expect to see workers streaming out of the gates with lunch
baskets. The only sign that it might actually be a prison is a pecu-
liar air about the men who are outside the metal fence cutting
the lawns and watering the flower beds. In their faded work shirts
and pressed jeans, they move with a curious slow solemnity. After
a few seconds, I realize that the reason they don't look up when

1

we pass is that they are trusties and probably don't want to see or to be seen. They have the special poignance of people who want to be invisible. And I think to myself that probably the secret of being a trusty is the ability not only to make people unaware of you but also to make yourself unaware of them, because if you allowed yourself to be sensible of freedom or selfhood, you would just throw down your rake or your hoe and start running and never stop until you were caught or shot down in your tracks.

John Thorne, one of George's lawyers, who is taking me into the prison, parks with hundreds of other cars in one of the three large lots just outside the fences. As we get out of the car, I realize that I am already exhausted from anticipations of many different kinds. Now that meeting George is finally at hand, all my apprehensions rise to the surface.

The only clue to the whereabouts of the visiting room is a small placard which states that all visitors must register with the desk sergeant. Inside it is like every other waiting room I have ever seen. We enter the door, and at the opposite end of the room, a man sits with an open register on the counter in front of him looking as if he were selling bus tickets. The room is filled with rows of high-backed, lacquered wooden benches. A small hobby shop occupies one side of the room. Paintings with ornate carved frames. Silver horses' heads on velvet. Rows and rows of cowhide purses. A large cash register right in the middle of the glass display case. Behind it a sign on the wall in gilt Gothic lettering: "NO CHECKS. NO CHANGE." On the other wall, rows of vending machines.

It is still early—we have come during the middle of the week so the room is almost empty. The only other visitors are a Chicano family, a middle-aged father, mother and their two small children, and a young woman wearing a short, brightly colored floral dress. The man at the desk seems happy to see us all. He remembers the names of the members of the Chicano family, and he smiles. After they register, he jokes with them a while. Perhaps because they detect something faintly patronizing in his manner, they go off and sit by themselves as quickly as they can, being careful not to give any suggestion of disrespect.

The young girl's turn is next. She gives the name of the prisoner she wants to see and her own name. The sergeant checks a card and announces that she is not eligible. The man she wants to see is married, so only his wife can visit him. The woman explains that she knows about the rules. The man's wife, who is divorcing him, has written the warden a letter specifically giving the woman permission to visit her husband. The woman herself has also written a letter, which has been acknowledged. The sergeant searches through another file. No letter. The woman's voice rises in hysteria. But before she loses control completely, the sergeant agrees to make a call. He speaks a few words into the phone and suddenly he announces that it's all right. It is almost too good to be true. The woman breaks down sobbing. A few minutes more and miraculously she is passed through the electric door into the prison itself.

Our turn has come. The desk sergeant seems to know John from way back, but his familiarity does nothing to reassure me. I'm certain that something will go wrong and I won't be allowed in the prison. I am almost happy that I will never be able to see George. I'd much rather daydream about him and be saved the disappointment of meeting him in person. After all, I've rarely met anyone who was completely what I wanted them to be. When you daydream a lot and read too many novels, the way I have, life is always a letdown.

The sergeant addresses John with a kind of roguish respect. After the endless procession of confused, imploring faces, it must be a relief to have a character like John pass by. At least he is someone to talk about. Because the case is just beginning to be well known and as George Jackson's lawyer John seems famous. In spite of his role in the case, and the militant symbolism of his costume—the gold clenched fist on the lapel of his denim jacket and the red star on his Chinese student's cap—it is obvious that John wants to be liked. That's usually enough to satisfy most people. From the way John jokes with him the sergeant must get the idea that if they should ever manage to get together socially, they would have a great deal to say to each other. After all, nothing extraordinary is happening, everyone is just doing his job. It is a perfectly normal thing to be going into prison to see

George Jackson. Everybody knows what side John and I are really on. After all, we are white, aren't we? Just making our living one way or another.

John explains to the guard that I am the person he called down about and for whom arrangements were made the day before. The sergeant makes another call and everything is all right. I am going to be allowed into the prison! I show him my driver's license and sign a few papers. We are going to meet with Jackson in the captain's office. We merely have to wait until he can be brought down from the maximum-security wing of the prison. Then the sergeant will get us an escort and we can be taken inside.

This is the first time I have ever been in a prison. Already I have a sense of it closing in all around me, laying claim to me.

The waiting room is beginning to fill up. Wide-eyed, brown-skinned boys and girls, all dressed up in their Sunday best, curl and squirm on the curved wood of the benches. George's manuscript rests in my lap in a large manila envelope.

Lost in my apprehension, I suddenly hear John suggest that we should get some cigarettes and candy for George, who will be missing his lunch. We stuff our pockets from the vending machines. I stalk back and forth across the waiting room, very concerned about how I look. I feel just as inadequate and badly put together as the baggy suit I'm wearing that I bought when I was fifteen pounds heavier. The excess material hangs in large folds around my crotch. I have on a loud floral tie, which I hope will deflect everyone's attention from my suit.

After a while, the guard motions us over to a door at his left. Another guard joins him. The door slides open and, with the second officer leading the way, we start along the walk that runs from the small reception building to a gate opening onto a larger building. As we walk through the door, I'm struck by the sudden, almost blinding sunlight. Birds are twittering all around us. The breeze is soft and warm. Banks of flowers line the walls of the building we are heading toward. They are almost too garish and effulgent to be real, like some kind of morbid growth that has leached away the very substance from all living things for miles around.

We have to wait for the door behind us to close before the gate ahead of us opens. Then we walk up a small flight of stairs and through another door into a large corridor. Glistening waxed gun-metal floors. A quality of light and color that reminds me of my high school days.

On the left a sign points to the visitors' room. I have a sudden visual sense of the scene. Families sitting together on fluffy stuffed floral-printed couches, eating from picnic baskets, kissing and hugging one another.

For many mothers and fathers, it must be like visiting sons who are away from home at school or camp, especially when, like George, the sons have grown old inside prison, locked away in an eternal childhood.

Our escort indicates that we should follow him to the right. He leads us down a corridor into a large empty office. "Jackson should be down in a minute." He closes the door behind him and we are alone.

Cletis Fitzharris, Superintendent of Soledad Correctional Training Facility: *

We have about 220 or 230 men who need to be locked up on a continuing basis until they are able to control their own behavior. And they are locked up for their own protection and the protection of other people, both inmates and officers alike, during one phase or another during their institutional careers because of their violent acting out or their behavior. . . .

"O" wing, where we put these men, has two sides, two sections. One is for isolation, which is a section for punishment of people who are convicted of breaking institutional rules. These men are only in there for a matter of a few days, up to twenty-nine days, depending on the type of infraction. The other side is for what we call maximum. These men have very little privileges. . . . In the upstairs "O" wing, they have additional privileges, and among these are access to educational materials, reading materials and this type of thing. . . .

As the men progress by showing their good attitude over a period of time, they are maybe moved into a different section, another wing, which is called "X" wing. Here again, they are given

* From an interview on KPFA, Berkeley, California.

increasing amounts of privileges, and they are permitted to have exercise in the yard, and they are permitted to take part in a little occupational therapy program going there. We have some academic education going in that wing too. And these men again are privileged to have schoolbooks and their courses are outlined by the educational people.

There is no shutting off the light. We have windows going out to the outside, and the sun comes through the same as from any window. On the fourth floor of "O" wing, there are six cells set aside for what are called "quiet cells." They are just like the other cells except that there is a vestibule in front of the cell, and the window in this vestibule has an iron flap on it, as does the vestibule door. So when a man is out of control and making all kinds of noise and cannot be persuaded to behave, he is put in here and the flaps are closed for the good of the rest of the men in the unit so that they won't be disturbed by anyone yelling all night.

There are no toilet bowls in these cells. They have what is called Oriental toilets, just a hole in the floor, and the flushing device is in the corridor behind each cell. The officer has to go in there a couple of times a day and flush it. Water is furnished by bringing it in a pitcher and filling a series of plastic cups because any glass or crockery or anything like this could be used as weapons against the staff or as a suicide device. . . . We have installed an electrically controlled flushing device so that we can eliminate the human element. We furnish water by giving the man five or six plastic Styrofoam cups filled with water so that he can have plenty of water to drink until the officer goes there the next time.

It is true that there is a minimum amount of light in these cells. But even though there is no light in there, it isn't completely dark because light comes through the cracks.

We feel that in the Adjustment Center setting ["O" wing] the man who is defiant about coming out of his cell or defiant about doing anything, stopping fighting or defiant about giving up some dangerous weapon or something like this, that we use a shot of tear gas as a humane way to move him and to bring him into control. This is used in opposition to getting in with four or five officers and fighting him and wrestling him down to the floor, with the danger of somebody getting hurt. The tear gas is not dangerous. It doesn't create any public [sic], I mean any permanent damage. We feel that this is the most humane way to handle people who are out of control and who are being defiant and who need to be controlled.

I can hardly recall an incident in the past six years, oh maybe a few incidents, where it has been necessary to use gas throughout the rest of the institution. But in the Adjustment Center and "O" wing particularly, it has been necessary to do that fairly frequently, maybe as often as on the average of once every couple of weeks.

For probably a year and a half or two years prior to this unfortunate incident in January, we had to have the inmates, the black inmates and the white inmates or nonblack inmates, exercise separately to keep them from fighting one another. And it has been necessary to kind of divide them up, assign the cells so that they won't be close to each other, that is, alternate them so that they won't be in a concerted group.

Now, unfortunately, it had not been possible for the men in "O" wing to exercise since we built "X" wing. At the time of the incident, it was a long time since any of these men had been out in sunshine and fresh air. We had diverted money from other maintenance projects and made this yard available to this group in "O" wing so that they would have some exercise. We asked the Director of Corrections and got permission for an officer to occupy a gun tower to keep trouble out of this yard. This is stated practice in Adjustment Centers in Folsom, San Quentin, Tracy and here. . . . We consulted one of the leading manufacturers of tear gas to find out if he would recommend tear gas for use in this yard and he actually made two trips here to experiment and we did experiment with a smoke bomb, but the air currents in this valley are such that the smoke would swirl, eddy and go into the hospital rather than stay in the yard where it would be effective. So he recommended against any attempt to use gas. The relative merits of a shotgun in opposition to a rifle were weighed. Even the inmates in "O" wing, when they were consulted, agreed that shotgun pellets don't have anybody's name on them. And you would get an innocent bystander as much as you would a person who was being shot at.

On the 13th of January, 1970, at about 9:15 in the morning, we began releasing one man at a time into this yard—one black and one nonblack—and actually the actual breakdown was, there were seven blacks in the yard, four Caucasians, two Mexicans, one Samoan and one Hawaiian. . . . We let them out alternately, and as they would come out they would group with their own, the blacks with the blacks and the nonblacks with their group. The story of the witnesses was that the blacks took some aggression, they moved towards the whites, the whites moved away, and finally that went on two or three times, and finally the whites took a stand and there was a fight. And it wasn't a scuffle like it was reported, it was a downright ongoing fight and three or four blacks had this one white man down and there wasn't any question that they were going to kill him. In the minds of the witnesses.

And the officers' testimony, that the officer blew his whistle as a warning, fired a warning shot, and then he fired . . . and this didn't stop it. He fired three more shots. And you understand that this is a swirling mass of fighting men and it would be pretty hard for anybody to pick out one guy and hit him. Anyhow, the net result was that the three men were killed and one was hurt. The grand jury reviewed all of the material, talked to many witnesses, not only our staff but the inmates as well. And not only the inmates of the Adjustment Center but the inmates working in the hospital and the medical staff who looked out the window of the hospital and could see what was going on. The Department of Justice was called in and they made a ballistics test. Reported that there was some fragmentation of bullets and the possibility, nobody can say for sure, [but] their best professional judgment is that the possibility is very great that a couple of the bullets were fragmented, there was a possibility that one bullet went through two people. In other words, it wasn't four clean shots hit four people.

The allegation about officers trying to start trouble between inmates of different races is kind of ridiculous on the surface. Why would the officers agitate some trouble and then have to go in and physically restrain people to stop the trouble? It seems incongruous to make that kind of an allegation.

It is not true because it is up to the officers to stop inmates from hurting and killing each other. And it wouldn't be smart to agitate something and then have to go in and stop it. We have racial disturbances, but I don't think that ours are as bad as they are on the outside. Our problems are not, in my opinion, a racial hatred for the most part. We do have some very militant whites and we do have some very militant blacks, but this isn't the big problem. These people are pretty well known. You know pretty much with what you are dealing. But what happens in many instances is that cliques or groups or gangs or groups of friends will get together like on the outside, and when one gang member is attacked by a member of another gang, then the two gangs go at it. It isn't a matter of their antipathy towards the race or color or creed, but it is a matter of sticking with your friend and backing up your friend's play. . . . So we don't think that we have much worse except that when men are in confinement like this and rubbing shoulders every day, there is much more irritant involved and so naturally you are going to be a little more edgy than you would be on the outside where you can walk away from some trouble.

Thomas Lopez Meneweather, inmate of Soledad Central Correctional Training Facility: *

I looked at the tower guard and he was aiming the gun toward me and I thought then that he meant to kill me, too, so I moved from the wall as he fired and went over to stand over Jug, all the time looking the guard in the gun tower in the face. He aimed the gun at me again and I just froze and waited for him to fire, but he held his fire. After I saw he was not going to fire, I pointed to where Jug lay, with two other black inmates bending over him, and started to walk to him very slowly. The inmate I had played handball with suggested that I take Jug to the hospital, so I kneeled so Jug could be placed on my shoulder, then started to walk toward the door through which we had entered the yard, and the tower guard pointed the gun at me and shook his head. I stopped and begged him for approximately ten minutes to let me take Jug to the hospital, but all he did was shake his head. Then I started forward with tears in my eyes, expecting to be shot down every second. The tower guard told me, "That's far enough." Then another guard gave me permission to bring Jug off the yard, and I was ordered to lay him on the floor in the officers' area and go to my cell, which I refused to do until he was taken to the hospital.

Hugo Pinell, inmate of Soledad Central Correctional Training Facility: †

On Monday, the 12th of January, 1970, I left for Sacramento County Jail again. It was raining like hell up that way so I figured the weather was the same at Soledad. Tuesday morning I was taken to court, but someone said it was a mistake, that I was supposed to appear that afternoon, so I was taken back to County Jail where I met other friends of mine. Well, me and my friends went to court that afternoon; when we returned, we happened to hear the news on

---

* From an affidavit filed with the Salinas County Court, subsequently published in *Maximum Security*, Bantam Books, 1973.

† From a statement filed with the Salinas County Court, subsequently published in *Maximum Security*, op. cit.

the radio where it announced the killing of three inmates at Soledad Institution while scuffling in the yard. Damn, for some reason I knew what yard that man on the radio was referring to, because I fell to my knees against my will, and tears rolled out of my eyes. Believe me, I am a man in every respect, but if you felt the tension we live under, you could easily understand a grown man crying. I was sad, angry and hateful. Gordon also cried and he wasn't even at Soledad and yet we know how it is for blacks in prison. Everybody stopped and stared at me, not understanding. I cursed people out for no reason because, after all, it wasn't their fault. I returned to Soledad the next day and I could smell death in the air. The tier was like a tomb—I was put in what used to be my personal friend's cell, W. L. Nolen. I asked what happened, and they told me that W. L. Nolen, Cleveland Edwards and Jug Miller were shot down like ducks in a pond.

A long desk against one wall dominates the captain's office. Guards with their faces almost pressing against the glass peer in at us through a picture window along the adjoining wall that looks out into the corridor. While I am bending over to plug in my tape recorder, I hear sounds like pieces of a crystal chandelier hitting against one another in a strong breeze. I turn and get up. Another person has entered the room, but he is hidden by John's body. He begins talking to John almost as if he had been in conversation with him even before he entered the room. Almost immediately John turns around and, at the same moment, the other man moves to the side and steps toward me.

"George, I want you to meet Greg. I told you all about him yesterday." The first thing I see are his chains. Momentarily, I shut my eyes. I didn't realize that he would be in chains. I look down for just an instant at his black shoes and his jeans, which have been worn down to bare thread, and feel my face growing pale.

I lift my eyes as he comes toward me. I know him from his photograph, but nothing has prepared me for his actual physical presence. He is young and slender. His face is smooth and unmarked, like a boy's. "I'm really pleased to meet you, man. We got a lot to talk about. I got a lot of questions."

Everything about him is flashing and shining and glistening and his body seems to ripple like a cat's. As he moves forward to take my hand, I literally feel myself being pulled into the vortex of his energy. There is no way I can look away. He gives me a sudden radiant smile of sheer sensual delight, the kind of smile you save for someone you really love. As we take each other's hands, I have a sense of becoming almost a part of his very physical being.

We bring chairs over to the long table and gather around close to each other. Before we can begin work on the book, John and George have some other matters to settle so I just sit back and listen.

All the time they talk George never stops smiling at me. I know it is because he is so happy to be having his book published. It is a smile which says so much. "What a fantastic pleasure to see you. What a fine rich time we are going to have together. I really love you." It is a smile that invites huge hugs and intimate contact of bodies.

As he talks with John, his voice swoops up and down in great arcs of feeling. Every least shade of meaning in his words is underscored by the music of his voice: mocking, ironic, insinuating, tender, boyish. His face is just as expressive as his voice, a perfect mirror of each changing mood.

With George, it is as if John has become a different person. In almost everything he says, I can feel him reaching out for George. When he addresses him directly, his voice gets heavy and he pumps out his words in the short thumping phrases that are characteristic of radical oratory. As he talks, John moves his chair closer and closer to George's.

John is very reassuring. He says only the kind of things that I'm sure he thinks George wants to hear. There aren't any problems at all. Even if there were, he'd be able to settle them. The lawsuit is looking really good. Angela Davis and George's father are getting along really well together. Since attending some of the early court sessions, she has gotten very close to the Jackson family. She is going to tutor George's brother, Jonathan. On her advice, Jonathan is going back to school. George is going to get out of prison for sure. John is going to be there waiting for him at the gates. He can't wait to see George and Angela get off somewhere alone for a few weeks.

"The magnificence of the two of you together."

There won't be any problems at all getting George and the other two accused men transferred to the San Francisco County Jail. Fay Stender, George's other attorney, and her husband, Marvin, who is also a lawyer, are going to get together with a judge who is a good friend of Marvin's and they are going to work everything out. And George takes it all in smiling. I sit there wondering how much George actually believes or even if it is a question of belief at all.

I know from George's letters that he doesn't expect to live. He has always believed that the prison authorities will kill him someday. Even if they don't kill him outright, he believes that the damage that has already been done to him in prison is irreparable.

I know John probably thinks of George taking all his reassurances back to his cell and daydreaming about them and taking strength from them. Because everything John says is kind and well intentioned. But what could his words mean to George, who is in such a different place, who lives inside such a totally different reality, the world of "O" wing?

It destroys the logical processes of the mind, a man's thoughts become completely disorganized, the noise, the madness, streaming from every throat, frustrated sounds from the bars, metallic sounds from the walls, the steel trays, the iron beds bolted to the wall, the hollow sounds from a cast-iron sink or toilet.

The smells, the human waste thrown at us, unwashed bodies, the rotten food. When a white con leaves here, he is ruined for life. No black leaves Max Row walking. Either he leaves on the meat wagon, or he leaves crawling, licking at the pigs' feet.*

The captain's office is on the ground floor. Its barred windows are partly open. Sounds of lawn mowers and songbirds chattering back and forth fill the room. At times they are joined by the dull rhythmic thudding of hammering in one of the offices next door. When John and George are finished with their business, they turn and look expectantly at me, waiting for me to say something, but

* *Soledad Brother: The Prison Letters of George Jackson*, Bantam Books, 1970.

no words come. George is sitting only a few inches away from me smiling with anticipation. It is as if I have lost my voice. I want to speak but I have no words. There is a long silence.

"When is my book going to come out?" George asks very quietly, as if to save me from further embarrassment.

"September is when I see it coming all together."

"Well, are there going to be any parts they are going to cut?" It doesn't seem to be a question as much as a statement of the inevitable.

"No! There is no question about that. If anything, we are going to make it stronger. What you've got to say is of interest to some of the people. There is no sense holding back. This is it! What's here we print." My incoherence is like a sponge in my throat. "There are a lot of questions about events that you allude to in the letters. Like what was happening in San Quentin at the time—."

John interrupts to remind me of the arrangement under which I am here. The weight of his voice tells me how important it is that I remember. I am supposed to be visiting the prison not as an editor but as a legal investigator. This is the cover story that has been devised to get me into Soledad. If the prison authorities find out about the book, they will do everything they can to stop it. John has already explained to me that the office is bugged. As if to reinforce his point, I can see the faces of the guards still at the window. But no matter how I try, I still find myself mentioning the book again and again, in spite of my awareness of the possible consequences.

To cover up my nervousness, I start explaining to George what I want the book to be. I hear myself making it seem almost as if he were going to have no part in it at all. His eyes lower and his face swells with rage. He bristles and thrusts his body toward me.

"Now look here, if there is any writing to be done in this book, I want to do it myself."

Everything about him becomes taut and coiled. I am not saying what I really mean. I have no intention of writing his book. But he reacts so quickly. Why doesn't he give me a chance to explain?

I try once more. "What I need to go on is something that I don't find too much of in your letters, the kind of circumstantial detail you get in a novel." In New York, I had decided that the letters needed a running commentary that could be put together out of George's answers to certain questions I had prepared.

"We can start here, but I would like to write that myself." I can see his anger bunching in his shoulders like knots of steel.

John's face has suddenly filled with a look of alarm. He seems to realize that everything is on the brink of falling apart. Twisting himself between George and me, he starts talking very rapidly, attempting to convince George that he should go on talking to me, if for nothing else, at least so we can open up some new ground.

There is a long silence and then George nods his head. The anger begins to drain from his face and his shoulders relax.

"We'll do this quickly then. How's your time? That's a ridiculous question. I mean, can you work on this? Because we want to develop it very quickly." Trying to talk like a legal investigator.

"Oh, yes! I can give you twenty-four hours a day. Well, twenty-one anyway." We all laugh. Everything is back to the way it was when we just met. He is all smiles again.

"Well, let's start at the beginning. Let's go back as far as you are willing to go. Take Catholic school. I think that was really very important to you. You refer to it over and over again."

George takes up my lead, chewing incessantly on the candy we have brought him, throwing his head back to catch a thought, coiling and uncoiling his body, screwing up his face as he goes deeper and deeper into his past. I can tell from his look that he has decided to give me a chance.

"I had no contact with any other children, all the way up until the day I went to kindergarten, except children in the immediate family. Let's say our extended family. You know, visiting relatives. We were living on the West Side of Chicago. My family was so afraid of the neighborhood they wouldn't let me out on the street. It was vicious. My mother kept me and my sister trapped on this little roof that adjoined the little second-floor apartment we had. We had a little door that opened out onto a roof. We had to do all our physical playing, ball throwing, on the roof. We were safe there because nobody could get on the roof except us." His voice recaptures his mother's sense of her children's vulnerability. "My mother kept us isolated from the community, thinking"—and he stretches the word out with irony—"that she was protecting us from physical and psychological harm."

He pivots in his chair and looks at me smiling, as much as to say, "Well, it's all right now. I'm giving you what you wanted. Do you feel better now?" Then he goes on:

"The first day I went to the public school, I saw white kids there, and it was just like seeing them for the first time. In my world, the world of the child, everybody was supposed to look like us." And he spreads his hands, as if to say, "Here I am." "Hair like mine. Nose like mine. Going to school was just like being sprung loose from a big trap, all of a sudden being let out after four or five years in the closet. I walked up, felt some white guy's hair, looked at him and said, 'Hmmm.' I rubbed his hair and said, 'What the fuck is wrong with you?' I didn't say it like that, but you know." He lowers his voice to soften his words. "I did that a couple of times, and later that same day somebody found me with the back of my head split open. Somebody hit me with something hard." George squints his eyes to mimic the sensation of pain. "And I was lying out in the street. Somebody scooped me up. I must have had some kind of ID or something because somebody took me back home."

As George describes his memory of the incident, his whole manner becomes paternal, as if he were looking down and smiling at a child playing on the floor. "I didn't know much about the situation then. I was just a baby. My mother was trying to protect me, but you see the results. This protective thing with a black is so strong, I think it is detrimental." As he says the words, he pulls them back with his voice as if he is uncertain about how I will accept them. I realize he doesn't want to talk denigratingly to me, a white man, about blacks, and yet it is obviously important for him to say certain things about black women because they are so much on his mind.

"After kindergarten, I went to Catholic school," George goes on, "and it was completely artificial. I didn't understand it too well when I first went there. I was just a baby, of course"—as if to disclaim any responsibility for political immaturity.

I'm smiling back at him now. Trying to show him with my eyes all the things that I can't say. And he is smiling back at me as if to say that everything is really all right now. "I like you. Don't worry!"

"But the thing that set me off was the difference between what they were saying and doing. Several times when I was a child, I caught these nuns and priests doing things that would be considered lewd"—and from the way he says the word I can tell that he doesn't use it very often; he enunciates it tentatively and draws it out as if he enjoyed the feeling of his tongue pressed into his teeth—"lewd and immoral, against their own code, anyway. The thing that they projected, the things they said in class, just didn't agree with me and the way I felt. That was my biggest problem when I was a kid. The whole class would stop and the teachers, the nuns and priests and I would start fighting, arguing, and hassling."

He is so proud of his memory of himself. He really likes the child that he was. As he goes on, I find it hard to believe that he hasn't spent the last few days rehearsing his story. He is almost too controlled and articulate.

"A school like that is really right out in the open fighting for control over your mind and your total existence. I understand now. Every chance that I got in the classroom or in the yard—no, not the yard, it wasn't a yard, it was a sidewalk—'yard' comes from being in prison too long. . . ." His mistake visibly pains him because it makes him realize that he is almost completely engulfed by his life in the prison, that it isn't just words. He pulls back in his chair and takes a deep breath. "Every chance I would get, I would fight. Out there on the sidewalk where we played (later on they built a gym) we'd have our little confrontations with the nuns and the priests. Because I found out right out front that they were chicken. They were scared. They'd have recourse to the stick, the whip. They tried to use it on me once when I was young. I just grabbed it and hung on. And we had a big thing. They were paddling the rest of them, but I found out that by resisting I didn't get paddled. By resisting, they didn't come back at me, they didn't try to come back at me." As he talks, he moves his chair closer to me, shaping his words with his hands.

"You showed them that you wouldn't take it, so they didn't give it. They only give it to those who are vulnerable."

"There was a little store on the corner that they wanted to get rid of. I can't quite put my finger on the real reasons. Probably they wanted the property that the store was sitting on. Well, anyway, the store wouldn't let the school buy the property. The nuns and the priests were just about to have a stroke, you know. It just so happened"—he gives me an arch look with his eyebrows raised—"that the store was owned by some blacks. All right, the teachers—I mean the nuns, they didn't deserve to be called teachers because they didn't teach me anything—they had a real propaganda campaign going against this little store. It was a big thing with them. In every class, at every opportunity, they would make it their business to downgrade these cats who were running the store. They didn't want us to patronize it so they would make sly little innuendoes about what was going on in the back of the store. No moral sense. Only out for their own power."

For a few moments, we are silent. The lawn mowers whirr outside the windows and the sound makes me remember cutting lawns when I was a child. The scent of newly mown grass fills the room.

"We were poorer than hell. My mother doesn't like to admit it. She had some pretensions, so there was always a big difference between the way they dressed me and the way they dressed the other kids in my school. We had to pay tuition. It wasn't much, you know, but we had to pay something. Once I had given it to the nun and she'd stuck it under a book up on the desk. And I'm thinking about the money and the other kids not having to pay to go to school. Well, the way it ended up, I took the money back. Well, actually, I stole it. She accused me of it. I just stuck to my guns. Just stood there and lied my head off. I believe from that moment, from that moment on, I believe it's from that day on . . ." And George stops as if for the first time he realizes the full significance of that event. He shakes his head to mark his sudden awareness that his rebellion had begun so early.

"How old were you?" I can see that George is excited by the memory of stealing. I am excited too. It is almost as if the idea of stealing were sexually stimulating. Like seeing a woman lifting her skirts. One immorality must lead the mind to another, and from there to everything that is forbidden.

"I don't know, I can't put my finger on it, it's a long time ago. I believe that from that moment on I decided that that was the way I would get back at them. At first, I didn't have it in mind to pay her back. But she stuck it up on the desk like she trusted me. Like I was a well-trained dog, you dig? She turned her back. I was sitting in the front row. They always used to stick me in the front row when they had visitors. They used to want to show me off for some reason. It would take hours combing my hair, brushing my hair and washing my face and hanging little things on me." He turns his head roguishly and rolls his eyes as if no one could ever imagine anything as ridiculous as trying to pretty him up.

"Why do you think they wanted to show you off?"

"I don't know. My mother was proud. I was an ugly little thing, you know." Disclaiming his incredible charm, which is dazzling us both at this very moment.

"But she couldn't control where you sat in class. Why did the nun want to put you in the front row?"

"I was in the choir. They always used to put me in the front row of that too. But now I'm the guy, I'm the guy that's throwing stuff, sticking out my tongue and so forth like that. I don't know. They put our choir on television once. They put me in the front then too. In front!"

He roars with laughter again at the absurdity of trying to show him off. Who could ever accuse him of being a teacher's pet, and yet . . . he glitters just like one of those wondrous multicolored snakes that I see in my dreams sometimes and that seem so much like gods in disguise. Who could ever imagine that he spent all his days locked up in a seven-and-a-half-by-eight-foot cell and that he is beginning his tenth year in prison?

"I think the ripping off, taking things back and so forth started right there, and it went on from there. And my mama doesn't like to admit it, but I've been robbing all my life."

I find myself looking at him as if I am trying to memorize every feature of his face. The brown tawny skin. Patches of stubble.

George catches me looking at him, really seeing him. I can see the awareness in his eyes. His face becomes even more liquid and mercurial. He is still just as seductive as he must have been when he was a child.

"We were constantly under attack in the area where we lived. This was between West Madison and the South Side of Chicago. Now it's called the black belt, because of the huge concentration of blacks there. They got off these trains coming up from the South and never got any further than the Sixty-third Street station. They'd just spread out around there.

"That's the thing that developed my consciousness of the fact that I am black, very, very early." He moves and the chains on his legs and his wrists rattle. He begins to make a large gesture and the chains restrain him and he looks up apologetically. "I knew right from the beginning that I wasn't supposed to compete against blacks because of the neighborhood. If I'd go two blocks outside into the white neighborhood, man, I'd never get back without getting involved in some kind of encounter, physical violence. The lines were clear. Now those whites were just as poor as we were. The adults, the poor adults, all lived on the same level. And yet they'd fight each other, threaten each other. Sort of like there was a mutual kind of hatred."

I can see the pleasure he takes in the precision of his analysis. Every so often he looks off and lowers his eyelids as if he is focusing on a very distant object. "The youngsters just wouldn't mix at all. Now after a certain age, the guys would mix together. You'd see them in bars and so forth, in restaurants, over on Madison. Madison is the main drag running east and west."

A bell rings and the corridors outside the window are suddenly filled with men. As they pass by the window, they glance furtively into the room.

"The kids you were hanging around with, how did they feel about things? Were they at the same place you were?"

"I hate to say things like this, because it might sound egotistical, but I say, No! They were aware of one thing only—that these cats come over and kick our ass, and we were to make preparations for them. Do you know what kind of effect violence like that has on a guy? You would start to fight and little zip guns would start cutting bullets through the air. And there would be hatchets and so forth with little embossed handles. It was vicious.

It was war. You know, right in the very beginning, it was a god-damn war." George breathes heavily.

"There is a lot of killing going on in the ghetto. A guy learns to run and make the fast break. There's not much that stands be-tween the black male and dying except cutting a guy's throat or running, making a credible defense on running. The heart of the fight is to tire the guy down so that even though you may be whupped eventually, he'll be too tired to kick you when you go down."

I blink and jut my face forward, totally unprepared for George's acceptance of the inevitability of defeat. He pauses and reaches back for a more pleasant memory.

"I've had one or two close friends. A guy named Joe. I think he's in the pen somewhere back East. He was really great in the old school in the old neighborhood. He was a couple of years older than me, which means a lot at that age. When kids are nine, ten, eleven, twelve, a couple of years means a lot. I think I learned quite a bit from Joe. When I was a small kid, we started robbing people, and stuff like that, you see. It's not too nice, you know. I'm not proud of it, but I will tell you the truth."

"Be proud of it. I mean, really."

He smiles back at me appreciatively.

"We would go to the other neighborhoods, you dig? We were hard up. We didn't have anything. Cats were hardly surviving. We'd look for paper boys. I was a kid and they were kids. We'd take them on. We'd start a fight. If they'd lose, we'd get their money." And he laughs because it had been such a foregone con-clusion that the other side would always lose. "Yeah, but that's robbery," he challenges, testing me.

"Yeah."

"Because we knew right up front that we were going to win. Two or three of us, you know, one of them."

"But they had it, you didn't."

"Oh, I can understand. Anyway, they were just as poor and fucked up as I was. They were in the same position economically. I didn't understand it then. I understand it now. Because the same thing that happened to them would happen to me, too, if I'd got-ten robbed . . . but those were the things that happened."

"Did you ever read *Dark Ghetto* by Kenneth Clark?" I ask. "One of the guys is rapping and he says, 'The way the man has us, it's just dog eat dog, you know.'"

"I can understand the problem. Some of the things I have done, I feel awful sick. I feel awful sick at some of the stupid things I've done, vicious thoughtless things I've done. I feel bad about them."

It seems to give him real pain to remember. He has more compassion for the people he has hurt than I have for those I have hurt. George's words have stirred up an old and painful memory of throwing stones at a poor idiot boy who lived in my neighborhood, stone after stone until finally one of them hit a tooth and blood spurted out all over his chin.

"What would you feel bad about? I mean, like ripping off those kids?"

"Yes, of course I feel bad about that, man."

I shake my head because I can't understand how someone who is suffering so acutely can still feel remorse for the things he has done so long ago.

"But who do you really blame?"

"The cats who built that neighborhood. The cats that structured it so that sort of thing would happen. Daley and guys like that."

"They are your real enemies. You can forgive yourself."

"Yeah, but one thing I can't forgive myself for, for not knowing then, for not taking the time to think about it at the time. I could have done better. I have made mistakes even recently.

"The lines are drawn in school, the lines of race, neighborhood. After that it is the economic situation. A lot of times my mother would sit back sniveling or drinking hot water. In Chicago we had nothing in the house to eat and so forth. I started feeling guilty about sitting there eating, that's why I left home so early."

When I was a child, my mother had bought steak so she could give me the juice. Everyone else in the family ate macaroni.

"When was that?" I ask.

"Oh, when we first got out here. I've never really lived with my folks since we've been out to California." The favored son always has to run from his mother.

"How old were you then?"

"Fifteen."

"Fifteen? You really went out on your own?"

"With periods, you know. I'd come back to the house and spend two or three months, then a month or so on the streets. I did a year in jail, fifteen months in jail. Off and on, but I really haven't been too close to my family since we came out to California."

"As the years went by," George goes on, "the lines got more and more distinct. It got so bad that at one time up at San Quentin, at one stage in my little experience, I would have pushed the button if I'd had the chance. You dig what I'm saying?"

I know. Destroy the world. Take everyone else with you. I had daydreamed about it a thousand, ten thousand times myself. We both pause to let the full significance of our memories sink in.

"The more I understood, the deeper I looked into the economic and social situation, the more desperate I got. I knew all those cats were just running off at the mouth. They didn't know what they were talking about, the guys that were talking about reform. Do you know what they called these joints at one point?"

"Reform schools?"

"Aw, listen, man. It's just so ridiculous at every stage. It just goes on being the same thing. I'm telling you about the nuns and the games they play with each other and the sex thing, you know. It's just the same as inside the prison. The cops talk reform, but at the same time they bring in narcotics or weapons and stuff like that. You dig what I'm saying? It just leaves nothing to your imagination. Guys go for it because actually they have to submit. They are not being reformed or rehabilitated. They are just submitting to a system that they feel that they can't change." There is a tone of reproach in his voice as if he had expected so much more.

"What was your opinion of cops as you grew up?"

"It started with the impression of big boots, of long high shiny boots like the German General Staff used to wear. Long tall boots and the night stick. They would hit me right behind the ear. Do you know where that spot is? Do you know how it feels?" But I don't know and I look confused. "You know, right here. Feel it."

Very self-consciously my fingers probe his skull for the small knot of bone. It is strange to be touching him that way, so intimately. I guess I had imagined him to be untouchable in some way. "Right there, there's a little thing in the forehead and they can kill you if they hit you there. Right up here, the right kind of snap can send little bone splinters right into your brain. Now this is what they are aiming for."

But I can't think about what he is saying because I am still so overwhelmed by the strangeness of touching him. "You know that now. But when did you start to realize that they were really trying to mess you up as much as they possibly could?"

"Well, I didn't learn the fact that they could kill me if they hit me there until later, but I definitely remember all the times that I got hit there. You can feel the results right here." The memory grabs hold of him, and he stops to light a cigarette, inhaling with a deep sigh.

"Getting back to when I was growing up. The big thing was to follow the leader. If a cat couldn't follow the leader, he was in trouble. But the leader would have to do some really daring things to stay the leader. Like, well, if you've seen the area, you know what I'm talking about. We'd get up on the roofs and there would be spaces, passageways, gangways, leading from the front of the house to the rear. And up on the roof, you have a situation with cats running. You got this space of about ten feet between the buildings. You can't even stop to think. You just got to jump. If you stop on the edge of the roof, it's all over, because the edges of the roofs are all broken and crumbly, and if you try to stand on the top of them they crumble. So you've got a huge jump." He smiles softly because there is such a sweet sense of freedom in his memory.

"Well, those were the kind of normal things we liked to do. The only place we had to play the games, the ball games that kids like to play, was right there in the alley and behind the house, and it was vicious and my parents didn't want me out there. They didn't want any of us out there. And when they'd catch me out there (you know sometimes I would be gone for hours), well, suddenly something heavy would hit me and I would be driven back to the pad. Well, when I got back to the house, my mother would sit me down and make me read. This is about the time my grandfather started to take an interest in me."

"He is the man referred to as Papa in your letters, the one you were afraid they had let die of neglect?"

"He had just come up from the southern part of the state, Cairo, Harrisburg. He was staying with my mother and father at first. My father started to hassle him. My grandfather almost jumped my father once, and my father never forgave him. When he got older, he just wasn't taken care of and he died of old age. We were living out here. He didn't have anything at all. I got really long scratchy letters from him." George's voice is heavy with grief for his grandfather.

"Did you get a chance to go back and see him before you came here?"

"No! But we were real close. He didn't have any competition really. He was competing with my father for possession of my mind, but he won every time. My father just gave up."

"And you did the same thing your grandfather did for you with your brother Jonathan. You fought for his mind. Right? I could see it in your letters. That's the most beautiful thing I know about you, the way you are with your brother."

George smiles and almost curls into my words. "But in the case of Jonathan I was fighting with both my father and mother. I didn't think they let you have any of those letters."

"I got the letters."

"I'll bet you didn't get all of them though. I told her to hold back some of the early ones because they were so bitter that I didn't want anyone to read them."

"You mean that? You don't want anybody to read them?"

"No! No! Because you see, when a guy comes under attack constantly, constantly under attack—I've never lost my control or my grip on my mind—but when a guy comes under attack constantly, when he has to be careful and watch almost every guy who comes within arm's reach, it does something to him, you see. I mean at one time I just felt that there was no possibility of any white person ever liking me."

"Uh-huh!"

"You hear what I'm saying?"

I hear and I don't want to hear at the same time. I close my eyes just for an instant, imagining the things he has been forced to do. He shakes himself as if he is awaking from a nightmare and goes on.

"You might not be aware of it"—going back to the police—"but the pigs have a regular procedure; if they want to clean up the books, they pick some cat up, just for a suspicion of anything. Then they've got a whole two or three months to hang it on him. Then they just push it right through the courts. Just hang it right on him. Make him confess."

"And you're always guilty."

"Always." The book is always closed. The door is always shut for blacks. "Man, I want to tell you, the first thing a guy starts thinking about when he is busted if he is black is, can he make a deal? Can he cop to something lower? Because there is no possibility of him getting off completely or pushing it all off him. He's born guilty, that's the way it is." He lights another cigarette. The ashtray is already overflowing.

"You said in one letter that the cops stopped you five times in the space of two blocks in Los Angeles."

"Has that ever happened to you?" George looks over at me quizzically.

"It has happened to me a couple of times. I remember one time being picked up late at night on the banks of the Charles River in Cambridge. The police car had driven right up on the lawn to the bench where I was sitting, and they accused me of being a cocksucker. They would have taken me in if I hadn't convinced them I was a student." They'd also threatened to take me down into the basement of the station house and beat me. I still remember my sense of surprise when this car suddenly pulled up right beside my bench. But I was white and a Harvard student, so they let me go.

"It happened to me all the time. One time they made me lay face down on the concrete when they searched my car, on the theory that it would take me longer to get up and start fighting than it would for him to draw his gun and shoot me."

"I was talking to a black guy in Cleveland," I interpose, "and he said if you walk down the streets of Cleveland in a white neighborhood they shine a 'nigger light' in your face. And I thought: nigger light, not searchlight or flashlight."

"Well, it is so pervasive . . . and listen, cat, you know what, man, if a cat doesn't understand protracted warfare"—he goes off into peals of deep rasping laughter—"it makes you think that man is useless. And rather than letting him loose in the world, well, you just want to tear all this shit up." He has a broad smile on his face, but his eyes are very sad.

"When was the first time you ever got busted?"

"In Chicago. Snatching somebody's purse or robbing a market. They took me down to the station, kicked me in the butt and released me."

"Did they really kick you in the butt, literally?"

"No, man, don't act like that." For the first time he is really hurt. He'd thought I understood. Suddenly he feels that I have only tricked him into telling me about his life when I really don't understand at all.

"No, tell me. I want it on the tape." Trying to show him that I really am with him and that I do understand.

"Yeah, they kicked me in the butt, busted me in the side of the head, everywhere else. See, they do this physical stuff where you folks can't see it." I wince at the way he sets me off with all the rest. "You come up with busted ribs two or three days later. Wondering why your sides hurt, why you're pissing blood. That's my strongest impression. Those tall black boots. And those sticks busting the side of my head. They hit you, and when you are down, they kick you in the ass and in the ribs, kidneys and groin. Once I took somebody's leg and bit it. It's beautiful. I liked it. You know what? It's got to be that way. The only way was to fight back."

He goes on: "Someday I'd like Angela Davis with me. That would be fun." Someone to admire his style and appreciate his courage. "I never met a more vicious woman in my life. I mean, she has nerves, she just reeks of the stuff." He pauses, and then continues: "The thing is, you got to learn how to run, and I learned that very early. My mama will tell you about it. When everything got hot, I'd run, head back East."

"You said in a letter you crossed the country three times."

"Yeah. One time me and this cat just left and hoboed. We got to this hobo jungle and just starved there."

"You were in a hobo jungle?"

"Yeah."

"How old were you?"

"My grandmother died. I was, I think, about thirteen."

"Were you able to protect yourself?"

"Yes." As if it should be obvious to me.

"How?"

"From whom and what?" He really doesn't know what I mean.

"In a hobo jungle, you protect yourself from the hoboes."

"You've got it just about backwards." He roars with laughter. "They were trying to get rid of us."

"Get rid of *you?*"

"You've got it backwards—what's happening. Because those guys, they're all beaten, broken men, you know. They're not aggressive at all. We'd bring stuff in that we stole and they were scared to death. I mean, they steal little things like food. But when they see knives and guns, they want to get rid of you. You've got that thing just backwards."

And I realize that I will always get it backwards. He really is a different order of human being.

"Well, you know," I go on, "I tried to figure that out from what Ernest Hemingway said about when he was a hobo in a hobo jungle. He said you had to have a gun or a knife and be ready to protect yourself at all times from the other hoboes."

"Well, that was in the thirties, when they were rough and vicious."

"Right."

"Anybody was a hobo then, in the thirties. Now those were the times that produced Dillinger and Barker and others. Times have changed.

"The problem is that parents just don't know about such things. How can anybody teach me things when they don't know about them themselves? That was why I rejected my father. He tried to give me his way, the way that had given him a kind of survival. My grandfather gave me a different outlook. My father didn't go to school. He was just cut loose. He knew nothing of the forest, of the jungle, just the trees around him. Up to a point, everything he knows . . . well, my mother interpreted everything for him. Indirectly, she formed most of his attitudes. Most of the time though, the reason for black female domination is that the father leaves, goes about his business, struggling. Leaves the responsibility to the woman by default. Makes it on his own. Too hard to stay. But when the man and woman stay together, usually the case is—this comes from hundreds of years—the woman dominates because she hasn't been the target, the victim of the same terrorism that my father and I know. I mean, nothing stands between me and getting killed. Nothing. You know, in a bourgeois society women aren't considered dangerous, and you get this sex thing.

"So it is natural for women to take over the running of the family. And my mama ran the house. No two ways about that. Because my father was usually off somewhere working. And when he was home, he was too tired to do any fighting. So she took over."

"That explains a lot of the attitude toward women that comes across in the letters."

"Yeah, I'm trying to get my mind regulated; I'm preparing myself for war. I want to get my mind regulated so I won't have any weaknesses of the flesh. I got no women around me, you know. I'm deprived of women right here. Right now, immediately. Well, if I do all right and survive, then I can do without them and survive until I get my little job done."

Talking about women makes him nervous. He moves his shoulders and adjusts himself in his chair, like a bashful adolescent looking in the mirror, preening in his awareness of someone watching him. I don't really understand what he is saying, but I don't feel I have any right to question him. It is so hard for him to admit that he lacks the power to do anything. I can feel his wounded pride. As if to say, "If I can't have them, then I don't want them. And besides, I have something else much more important to do." But I can feel his pain, like a taut noose around his words.

"I understood right from the very beginning that my mother used to make this cat jump on me. I'd do something and he would come in. 'George did such and such.' And ten minutes later I have to dodge."

"That's the threat all mothers seem to use. 'I'll tell your father when he gets home.'"

"That's why I love Angela, because she is so different from the rest of them." I know this remark is partly intended for my benefit, to show me that even in his situation he still possesses extraordinary power over women.

"But weren't you uptight some time ago?" As if he could ever stop being uptight until he got out of jail.

"I was uptight against my mama. I turned against my mama because she would come into the visiting room preaching about accepting things that I can't change. That was the same thing that these cats in the institution were telling me. There were signs all over the place saying, 'Lord, help me to accept the things I cannot change.'" And the idea that he could ever endorse such a sentiment sends him into gales of laughter.

Talking about sex has made him so nervous that for a moment he loses track of what he wants to say. "And that was the whole thing. I think there was a little more to it: 'Help me to change things, change and accept the things I can't change.' Or some shit like that. But what I want to know is, why can't I control my environment? What is it in my environment I can't change? Nothing. I proved that. If I'm a man, I'm supposed to have control of my environment, see, a little bit more than, a little bit more than I've had anyway, *a lot* more than I've had."

It seems as if everything stops for a few minutes. The room becomes utterly silent. We both become aware at the same moment of George's chains and the bars on the windows and the angry faces looking in at us.

"You know what? I knew that my father was innocent because he's so naïve. Both of them got together one day when I was in prison in Tracy. I had been fighting and they came up to see me. And my parents asked what happened. And I explained it to them, that the guards are wrong. And they said, 'What do you mean, the guards were wrong?' And they reminded me that the guards had the law behind them and they had guns, you know? That didn't make a damn bit of difference to me. They were still wrong.

It didn't make it right. And they asked me what I told the bull. They knew it was something vicious. And I told them. The bull was questioning me. He was asking me questions. I said, 'What the hell is wrong with you, what makes you think I have to answer your questions?' And that stopped him. 'What makes you think that you can question me about anything? It's none of your business what happened, you know.' And I told them that, see, and they just almost fell off their chairs, you know? 'Why would you say that to a policeman?'"

"They thought you should ingratiate yourself, right?"

"No. I'm going to tell you exactly what my father told me, or my mother told me. One of them said the first half, and the other said the last half. One made the statement and the other one reiterated it, you know? But I knew that my father was innocent because this cat never had an idea of his own in his whole life. He never had an original thought. Not one whatsoever. Everything was forced on him. Poured into his head." I feel George re-experiencing his sense of his father's shame.

"They told me, before they left, that if it would help me get out of the joint, that if it would help me get out of prison"—his repetition is like taking a deep breath so that he can go on, because it is still so painful to him—"that they would like to see me crawl from the chair that I was sitting in right back to my cell on my hands and knees. And I think I sort of resented it righteously from that day on. Because all I asked her was to understand.

"But I'm just not going to kowtow for the motherfucker. Excuse me. I'm just not going to do it, see? You see, I know that these cats don't like me, you know, and by kissing their ass, you know, and by trying to get along with them, I'm not going to help the situation here. It's just not worthwhile, just not worthwhile. They've got to understand that, though I love life, it is not worth living. I just can't be like my father."

I realize he is terrified of being like his father, that it is almost as if he regards his father as the carrier of a fatally contagious disease which will break out in him, too, unless he is eternally vigilant.

"I can't be like my father. It's just not worth living if you can't look at yourself. So I figure things out for myself. I got the thing going in the pen. Other brothers don't like to investigate, who don't read, not aggressive. I've got a little thing going with them, trying to bend their minds in the same channels as mine."

"I saw that right in the beginning. You are a natural-born teacher."

"I hope that I don't seem—it troubles me sometimes that I might be what you call domineering. I hope that's not the case.

"Now my mother could hardly keep food in the house, but she sat around mooning, pining and calculating on how she's going to buy something out of *Vogue* magazine. That is what they are talking about when they refer to the rat race. Senseless."

It seems to me that George's resentment has deeper roots than simply childhood memories. For a man who has grown up in prison, and who has remained there long after the age when he would normally have left home and married, continued dependency on his mother must be intolerable. He is like a boy who has been kept in camp until his hair has turned gray still getting packages from his mother. Her visits must be a reminder of his imprisonment in a kind of perpetual never-ending childhood.

"Yeah, but that is what has been done to people," I answer.

"They just don't understand. It is not those people, they just have to be helped to understand."

"That's a big job, a beautiful job."

"That is why I love Mao, because he understands protracted warfare. That's a guy, not one minute in his whole life did he deviate. You just got to respect people like that. I do. I have to and I love him. His grasp, his understanding of life. Mao is the universal man. He sees himself in relation to China for one. But now that doesn't inhibit in any way his understanding of himself in relation to the world, the universe, the universal man."

At first, this sudden jump from his mother to Mao disconcerts me. I am not prepared for how deeply politics is involved in every aspect of George's life and how his politics grows directly out of his personal problems. But I try to show him that I understand.

"The family relationship in our society is part of capitalism. The president of one of the companies where I worked was very much interested, when it came time to hiring a guy, in whether or not he was a family man. Now you know what that means. Is it necessary for him to work? In other words, does he have the guy right in his pocket? Because if he is a family man, that guy has to have his paycheck."

George laughs with understanding. "It's a sweatshop. That is the principle that allowed the sweatshop and the whole economy to function. When slavery was moved out and the country emerged from the agricultural thing and went into the industrial thing—I might be reading history wrong—it's my impression that the Industrial Revolution went down in the U.S. with the Civil War. The industrialists took over the political structure of the country. It's my impression that when child slavery was abolished by the industrial North, their reason wasn't any feeling of love. It was the economic motive that was important. They wanted to move the men in the United States into a different kind of slavery, the slavery of the sweatshop, where you don't own the guy outright, you just own the means of his existence and consequently through that you own him."

As George talks, he seems to gain strength from his argument. As he subsumes more and more into his theory, his physical force seems to grow proportionately. Listening to him, and watching his body tense and swell, I get a sense of how much his ideas have nourished him over the years, and at the same time I have a sense of how my own ideas have served only to muzzle and cripple me.

I add, "You know, they get people in this country to conform in such a filthy way, through their most generous impulses. Mothers and fathers interested in their kids mortgage their whole lives, work themselves to death, to give their children things they don't even need."

George replies, "That's so sad. As long as it is important to me to be successful, as long as success means money or control of money, it means I'll just step on anybody—my mama, my brother, anybody—to get hold of some money because I want to be a success. If I fail, if I fall short of success, then the whole world, the whole society, turns against me."

"You are a failure, even to yourself. You are a flop, man, against yourself. You have no right to exist any more."

"It is crushing for a cat like me."

"So many people are crushed in this society."

"I understand it, man, you see, because in all my experiences inside and outside the joint, I've understood that a man is judged by whether he bets at the two-dollar window or the fifty-dollar window—you dig?—and it is humiliating for a guy to walk up to two-dollar windows. So cats pretend, even though they may have nothing but fifty dollars in their pockets. That's sick. Somebody has got to do something about this shit. All the potential wasted. You know this country could feed the world. Stop the waste, clothe the world." He pauses and then changes the subject abruptly.

"Tell me about yourself. What sort of things have you been into?"

For a moment, I'm astonished and speechless, the question is so unexpected. I'm so unprepared to talk about myself in terms that I think George could understand. Even before I speak, I have a sinking feeling, as if I am about to lose all the intimacy we have reached together. What is there I can possibly say about myself which will retain his respect?

"Doing? Well, I was a typical victim of the slave mentality." Reaching for some concept that might impress him.

"Just give me a few sentences, run it down." He won't let me evade him.

"I was trying to make it the man's way, right?" He must know that I never really talk this way except when I am with blacks. "I was trying to get ahead. Make myself safe."

"Ah, that's the key word."

"And I thought if I pleased my employers—anyone who had more stature and power—they would take care of me. And that would make me happy. That was the syllogism. But it didn't work out that way. I just found myself getting more and more miserable. So I decided to start thinking for myself, right? But all this happened only after I left my wife. My marriage was part of my conformity. I got married because I thought I had to be married to be a real man and a responsible member of the community. But it just didn't work. I just got more and more messed up. So I left my wife. And it hurts, because I left two kids too. But since that time I've been able to start understanding."

After I finish, I feel relieved, as if I have passed a test, because

I have found the right words. But my hands are shaking because that isn't really what I wanted to say at all. Because everything I have said is so abstract and meaningless. What I really want to say is: "Oh, man, I am so lonely. Nothing has ever seemed to work out the way I've wanted it to. And I'm really glad you have accepted me as your friend, because I respect you so much. And I've really got to do some thinking about my life and find out what's wrong." But I can't say it, and I can't even bear to look at George.

"If I was alive, existing in the black community to the age I'm at right now," George says, "what kind of an individual do you think I'd be? With no time to think, you've got to hustle all the time, be aware. I'd be an animal, the worst type of animal, the human animal. The most predatory and vicious animal." He shakes his head and closes his eyes.

"Not now," I say. "You might have had a chance in the last few years."

"I wouldn't listen to people, that was one of my characteristics. I automatically doubted anything anyone might say. I might not have listened even if I had had somebody to teach me. I might not have listened."

"But that skepticism really saved you."

"Man, I turned against the world a long time ago, right from the beginning. Maybe if someone came from a different planet somewhere, I would listen to him."

"It is really hard when you turn against the world, that really is hard."

"I saw people in their weakness," George goes on. "I didn't see their strength. I couldn't discern, I didn't see the light."

"But you know what they weren't giving you. It's hard to see their strengths when all you see is the weakness they are giving you."

"The thing that my mother and father had going all their life, it seemed as if they were miserable all the time. And I'd never entertain the idea of doing a thing like that. And so the way I read it in my mind, the man-woman thing, is that if I can find a female guerrilla, that's beautiful. But if I can't find a woman who can accept Marx and accept Che Guevara's outlook, she certainly couldn't respect my life. Marx's mind and Che's achievement. If she couldn't accept those, we could never get along. A woman like my mama, who worried about the hairdo thing with me, I could never identify with a thing like that.

"But that's what knocked me out about Angela. She wasn't just hostile at first, she wasn't just hostile or defiant. She had a plan, a message. We've got plenty of aggressive, hostile women, but they have never actually isolated the enemy."

"How did you meet Angela?" Everything about their romance seemed so improbable.

"I read an article in a small black tabloid and I asked my mother to call her. But Angela didn't even return the call because it was just one of hundreds that she was getting, and most of them, you know, she didn't know the people. I guess they were what you call crank calls. You don't come out when you're a professor on the campus and say, 'I'm a Communist,' and not get crank calls and letters and every other thing, you know. She was just flooded with them. Just flooded."

George's chains rattle violently. I think I can guess what he is feeling: *Was I just a crank to her too? Does she think I am just a crank still? Is she just humoring me?*

"You know, I couldn't possibly accept any other black woman— you know, accept them as human beings—unless, of course, they were part of my goal."

We are silent for a few minutes, then George goes on. "My father was a child of the depression. I went to the neighborhood to investigate in 1958 and 1959. I talked to some of the people in the neighborhood and investigated the area. He would never talk about it. This is, the cat, I don't think I've seen him smile more than about five times in my whole life. I just got sick. And I felt sorry for him all along." And then, almost as an afterthought, to balance his pity he adds: "I just love him. I heard a lot of comments about his past from my mother, her side you know. I just got half-truths from my mother. So I went back to investigate his side when I was on the street in '58. His folks abandoned him during the depression. His father and mother hassled all the time. You can imagine what they hassled about. Finally, they just split up. The system was attacking both of them, but actually the brunt of the attack was felt by my father and his brothers. His mother finally abandoned him. From all indications, she just walked off and left him standing on a corner in East St. Louis. Lester and his brother ended up on a little farm."

"How old was he?"

"He's about forty-seven now. This happened in what?—the thirties. You know, he was just a kid of thirteen. Him and his younger brother ended up on a farm of one of their relatives. I think it was his niece or aunt, great-aunt I guess. They lived up on a farm in Lake Charles, Louisiana. They still aren't doing too well, but people in the countryside learn how to feed themselves off stuff like purslane and dandelions and stuff like that. Rabbits and —what are those things that look like rabbits?—possums. But anyway, something happened to him back then, something went desperately wrong with his head.

"He's a broken man now, but you see, I've always entertained the idea that this cat could change, you know? You could touch something in this guy, a responsive fiber in this guy's mind. You know what really gave me the indication that that was possible? At about forty years old, this brother went back to school to pass some kind of mathematics business course. But he did it and he did all that with the idea of improving himself. You know, just something for the immediate present. He wanted a job as a clerk in some drugstore. He had a job in a confection and drugstore. A friend of his offered him a new job if he would go back to school to learn something about mathematics. But the friend didn't come through with the job. They wouldn't give it to him. He wouldn't talk about it. He was always like that. He would never talk about his mother and stuff like that. I'd ask him a question, but he'd always find a way not to answer."

"My father was an orphan. Once I asked him why he never ate oatmeal. He said he still remembered it from the time when he was at the home. He just couldn't eat it ever again."

"I'll never eat another cookie in all the days of my life," George says. "That's all they ever serve here for dessert. Look, I wanted to understand this guy, you know? Certain things went on. I'd do certain things and they would invoke very violent and

hostile fear responses. I just couldn't understand. This cat terrified me."

"You terrified him."

"That's really the case," George says, surprised that I would
understand. "I was just a child. This cat would attack me when
I'd do certain things just like he would attack a stranger. But
then a couple of hours later he would do something that would
indicate that he dug me. So I'm saying all along that there is
something wrong with this guy. How come I can't get close to
him? I'd ask my mother. I'd come to my mother about the relationship me and the guy had when I was younger. It came to a
point where we just fell out on each other, started competing
against each other. I did something stupid. Stole his car a couple
of times, an old wreck, I stole it a couple of times. And I took
it out one time—I figured I'd drive my sister to a church. I was
supposed to go to church myself, but I just left them and split.
I came back about twelve o'clock the next morning, twelve-thirty,
one o'clock the next morning, and he was waiting in the door for
me, and he punched at me. And we were struggling just like two
strangers." The way he says it reminds me of Jekyll and Hyde.
Two halves of one self, struggling for supremacy.

"And I didn't understand too well, but I was trying. And he
didn't understand at all. You know, the thing about it is, right
in the beginning he learned that if he showed any type of affec-
tion, or if he showed any type of understanding, somebody was
going to step on him, walk on him, you know? The absence of
the smile. That's a defense mechanism. Not give anybody an
opening to use him, and I imagine he got used to plenty as a kid."
And George knew. He had been there himself. In one of his letters, he had vowed never to feel again.

"Lester loves Jonathan more than he loves himself," George
continues, "more than he loves anything, but Jonathan doesn't
know it. You see what I'm saying. Jonathan doesn't know it. My
father and I started being close when I passed twenty-three. When
I was in San Quentin, one of the bulls, one of the cats that wasn't
as sick as the rest of them, told him that he should try to show
interest in me, and he started visiting me about once a month. And

we started writing. But prior to that time, it was nothing but competition."

How bitter it must have been to know about the guard's part in his reconciliation with his father.

"How do you dig that?" George asks. "What do you think he was doing?"

"I really think he was scared of you, scared of you doing things he wanted to do himself." Thinking of my own father's fear that I would do something that would get him into trouble. That I might do something that would rub off on him.

"That occurred to me a thousand times, you know. It might have been mixed emotions. He was just mixed up. He felt that I failed him. He wanted to prepare me for stepping into the black bourgeoisie, and when I rejected that, he rejected me. But now an element of what you say was positively there also. I could read it in his conversations when he was in the visiting room, when there wasn't anybody else in the visiting room but him and me. No other members of the family, that is—just convicts. I would just sit and listen because I wanted to make him talk. I wouldn't say anything. The things that he was reaching for indicated that he has got something that he could change. I think this incident here is going to help change him."

At first I don't understand what incident George means, but then I realize that it is the murder charge.

"I think he's going to come out of it a lot different. I mean, it's going to be very educational for him. In five or six letters, he has already alluded to the constabulary here as pigs. That's a giant step right there."

George becomes very agitated, squirming in his chair, because it is so important to have his father understand. It is as if he is squeezing the emotion out of himself because it is too heavy to bear.

I add, "You know yourself that once the door opens, it never closes again."

"When I was growing up," George continues, "we were competing. He even wanted to direct my mind. And I knew beyond the shadow of a doubt that he didn't have the qualification to direct my life. I just knew it. So I rejected him and he rejected me." I could sense that his bluntness was his way of dealing with the pain of his memories. "Actually, I've always done what I wanted to do all my life. When it came consequence time, I'd just catch a fast freight out of town. He just didn't dig that stuff. He's a settled type guy. He just gave in right in front. He gave in, and he felt that was the right procedure, the best procedure for survival. I always disagreed with him. So anyway, he wanted to bend me to his way of thinking. But in a way, he might have been in agreement with some of the things I did. I know I recounted some of the incidents after they had happened. You know there would be a few years in between. I'd talk about them and I'd see the shadow of a smile. You know, at least there would be no bitterness.

"But one thing about it, all the way down the line, he has always been loyal. He has never abandoned me whenever I got into something. I don't care how long it's been. And mostly all the time I was wrong. I don't say I'm wrong for rejecting racism in America, but my procedure, my method, was wrong. I shouldn't have been robbing some supermarket. I should have been plotting on Howard Hughes and getting a million dollars. I was stupid, wrong, but I didn't have anybody to help me. I had no instructions. No guidelines. Nobody was laying down any kind of truth then. Not a chance. Those were the dark ages. Even my grandfather didn't offer any specific remedy. No remedy, no prescription. He was just like every one of us. Just like most of us. But I can understand my father. My father didn't want me to get killed. My grandfather was just the same. He didn't want me to get killed either."

"And your mother?"

"Yeah, well, we're talking about the men." George is faintly irritated that I have changed the subject. "But . . . well, my mother was the same way."

"If you read a lot of black literature, you can't help but be impressed by the tremendous amount of resentment against the black mother who holds the son back and presents a false image of the world that doesn't prepare him for the problems he has to face. A lot of speeches. 'Behave yourself.' But then, it's out in the world, naked as a lamb."

George takes up the theme. "The best of all possible worlds. That's a defense mechanism. The reason is that my mother didn't want to cry over my grave, cry over my grave. Meekness is a defense mechanism, an adaptation for survival. My whole purpose in all these years of writing letters to my family was the effect and the affect on them. And then, too, I always wanted to put certain things down on paper because it helped me to clarify things in my own mind. I really felt that maybe I could help my father to understand, to observe his environment and understand it. I felt that if I couldn't make this cat understand, how could I make twenty thousand cats who don't feel nothing for me as an individual understand? So I just kept on trying. We had terrible things. He just went all the way out on me one time. I mean, his mind just slipped on him. Thirty years just slipped away from him. He was talking to me as if it was thirty years ago and completely removed from where we were. He lost touch with reality altogether and started talking to me like I was someone else, like I was his brother Damon. Altogether, he stayed in it for fifteen minutes."

"That must have really scared you."

"Aw, man. I felt so sorry for that dude. He was sitting there talking at random, ranting about something, about experiences not in this day or time. When he snapped out of it, he said, 'I'm sorry, you looked so much like Damon.' I mean, they have driven that cat crazy."

"He's not alone, though. It is the experience of a whole generation."

"It's not just a matter of generation. It may be that there's not one normal black in this country. Not one of them has survived intact."

I have sensed this in many blacks that I have known. As I sit there with George, they pass in front of my eyes. What George says is like a sudden stab of pain, because I know he is including himself among the damaged men.

"Even in this case," he observes, referring to the accusation of murder against himself and the other two Soledad Brothers, "we can't get along with each other. The ego is coming in, man. I mean, just little things, you dig? You have to be so careful not to interpret the little things convicts say as a challenge. When it first strikes you, it seems like a challenge. I have been dealing with the black psyche all along. There is a thing that turns us inward. We are scared to direct our rage at the real enemy."

I think of the blacks I have seen in court when I served on juries. Huge men with deep resonant voices like drums who became almost totally inaudible when they testified, looking imploringly at their white lawyers for guidance.

"Now, look!" he exclaims, gesturing with his fingers. "When we are separated, somebody can get in between, like this." He holds his fingers apart. "You go out one at a time! But now, standing like this"—with his fingers close together—"nobody can get in between you. The guy is forced to respect you. He can't destroy you without some risk to himself. If it is understood, if you make it understood, that if the man attacks you it's going to be at some risk, then you get some effects. Something has got to happen. The problem is that we got to direct it. That's the whole problem. Outside there isn't anybody to direct it. They aren't teaching the lessons. There is a big lesson about war and the reasons for that war. The people have got to be told. We are at war everywhere and people have got to be told. We got to instruct them. Structure something. It's just like Mao. We got to get behind cats like that now. They said the Chinese could never be united, but look what happened. I think we got a cat like Mao in Huey Newton. He's the only one who comes to my mind when I think of Mao. People like that help to resolve the kind of thing that is happening between me and John Clutchette."

The mention of Clutchette's name reminds me that in just a few minutes I will be meeting John Clutchette and Fleeta Drumgo. I find myself hoping that perhaps it won't be possible for some reason or that someone will forget, because I feel so good with George now and I don't want it to end, I don't want any intrusions.

Suddenly John Thorne's voice breaks in to ask George if he notices something. George nods and John explains that we have the honor of being guarded by the captain himself. As I turn to look at the window, I see a man's face suddenly disappearing.

Listening to George I have begun to sense the unique quality of his political commitment. For myself and all my friends, despite moments of intense passion and rage, politics is still only a form of play, of theater. We put it on or take it off at will like a costume. But for George, politics is a matter of survival. It is like a heavy bandage of muscle over all his pain and disappointment. Everything—his blackness, his rejection by his parents, the destruction of his hopes—is transformed by his politics. And when something touches too close to the nerve, opening his wounds, he reaches out for it.

"It's not coincidental that cats like Martin Luther King—I'm giving Martin Luther credit and a lot of people don't give him credit. I think I see a little bit more to that brother than other people see. The appeals he made about poor people and the machine that is crushing us."

"He was starting to get with it."

"Not just starting, he might have been there all along. But he used a delicate approach so he wouldn't kill the people. He wanted to connect, shock, introduce some brand-new explosive Marxian ideas to guys, sharecroppers and provincials, but he went easy because he didn't want to get them killed because they would get mad, too mad right out in front, and they're not prepared for a fight. If—I'm not saying 'if'! . . . that guy was just like me. He was just using a different approach. That's the way I am going to write about him. As a Marxist using a different approach."

Suddenly the door of the room opens with a sharp noise. I jerk in my chair. I feel as if I am being awakened from a deep sleep because I have been so lost in what George is saying. The man who had been at the window just a few minutes before enters the room. John asks him about bringing in the other two Soledad Brothers. The man tells us that if we want to see them right away they will have to miss their lunches. When John persists, the man's eyes look us over with sneering disdain and he leaves the room.

George glares at his departing figure. "He's a desperate guy. Real vicious. But whenever they have somebody who is going to come into contact with free people, they won't let him use his tusks. Public relations, you dig? The guy in the visiting room. They always pick a guy with a straight face, you know. A small guy with a straight face or an older guy. They hide guys like you see out there in the hall"—the ones who were still standing at the window peering in at us—"Vicious! They hide those types, see. Public relations."

I feel that my time is running out and I want to find out more about the actual circumstances of George's life in prison.

"What is the physical layout of your cell?" The instant I hear the question coming from my mouth, I realize that it is just like dashing him down into a pit.

"Now, the cell is eight and a half by seven. We got a toilet right in there with us and a washbasin. That's what they call it. The bed runs across this wall." George begins to draw the layout of his cell on one of my pads.

"Yeah, tell me about this as you draw it."

"This isn't traced out right. This is the bed. Next to the bed you have a washbasin and toilet. And this is the area that I work out in."

"That's something you write about a lot. 'I've got work to do in the cell.' What does that mean? Are you referring to reading and writing?"

"Well, a cat after ten years and no sex, man—push-ups, that's why I'm in such good shape, you see. A thousand and one times on my fingertips."

John suggests that I feel George's arm so I can sense the results of all those push-ups. I am still shy, but George offers me his tensed arm and I take it in my hand and it is like a horse's haunch.

"I almost can't believe that," I say.

"Right, it takes me about forty minutes."

The door opens and there is a rustling and a sound like a xylophone. And it seems as if the room is suddenly filled with people. Two black men in handcuffs and shackles, one very tall and one of medium height, come forward very diffidently, greeting John and nodding at George. They start to smile. The closer they get to us, to our side of the room, the broader their smiles become. As I look at their faces, it is almost like seeing them walk from darkness into light.

It is only then, when they are in the room and sitting down in chairs beside us, that I begin to feel I am actually in a prison. They seem to bring with them part of "O" wing. It is as if they had an aura of confinement about them. Terrorized and muted, as if they had been locked away in darkness for weeks on end. They sit, almost motionless and apprehensive in their chairs with their hands clasped, just moving their eyes enough to check out the room and observe guards outside the window. John Thorne introduces us and tells them a bit about what I am doing.

I reach out to shake their hands, and, to my astonishment, Fleeta Drumgo takes my hand with a sudden and totally unexpected thrust of strength and maneuvers my fingers into a Black Power handshake. When I realize what he is doing, I respond and we stand there, hands clasped together. I have a sense of literally exchanging power with him, of being absorbed completely into their fraternity.

John Thorne and George go off to one side to discuss an affidavit,* and I am left with the other two brothers. John and Fleeta look at me, waiting for me to speak. I have nothing to say, I feel abandoned by George and John. Finally I ask them what is happening.

"Where do you mean?" John Clutchette replies.

"I mean, you live in this hotel. What's happening?" I hear my words and I can't believe myself. I can't have said them and yet I did.

They turn their heads slightly toward each other to establish that they have both heard me correctly. Then they begin to describe their lives. They know I want to hear about the atrocities they have suffered. I suppose that all their visitors are the same.

John Clutchette begins to tell me about life on "O" wing, about how one man had been tear-gassed to death in his cell, even though later the authorities claimed he had died of a heart attack. Most of the day they are locked in their cells. Whites on the way to and from the exercise yard throw excrement—urine and shit— into their cells. Fleeta has strung a blanket across the front of his cell to protect himself from their bombardments. From the way he is blinking, I have a sense of him living in darkness—in a sort of cryptlike dungeon, a small room in total darkness with spiders crawling everywhere.

* This was made public after George's murder. In it, Allan Mancino, a white convict who was in prison with George, described how the captain of the prison had attempted to persuade him to kill George.

The white convicts—the tier tenders—mix ground glass and soap powder in the food they serve them. Sometimes they put excrement into the food.

The only jarring note is John Clutchette's fingernails. I can't take my eyes off them, yet I don't want him to see me looking at them. They are almost an inch and a half long, like the fingernails of a Chinese courtesan.

While we talk about what is being done to them (George tells me later that 'They never pulled any of that shit on me'), George is telling John Thorne about his plan to get the white cons on "O" wing to join with him in an action against the prison. This is just what his prison record had suggested he would do: "A dangerous freewheeling convict leader who was trying to organize convicts to challenge the administration itself for control of the prison." Listening to him, I see him in my mind's eye trucking along, wary, belligerent, rising up on his toes like a boxer about to deliver the final crushing fusillade of blows—arms, shoulders, legs quivering, straining for battle.

After John finishes going over George's plan, they pull their chairs back near us. John Thorne asks John Clutchette and Fleeta if they want some coffee. Then he goes to the door and raps on it. After a while, a guard comes. I can't hear their conversation, but the coffee never arrives. I realize that John thinks he can control the whole prison with his hearty cheerfulness. It is such a nice, thoughtful thing to try to do that none of us can bring ourselves to note its failure. As we talk, all three men move and the sound of their chains is loud in the room. Although the sound must have been almost continuous, I become aware of it only during the pauses in our conversation.

By now we have been together for almost four and a half hours, and a heavy silence comes over us. Even though the sun is still shining outside, it feels suddenly dark in that room. When a guard enters to tell us that our time is up, I think we are all ready to say good-bye. I don't want George to leave, but I don't have the strength to stay with him any longer. And suddenly, before I even realize it, they are gone, and John Thorne and I are alone in the room.

Men in shackles and chains seem so humble, bowed over by

their constricted limbs. They just disappear out the door where the swarming guards have been watching us through the window. Suddenly the window is empty too. All the guards have left to surround the three men. We remain in the captain's office with an acute sense of solitude, waiting for an escort to take us through the other door, that leads past the surreal grass and plastic flowers to the parking lot outside.

John's office is empty when we return there. He gives me the grand jury testimony on the murder of the guard to read while he goes off to shower. For a while it seems as if I am still back in the prison. I have a lingering sense of George's presence nearby, and I find myself smiling there in that dimly lit room because I have found a friend. I want to sit there and daydream about him, but I have to force myself to read the grand jury minutes because it may be the only chance I will ever have.

Thomas York, inmate of Soledad Central Correctional Training Facility:

On Jan. 16th 1970, I was an inmate at Soledad Training Facility. At around 6:30 I was in my cell sitting, laying on the bunk; and after about, I'd say, fifteen or maybe twenty minutes after having laid there the guy next door to me came up to my cell door and knocked on the door and he started talking. So after about ten minutes of talking, while standing with my door still closed, I got up and opened my door and he placed one leg between the door and we started talking. I got up and I was sitting at the time. He suddenly stopped in his conversation after we had been there for about fifteen or twenty minutes talking, and he said that, "They've got the guy," something to that effect. And when he said this I thought that he was probably just referring to some of the other inmates fooling around on the tier, what have you. But he repeated the same thing and I saw the expression his face and I knew he was serious then. So I got up and I looked out, I looked out the door, and saw what was taking place. And I immediately said to him, "You better make it, I'm going to lock down." So he left and I locked my door and I saw what was taking place.

The first thing that I noticed was that an officer was being held in deadlock. And I saw an inmate hitting the officer in the face while he was being held in this position. This punching went on for—oh—two, three minutes. Then, this gentleman disappeared, the one that was doing the punching, and the guy that had him held in this deadlock continued to apply pressure around the neck area. And there was another man standing by. And he continued to strangle him, I would say, until I could see the body going limp. The names of the men who were involved were Jackson, Clutchette, and Drumgo.

After the man Jackson, that had him in the deadlock, I could see the officer's body trembling and finally it seemed like it just went limp, he—this subsided. Clutchette stepped up behind both of them. At this time my view was blocked, I couldn't see the officer. I could only see the lower part of his leg, so to speak. And I don't know what he told Jackson or if he told him anything, but finally Jackson released the officer and he fell backwards. Jackson disappeared to what would be my side of the tier, on the west side. And Clutchette went into his cell. Jackson then came back out of his cell, or wherever he was at, and started judo chopping the officer in the throat. And after he battered him for a while he then went into Clutchette's cell. And he returned and pulled the officer's flashlight from his waist— After he beated him for a while, he went back into Clutchette's cell. Clutchette then came out and picked up the flashlight. Jackson then returned and lifted up and slid him over the tier, the third tier. I seen him falling, he hit the—the rail of the second tier and tumbled over; from then I couldn't see anything else.

Larry Thomas Eskew, inmate of Soledad Central Correctional Training Facility:

On January 16, 1970 I was standing outside my cell talking to my neighbor at around 6:30 in the afternoon and I heard a strangled yell and I turned around and looked towards the corridor end and I seen the officer being assaulted. He was being held by one inmate and he was being attacked by two others. One inmate was hitting him in the face; then he stepped back and another inmate he run over and started hitting Officer Mills in the face. The names of the three inmates were Fleeta Drumgo, John Clutchette and George Jackson. After I saw what was happening, I told my neighbor, "I'm going to my cell."

And so I went in my cell and I got a hobby box I had and I took out a small X-acto knife, and I went back to the door and as I went back to the door, opened the door open, and then I seen Officer Mills was on the floor then. And Jackson was down on his knees, he had Officer Mills' flashlight and he was hitting him in the face with it. Jackson laid the flashlight down beside the Officer Mills and he got up and he walked to cell 302. This is where Clutchette lives. And he went in the cell and then Clutchette came out after this, you know, just momentarily or just a minute or two after. He came out and he went to the body of Officer Mills and he picked up the flashlight with the towel that he had brought with him. Then he walked back to his cell, took the flashlight in the cell with him. At this time I thought Officer Mills was already dead. And there was some activity somewhere on the tier and I turned my light out, so I stepped back away from the door so, you know, anybody coming by wouldn't see me at the door. Then I stepped back to the door and Jackson came out of Clutchette's cell, 302, and he went to the end of the tier and at that time the door opened again at Clutchette's cell and Clutchette leaned out with his towel and he was wiping something on the front of his door, you know. And so I was watching Clutchette and then somebody came by, I heard them come up on the stair on my side and start to come by, so I stepped back again and a guy walked by. Then when I stepped back Clutchette was just going back in his door. He was kind of leaning around his door like this, you know, and he just leaned back inside and shut the door. And then I looked down at the end of the tier and the officer was gone and Jackson was just standing there.

Q: What do you mean the officer was gone?
A: Well, Officer Mills was laying on the floor and later on, when I looked back, you know, in that period there when I looked back, the officer was gone.

Thomas Worsella, inmate of Soledad Central Correctional Training Facility:

Well, when I came out of my cell, like I say, I looked over to the right hand side first went to my right, and there was some glass down there already, it was broken, and there was nothing going on. And when I looked to my left this Clutchette and Jackson were standing over this—I still call it the body; I did not know who it was; I'll just say it was a white person, all I could see at that time was an arm sticking up. About, well—if he was lying flat on the ground his elbow would have been up like this. They were both standing over this body. And when I just looked up they immediately started walking to Clutchette's cell, which was 302, I believe, and Clutchette opened it and Jackson handed him a rag—I don't know if there was anything on it or any blood or anything; I didn't see anything—but it was a towel, he handed it to him and Clutchette went into his cell. Then Jackson walked back over to the body, whoever it was—I didn't know at this time—and I don't know if he picked up the flashlight but it looked like the flashlight to me, or he had it in his hand at the time, but he lifted the head, seemed like he lifted it just like a baby. Then I seen him come down—I watched him three times come down with blows which would have been right in the head or in the facial area somewhere. And after this I seen other inmates running to their cell and I just turned around—I didn't know what to do. I looked on the tier and there was a colored inmate passing me at that time and he had a rag wrapped around his hand and I thought that he might have a knife and I backed up towards the tier and he passed me and some people started running to their cells and I just opened my door and locked up in the cell. And then I came back to my window and looked back up there and Clutchette, the one who was in the cell, came out of his cell and he was wiping his door off with another towel, wiping the wall around his cell area off. And then he went back in his cell. Then I went and laid on my bed and that's all I seen. I heard the sound of the body coming over the third tier but I did not see it.

The next thing I know, John Thorne is standing beside me dressed in a floral dinner jacket with a ruffled shirt and love beads hanging round his neck. Still stunned by the testimony, I go into his bathroom and wash my face. Then we drive over to the house of the tax lawyer, Harry M., who has set up a Bahamian corporation that is going to receive all the funds from George's book. On the way over, John tells me how successful this man is—his clients include some of the most famous movie stars in Hollywood. He is so powerful and brilliant that they actually travel from all over the world to San Jose to see him. Perhaps that is why we sit in the driveway of his house waiting for him to emerge instead of going right up to the door and ringing the bell. While we are still outside waiting, John's girlfriend arrives in her car and we wait together.

When Harry and his wife finally come out, we transfer to his limousine. On the way to the restaurant, John and Harry talk about a will that is just being probated and how to make sure that John gets a suitable fee. But all I really remember is that they talk a lot about how to make money.

We go to a restaurant called the Peking Duck, where they know Harry well. He has ordered ahead. We drink a great deal of champagne, which is opened ostentatiously. Then we nibble on crisp slices of specially prepared duck which we dip into six different sauces. At some point during the meal, Harry asks me if I think George could have really written the letters. He is skeptical. For a long time I just stare out into space. I can't say what I really think about someone who would ask such a question because Harry's tax expertise is supposed to be important to the defense. So I simply reassure him that there can be no doubt whatsoever about the authorship of the letters. Still, he shakes his head and continues to mutter his doubts. I get very drunk. On the way back, I fall asleep with my head on John's girlfriend's lap, and she lovingly strokes my hair. And it is as if I am a child again in my mother's arms.

Soledad Prison
The Second Day
June 19, 1970

"I've been the victim of so many racist attacks that I could never relax again. . . . I can still smile now, after ten years of blocking knife thrusts, and the pick handles of faceless sadistic pigs, of anticipating and reacting for ten years, seven of them in solitary. I can still smile sometimes, but by the time this thing is over I may not be a nice person. And I just lit my seventy-seventh cigarette of this twenty-one-hour day. I'm going to lay down for two or three hours, perhaps I'll sleep. . . ."

—Soledad Brother

The next morning, I get up early and drive down to the prison alone. It is as if I were going there for the first time, past the hills that run parallel to the highway and the plum orchards and vineyards and artichoke fields. They are all new to me because I am seeing them without John's face beside me and without the sound of his voice in my ears. The day before, although the sun had been shining, it had been as if everything were covered with a dense impenetrable fog. Now I see everything with almost microscopic clarity.

As I near the prison, I am reminded of the beach. Perhaps it is the vast expanse of sky and the sandy soil. Although, actually, it is not so much the beach that I am reminded of as the flooding night seas of tidal waves and drownings that I inhabit in my dreams. And going down to the prison is like a dream because it is so unexpected and unprepared for. I have a sense of being unable to find my bearings. Driving the car, I feel as if I were being swept forward by a wave. It is a little bit as if I had slipped into my unconscious. And my sense of George is as of one of the characters in my dreams, one of my representations of myself. Because I think that is one of the things we do in dreams: we put ourselves inside other people so we can understand them, feel their lives as they feel them. I feel as if I have dreamed of George all night long, and as though I am still dreaming.

The road seems so different that I am sure I have lost my way. I am doing everything I should do—willing myself to find the way in spite of an impulse to get lost so that I won't have to go inside the prison again. I turn off the road at just the right point and swing in through the main gate past the bronze plaque with the prison's official name. Now I realize that there are three separate parking lots instead of just one. I am reminded for some reason of the times I used to go with my family to see the deer at a special park. As I walk from my car to the visiting room, I realize how much more real everything seems today. The macadam under my feet with the tiny stones embedded in the tar. The cars with the sun reflected from their polished metal surfaces. Yesterday the visiting room had seemed completely distinct from the rest of the prison. Now I see that the entrance is actually almost hidden away in one of the walls.

The same desk sergeant is there, but we pretend not to recognize each other and there is a definite coldness between us.

This time it seems like it takes forever for me to be admitted. I wait and I wait and finally a young guard comes through a side door and asks me if I am the investigator who is going to see Jackson. After I identify myself he takes me with unexpected courtesy and deference through the electrically operated doors into the prison. Convicts are everywhere, swarming in the halls. Even though none of them even so much as moves a head, I can feel their eyes turning toward me as I pass.

Instead of going to the captain's office, I am led up a flight of glistening waxed stairs to a small room which is totally bare except for an old school desk and two straight-back wooden chairs. The guard holds the door for me to enter. "It will still be a while before they can bring Jackson down because he has got to come from quite a distance." Then he leaves, locking the door behind him. I try to imagine that I am alone in my cell, and I am lost in thought when the door opens and George enters.

To the guard's astonishment and to mine, George opens his arms to me and we embrace, and I can feel my face glowing with deep pleasure. "I'm really glad you got here, man. I was afraid you wouldn't make it," George says. Still smiling, I empty my pockets on the desk of the candy and cigarettes I have brought with me. We move the chairs around so we can face each other. I can sense our anticipation of each other.

George is wearing a blue sweatshirt and a pair of dungarees. Immediately he notices my awareness of his clothes. "They are really getting vicious around here. Look at the way they made me dress."

I don't understand because I am not aware that prisoners have any choice about how they dress and, in any case, I don't see how someone like George could possibly care.

For a few seconds we look at each other and shake our heads, the way men do when they have accomplished something extraordinary, and when they are searching for words to open up their feelings. We both know that something happened between us the day before, an improbable and almost indescribable intimacy. And our initial silence is a mutual attempt to recollect and revive that friendship. We are both concerned that it might have disappeared or that perhaps it never really existed at all. Or, even worse, that it might have been one-sided. Each of us is afraid of rejection by the other. With John in the room, there could be no possibility of George and me really confronting each other, but now we are almost excruciatingly aware of our isolation together. A single guard stands at the window, and sometimes even he disappears.

"Well, after I left you yesterday, they tried to send me through the Adult Authority Board formality.* At first, I didn't really understand. I didn't remember. Nobody reminded me that I was going before them. About three months ago, they sent me papers like they do. This is the formality. They send you papers to fill

* Parole Board hearing.

out, to explain your stand and describe what progress you've made. Well, I didn't fill out the papers because I was right in the middle of this case. So they took me completely by surprise. They separated me from the other two Brothers and brought me up here and put me into the gatehouse. I still didn't remember or understand what was happening. I thought it was some kind of ambush." He laughs, and his laughter is like an epitaph. "And I asked the guy, I said, what was I doing there? And he told me it was my annual Board appearance. You know, this is the tenth one."

I shake my head and close my eyes in recognition of what he must have felt and then look up at him.

"This is once every year?"

"It certainly is. So I told him that I didn't care to have anything to say to the Board. I sent them a four-letter word. I know he didn't deliver it to them. Let's see, cigarettes? You know they don't let us have cigarettes down there.

"This is beautiful. I'm tearing off the filters because I like them small. I'm not scared of cancer at all. I was born with one."

"Yeah." There is nothing else for me to say.

"So the Board sent me a message: 'We'll see you next year.' "

"They aren't going to see you next year."

"They sure won't. I think I'm gonna walk out of the courtroom. You take my original case. Inadequate counsel, which definitely was the truth. But even if I don't beat them, I'm not going to see them. I'm not going to see them any more." I realize that he is telling me that, one way or another, his life has reached its end. "There is no way back. You got to crawl in on your knees."

The guard who escorted me into the prison opens the door. For one awful moment I think he has come to take George away. Instead, he asks if we want anything, and when we demur he leaves the room again.

George notices another face at the window. "That one guy"— gesturing with a flip of his chin—"he's just started working here. He's black. There, you can see him now. He still feels a little guilty, but in a few months he'll want to get out. Not very many of them come in that way. But in a couple of months he'll be corrupt. The convicts will help corrupt him. If he doesn't get corrupt, they'll make life so difficult for him that he'll have to leave, right? Well, see, the convicts are corrupting—right?—and the police are corrupting, you see, because they're constantly bombarding him with anti-convict, anti-inmate talk. Like: 'Every guy you see, he'll stab you in the back, steal your wallet, lie to you.' The bad experiences he is bound to have with some convicts are going to confirm everything that the cops say. In a couple of months, he'll be a dog just like all the rest of them. He'll have a defensive attitude. Can you imagine? They're the cats with the guns, the fences, barbed wire and the wall. And they've got the defensive attitude."

We both start adjusting ourselves in our chairs for the long talk ahead. "I'm glad that they put us up here, because I really feel like I am in prison. When I came up those stairs and the doors closed behind me, I really got that feeling, you know. My head began to slump. I really had a sense of being caged."

"I'm trying to count how many doors I passed through here." George takes up my lead. "Let's see, there's one from my cell, there's two before I get out of the cell block, three, four, five, five by the time I get to the hall, all of them double safety. You know how concrete and steel can hurt. It has no life, no intelligence." And he drops his chin and shoulders as if to pantomime the cruelty of inanimate matter. "You can't say the same thing for the guards. I don't know why guys let these people hold them. You know what it is? I'll tell you. It's not just the police. It's not just the concrete and steel, because you can overcome something like that. But it's the fact that the police can call in the National Guard, the highway patrol, to control any mass action. Every hand is turned against you, every person you see on the street is turned against you.

"Now there's guys here, I'm speaking about guys who have no recourse. If by chance they should spring, get away, break out. I mean, guys have done it. I mean, some of the guys have done it, left here, and some of them have led what you could call normal lives, even in spite of the bombardment from all sides and with the occasion or the opportunity to get in trouble, but have led what you bourgeois people call normal lives." He lowers his chin slightly and looks up at me. "But they get busted on a traffic ticket and, you know, their records catch up with them. Then there are guys with intentions of (they don't think too far ahead) just living, going back home. You'd be surprised, about ninety percent of the guys who escape from places like this go home. When they go home, the police are waiting right there for them. Or when they get home, their mothers turn them in, or their wives, and so forth." George shakes his head ruefully. "It's not just the law, the pig, it's the propaganda, the anti-education, the un-education. It's the total environment of the society. You know, the whole society has turned on him, that's the crucial point. And of course, that sets up reactions. You know, 'It's me against the world.' You hear that a million times. 'It's me against the world.' 'Fuck the world!' They tattoo it right on their arms, I saw one guy with it tattooed across his forehead."

"What? 'Me against the world'?"

"No, 'Fuck the world.' "

"He had 'Fuck the world' tattooed on his forehead?"

"You think I'm lying." George throws the words out like a challenge.

"No, I don't think you're lying."

"I'm telling the truth. Guys like that know that the world's abandoned them. They know that society has been neglecting them. They know that they're victims of something, some kind of wrong. But they haven't isolated what it is, or why. Give them enough time and they'll understand. Here is the whole thing: cats come in, and they'll do two and a half, three years, and they'll get out on the street and do two and a half to three months. Then they'll go right back to the joint doing another three years. Back in the joint they try to adjust to the fact that they lost something. They are confused and they try to entertain themselves with the fantasy of trying to escape. What they really escape is the necessity of having to do some thinking. I'm talking about the dudes with cowboy boots. They ain't never really had time to figure out what's happening. See, on the street they're just trying to outrun the parole officer. The parole officer has absolute power over their lives.

"If you are out on the street selling the Black Panther newspaper, the parole officer can just bust you. He will say that you have failed to maintain the right contacts. You failed to maintain employment. You failed because you were associating with undesirables. He won't say who they were or what you were doing. He won't put the political character into the write-up. But he'll send you back to jail."

Abruptly, he turns in his chair to face me, and looks me straight in the eye as if to say, "Who are you?" and "What are you about?"

"Do you understand that you can't have a peaceful revolution?"

It is like a Christian asking if I believe in God. I realize that for George it is really a way of finding out whether I am worth talking to seriously or not. I have been grappling with this question a long time myself. Intellectually I realize that the people who own the major part of this country are not going to relinquish their power peacefully. But the question is really whether I am personally willing to fight in a revolution. Whether I am willing to give up my own power and privilege and risk death for an ideal of social justice. And I answer more out of a desire to believe than out of an absolute conviction.

"Sure, I understand that."

George weighs my answer and then goes on.

"It's impossible to deal with a guy whose whole mentality is built around a gun. To him, that's the sex symbol. You dig, that is the thing that makes him a man. Physical brute-force power. The ability to squeeze off a .45 caliber and kill a guy, bust a guy's breastbone, you dig? Certain people are attracted to the gun-slinging jobs, and you can't reason with those people. You have to make them fear. You have to control them, grip them by the throat."

I hear these words and my body jumps. Involuntarily I remember the words from the grand jury testimony I had read the day before: "Jackson . . . had him in the deadlock, I could see the officer's body trembling and finally it seemed like it just went limp." I look up at George guiltily as if he might have heard my thoughts.

"There are a thousand different ways of using power. Now I am not suggesting that an untrained guy come up against a pig who has seven hundred hours of practice. I *am* suggesting that a small cadre of guys with the nervous equipment to handle weapons should be kept in the background, kept on a leash, and at the right moment, at the right time they should strike."

As George talks, his head is slightly cocked and the meaning of his words colors his whole expression. He rocks slightly back and forth in his chair. I have the sense of a cyclone gathering force before it lashes out. I am beginning to become a little bit uneasy. He is looking at me almost as if he didn't know who I was. I imagine with a tremor that he is replaying the scene of the murder in his head.

"And each strike should be spectacular for success. That way they will have to strike less often. You dig what I'm saying? When there is a guy who is leading the reactionary forces in a way that is real powerful and brutal and detrimental to the people's movement, then we should call on a guy who can handle this. Listen, there is only one kind of guy who is able to handle people like J. Edgar Hoover. He has a self-righteous attitude that you couldn't even dent in the next hundred years. He is not listening to you because he has figured he has answered all your questions already. You are talking and he is not listening. He is searching the rulebook, which removes the necessity for him or any FBI people to do any real thinking."

"Right, or to be human." I am becoming very much aware of how little space there is between us. I am looking at him, but I do not feel really with him. It is as if he were alone in the room, and I were looking at him through a window. I have this sense because I realize that he is not talking to me any more but just listening to himself.

"Right, or to be human. There is not but one way to reason with a cat like that! Whack! Get him where it hurts." George rises up in his chair.

With those words I flinch again. I am scared. George could kill me and I would have no defense whatsoever. I feel the enormous rage in him that seems to sweep away all reason. What if he decides I am not really a friend? We are all alone in that small room and the guard appears at the window only sporadically. He could never get to him in time to save me. George's fantasy of killing is so powerfully alive in that room that I feel all the normal restraints of human behavior have disappeared. A charge of suppressed rage surges and quivers in every word. It is like the karate practice that George does in his cell. Manacled hands cut sharply through the air. His voice seems like a noose tightening around the neck of a victim.

"Take his gun away from him," George continues. "Now that is just the first step, of course. A concomitant step is the destruction of the cat that made the gun. The people who make it necessary for pigs to patrol the marketplace. You have heard them talk about the thin blue line. You have to deal with that. Then you can get to the guy who built the thin blue line. We have to maintain some type of violence. I am against property rights. Our assault is going to be against property. Men will get hurt, like in all wars, you see, because someone will be there to protect the property. Men will get hurt, but essentially our war is going to be a war against property."

As George goes on, I get the feeling that he has removed himself completely from individuals. I feel obliterated by his words. It is as if he were driving me away, wiping me out. How could my life have any significance for him? Anger wells up in me, but I squash it down. I want to lash out at him and obliterate him, the same way he is obliterating me.

As we talk, heavy black clouds pass back and forth in front of the sun and the room becomes dark and then lightens.

"The point is this. Are we going to let those cats build a situation where the whole world is going to have to die? It is better to get rid of a handful of guys over here than let the whole world die. See, the military establishment in this country sits around and talks about wiping out 800 million Chinese. Now why should I have any qualms about killing guys like that? Madmen."

"You should have some qualms about that." I feel I have to say something. "No matter who, you are killing a human being. Take that responsibility on yourself when you shoot the gun. Because otherwise you dehumanize yourself in the act of killing, dig it?"

"I have thought about that a lot. Yeah, if I am going to kill someone, it is going to hurt me to kill him. I am going to kill him, but it is going to hurt me because he is a man. And do you know what is going to hurt the most? Killing a guy who is guarding something. Like a person who is guarding a railroad or something. You see, he thinks he is defending an ideal or something. It is going to be hard to kill him."

"Killing always has to be hard."

"That is why it is good to start at the top. It is good to have a small cadre to take out the big pimps and hoodlums. The guys who put grease behind their guns, like the Hunts, Hughes, Morgans, Rockefellers."

"Once people see that it is possible," I add, "once revolution becomes a reality instead of a dream, once they see a revolution as successful action, there is going to be a big change."

"That is a beautiful point."

"That is why the people who make it are so important. The people are going to learn from the humanity of revolutionaries."

"That is what I meant a while ago when I said about the small cadre. I am talking about the small cadre within the vanguard. Each one of their violent actions should be spectacular for success. If they fail, this is going to create an impression that revolution can't succeed. And that you can't be violent against superman."

I realize that we are talking on two different planes, but I don't know any way to bring them together.

"See," he goes on, "that is the first point about guerrilla warfare. I have an advantage over the cop out there. You see, there are thousands of us walking around. It's this guy's job to guard. We have an advantage over the establishment guy who has a uniform on. You can even put him in a suit and I can still distinguish him. Okay, he is standing there guarding, and that makes a target out of him. That puts the finger on him. Thousands of us go by. We are all supposedly ordinary citizens, but I am not ordinary, see, because I have something under my coat too, but I got it well concealed. I don't have it in the front where he can see it. He is watching, but he doesn't know me. I know him. Now I got an advantage on him, a terrible advantage. And the moment he turns his head, I have got him."

I think back again to the grand jury testimony. *"The guy that had him held in this deadlock continued to apply pressure around the neck area. And there was another man standing by. And he continued to strangle him, I would say, until I could see the body going limp."*

"That is what you are talking about when you say there are too many of you?"

"Sure, man. He has got a gun there, but there are fifty of us. He doesn't know which one of the fifty is after his ass." The idea delights him, and he grins from ear to ear. "In other words, he can't watch all fifty of us, and when he turns his head, I've got him. Since we have been trying to get rid of capitalism, the approach we have used is that killing is evil, immoral. But I know I can't talk to that guy and make him put his gun down. With that kind of historical amnesia you lose. You can't talk to the guy because he is not listening. Reasoning doesn't make any sense to him. Reasoning has never been a strong point of that particular stratum of society. They get no education, no refinement whatsoever. Things you be saying maybe go over his head. His whole life is wrapped around that gun, see, and when those guys meet at headquarters, that's their main topic of conversation: 'Don't listen to those people, those crazy guys, freaks, traitors, bums.' Those guys are really robots. They become automatons. That is what they really are. They come on teletype. There is one way to handle them, only one way to handle them—force.

"I figure this is how Mao sees it, a long protracted thing. But the longer we wait to get started, the longer it will take. I figure that these last few rights that they have allowed us, they might pull out from under us, they might just roll them out from under us, overnight, tomorrow. I'm prepared to go out and support long aims for political action, but with an additive, with one little additive—force, a little force. And I subscribe to this additive because I know the only way to start things is to help them get started right now. You see, long-range politics itself won't help the guy who is dying right now. It won't help the person who is going to die tonight or die tomorrow. It won't help the cats who are dying all the time." It certainly won't help George.

"That is what you said in one of your letters. I mean, living long, who cares? You have got to live well. You have got to live now. You only begin living by beginning to understand and beginning to act on your understanding. That is the only way to live. Until you reach that point, man, you are dying."

Of all the things I had read in George's letters, this had meant the most to me, the importance of not putting off living. And yet it has such different meanings for the two of us. I think of it in terms of throwing off my restraints and fulfilling myself. George sees it as a matter of life and death. As a black, if he throws off his restraints, he always has to be prepared for a battle to the death.

"You know," I said, "one thing I have always wondered about is why there have never been direct reprisals for so many things that have gone down. The killings at Jackson State, the murder of Fred Hampton. I mean, why haven't those people been dealt with before?" I know I am treading on dangerous ground because this is just what George was accused of doing.

"Nice people don't like to cut throats. The kids at Kent don't. The Panthers are human and they feel for their people. They're not in these things because they hate. They see things happening to the people they identify with. The trouble is they feel for people. They are righteous people and righteous people just do not like to cut throats." As he goes on I begin to feel ashamed of myself for even thinking for an instant that he might be a killer. "That is why we haven't had any throat cuttings. It just doesn't occur to righteous people. Just like us, we were just moralizing about killing. To deprive a man of his life is to take away his most valuable possession. It is a terrible thing, but you have to weigh it against the big picture."

I am completely worn out. The killing and all the talk about killing has become an obsession to me and I just want to scourge it out of my brain.

"Is this what you have been writing about to Angela? This revolutionary manifesto?" I ask.

"No, I have been writing her a lot of personal stuff. I get carried away. There are some references in it."

"You're neglecting the job."

"No, no, no. Never. I've asked her to edit those letters, taking out the personal stuff. I haven't written that much pertinent to this thing. Some of it I was holding back until we have erected some channels of communication. But now that people are going to cooperate, I have started on a monumental project in my cell. You can't just rush things. I am preparing my statements very carefully."

"You have time!" And almost instantly understanding their implication, I regret my words.

"Have you met my brother?"

"No, I haven't met Jon. I think I will meet him tomorrow."

"Don't ask him about his age."

"If he won't ask me about my age, I won't ask him about his."

"He is only a youngster. Don't ask him. He is seventeen this month. He is sensitive about being sixteen, because he feels he is a lot older."

When George starts talking about his brother, I hear a certain tenderness and concern in his voice for the first time since we entered the room. I feel my heart melting and I feel myself together with George again. I would like to put my arm around his shoulder because I am so relieved to be with him again.

"He has some of the regular problems that kids have, but he's beautiful. He is not lazy. He hasn't trapped himself. He has avoided that bourgeois thing, cars and clothes and stuff like that. He likes girls, but the only type he likes are ones who can match his enthusiasm for this thing."

"I hope he is successful in finding them," I said, "because they are not all that prominent."

"That's why I'm so taken aback by Angela Davis."

"Women have to be in the same place you are, or at least pretty close. They have to be ready to move and not hold you back."

George goes on: "She has got to be willing to watch all day and work all night. She has got to rob with me, steal with me, cut throats with me and everything that is necessary. And I definitely, definitely don't want to have to explain myself to anyone else. I don't want a woman to be overly protective. Never. That is a sore point with me. Will you have a chance ever to talk with Angela?"

I explain that I will be seeing her on Sunday at a fund-raising party.

"I wish you would convey to her that a long time ago I castigated black women in general because I was getting a lot of resistance and static from my mom and sister. And I was looking at all the rest of the black women I had ever known, all the black women I had been reading about. The only thing they can say, man, didn't make sense. They was just hollering 'Honky.' Now what sense does that make? They aren't isolating the enemy. No brains. No guts. So consequently I formed the conclusion that black women born in the United States are too corrupt for me."

"Could you tell me about life in prison?" I ask. George throws back his head and opens his mouth. Then the words just pour out.

"My first trip to San Quentin was in 1961. They locked me up immediately. I had to go before a committee before they let me out on the main line* because I'd had trouble in Tracy. I started off in Soledad, but I'd gotten into an altercation with the police there too. Tension had been building up inside the joint. The white guys were supposed to come after us and kill us. They dared us: 'Nigger, come out on the tier, we're going to kill you,' and stuff like that. So a group of us came out. The police, in an effort to protect the white inmates—and they did this all the time—would stop the blacks and search them. You understand the significance of that. If I had a weapon and I got caught, I would get a new case, a new beef, something to hold me in the joint longer. If a white guy was walking right behind me, he might have a knife which he intended to stick in my back, but he was not searched. When it came time for the final confrontation, I wouldn't have a knife. That was the situation. We were completely resentful about it. Instead of trying to control the tension, the guys who were running the joint tried to build it up. Our violence was entirely defensive. All the time we would hear ultimatums like 'Blacks can't come out. Niggers not allowed in the yard today.' So I came out one day with a small group of the brothers. We didn't have any weapons. We stashed them away where we could get to them if we needed them. But you could see the disadvantage. One guy came under attack. He got stabbed right under the heart and he almost died. We rushed him to the hospital and put a pressure bandage on him. We had to know about things like that. We had to provide ourselves with a

* General prison population.

course like you'd get in Korea for battlefield medicine. I've studied the army manuals. And because of that, I've saved guys' lives after they've gotten holes put in them or been burned by something like a Molotov cocktail. Now we put a pressure bandage on that guy and rushed him to the hospital.

"I got shipped away on that incident, to Tracy. The minute I got there they locked me up in the Adjustment Center.* It was at Tracy where the incident went down behind the TV. When I finally got out of the isolation, they put me in a wing with a lot of young punks. I guess I was classified as a young punk. Guys who used to do things for thrills and so forth. But I never did anything like that. There was a method to my madness all the way along. This wing was hostile and racist in atmosphere, extremely volatile. Everything ended up in a fight. Every little thing. Go to the showers, fight. Every five minutes, it was fighting. The TV room is where the fights originate and they end up in the shower room. The TV room was segregated. I can stand segregation if I can get my own side, you know. But I'm not going to go for segregation if I'm going to sit in the back on a hard bench. So I was out of isolation for just one week. During that week I was going to the TV room because I had been locked up. All these blacks were sitting in the back, big young strong brothers. And it seems like these brothers have got a complex, you dig? They felt that they were under constant attack, you dig? So consequently they were in good shape, because they were out on the track, lifting weights and boxing and so forth. Beautiful specimens, but their minds were gone. All they wanted was to go home. I wanted to go home too, you know. But goddamn, man . . ."

George sighs, and we are both silent for a long time.

"Great big brothers, young, healthy"—he sighs again—"but they let these white guys force them to the back. Well, rather than sit down in back, I stood up in front for the first couple of days. And one or two of them called me back there. 'I'll make room.' But I didn't go for it. About the third or fourth day—I can't remember exactly, if I thought about it I could remember—I went and sat down. And these guys—ha, ha!—these guys are trying to throw

---

* Special isolation and punishment section of the prison.

their weight around, I mean the white guys. These are just little bitty guys, you know. And Tracy is the joint for the youngsters. Cats from environments where it wasn't always necessary to be physical. But it doesn't take but a few pounds of energy to stick a knife in a guy. And they got numbers and they got knives. And that is where they got their artificial sense of security from. They attacked me when I sat down in the chair. Now I was not watching TV, I was watching them. I knew they were going to attack me."

I can sense him relishing his memory of the fight, moving his shoulders from side to side as if he were actually there and readying himself to go into the fray.

"The police were right there in the TV room, supposed to be watching us. There was also a great big sign in there saying, 'NO SAVING SEATS.' This cat walks up to me and says I'm in his seat. I had been sitting there for about half a goddamn hour. Tells me I'm in his seat. I just pointed to the sign. He left and came back with a bunch of guys. One of them paraded by me. When they were all just about in the middle, one of them stepped right on my foot. His back was to me, see. So he was out of the fight right away, you dig?" I assume that George means he knocked him out instantly the fight began. "Then me and the others start in the fight. The blacks in the back are hollering, 'That's his business, we're sorry, we tried to make room for him.' " George repeats their words in a piping falsetto. "You dig?

"The police took that write-up* out of my jacket.† The write-up was so black, so overtly racist. The cop who witnessed the fight was the one who had to do the write-up. He put in there that I was acting like I was crazy. Nobody does stuff like that. Nobody had ever done anything like that before. So he had to assume that I was crazy. That's what he wrote. When I got to San Quentin, they lifted it from my file, because it's not in my jacket any more. I asked Fay to check whether or not it was in there. They just twisted it all around. You know, they can do just exactly what they want to.

"After this I got sent to San Quentin, where they locked me up immediately. I had to go through a little disciplinary committee

* Disciplinary report.
† Folder which contains an inmate's prison records.

process. You know, you come before a group of local pigs there, and they decide what to do with you. They usually have decided ahead of time, but they put on a show of giving you a hearing."

George isn't only lecturing me. It is a lesson he seems to feel he has to hammer into himself over and over again. Never believe them. Never accept what they say at face value. Just by the way he emphasizes his words, I can understand his constant struggle against any kind of faith. He isn't going to be disillusioned again.

"So I let them go along with it. A guy asked me what I wanted. Where I wanted to work. I told them I wanted to work in electronics. I would like to learn something about electronics in school. The cat told me to be practical. See, there weren't any blacks at all in electronics or the electrical shop. They just wouldn't let us in there. They let one or two in one time, the white cats beat them up and kicked them out. You dig what I'm saying? So they stopped putting guys in there and they told me to be practical. I told them I was interested in something where I would have some time to myself and I could follow my own pursuits. 'Since you won't let me follow them, you know, since you won't help me follow my pursuits, let me follow them myself.' So they gave me a job sweeping the yard." He laughs, because their mendacity is so blatant. Who did they think they were fooling, anyway?

"You know, I submitted to it a long time ago. I just faced it. Racism is a basic characteristic of Yankee society. It is part of the thing, it is a way of control. I mean so long as we are squabbling, we will never get together among ourselves. That's the first thing that politicians learn, ways of breaking you down. When they break people down into single units, then they're easier to govern and control. In San Quentin some white guys called themselves 'Hitler's Helpers.' We were having a strike; they were strikebreakers. They were trying to lynch this black guy because he was part of the strike committee. They got ropes and knives and stuff and they were actually going to hang this guy from one of the railings of the third tier." From the way his voice tears, it is as if he is remembering the deaths of his own brothers and sisters. That one word "lynch" seems to push forward a sudden rush of compassion for all his mistreated black brothers.

"Police put them up to it. Most of the whites work with the

police. Without shame they work with the police. You know the old code from years and years ago when you didn't even talk to a cop, they broke that down a long time ago. Nowadays a cop will walk up to a con and say, 'You know, man, you're white and our politics is such and such, you see.' And this is the same cat who will shoot them if they so much as look at the wall or cross the line in front of it (you get shot even though you haven't even touched the wall). But cons will play along with the pig anyway because they are both white.

"They were hanging this guy when I walked in and saw it. They had a rope around his neck which they had tied to the railing, and they were about to throw him over. Listen, there were twenty-five or thirty of them and they charged me with assault. They charged me with assault and not one of those guys had any charge at all levied against them. It's right in my record. All you got to do is look at my record and you'll see the beef right there. They paint me as a wild, savage, uncontrollable, racist nigger dog. You dig what I'm saying? In the record it reads that I started down one end of the tier and just started beating people, kicking people and throwing them over the tier for no reason whatsoever. Now there is a slight reference later on to the fact that I might have done it to revenge an attack made on another black man."

He pounds the table with the tips of his fingers. He knows he has done the right thing and he couldn't do anything else. But what good has it done him? There is no reward for righteousness in this sorry world. His realization of this triggers a rush of despair, which he almost immediately transforms into anger. I can see one emotion passing into the other like colored slides.

"They paint that stuff the way they want it, I wasn't revenging that guy. That guy was getting hung. You dig what I'm saying? These guys have got to be stopped. There are certain types of men who can't handle absolute power, you see. You know that the pigs who are attracted to these joints couldn't possibly handle it. The whole idea of prisons will have to be changed so drastically, so radically. Prison is actually a poor place to start. We have to start in Sacramento. We've got to start with Washington, D.C." He pauses to catch his breath.

"In your parole reports, they describe you as a bad management risk."

"They got a lot of those in here. They want you really to leave here a broken man. When you are broken, then they will let you out. Say, do you have any aspirin? I get a strain behind my eyes."

In many of his letters he writes about his headaches: "I was born with terminal cancer, a suppurating malignant sore that attacked me in the region just behind the eyes and moves outward to destroy my peace."*

And as we sit together, it suddenly seems that he is all pain, utterly raw to the touch, and as if everything he has done has just been a way to stop that constant pain. I don't have any aspirin. I have nothing for George's pain but a vast sense of responsibility. I pound my foot and nod. I realize that George isn't asking me for an aspirin as much as he is simply telling me about his pain.

"There is a total wall of hostility in this place. Sometimes the pigs beat some guy to death in an emotional rage. Sometimes they just do it because it's their nature to be sadistic, protected by the DA. They beat a guy to death. His head might swell up to three times its normal size, and the doctor will say something about a heart attack.

"That's what happens whenever you don't have the consent of the governed. You have to rule through fear, terror and repression. People on the street accept it and apologize for it. They say we have to hold the guys like that because they are preying on us. What we have to do is to stop and consider that we give those cats absolute power. There is no man in this country who wouldn't abuse absolute power. But it's particularly cats like we got here who will abuse it. You give cats like these absolute power and they are just going to go wild. That is just what is taking place in here. Guys from the very lowest segment of American society, the segment that has no sense even of the need for education or enlightenment. They are the ones who get the power and they get a paycheck too."

I can sense the infusion of strength that flows into him from his

---

* *Soledad Brother.*

intellectual control of the situation. I ask how it is possible for inmates to get together under these circumstances.

"It's difficult. This Parole Board thing, tied in with the fact that that cop out there can stop me and give me an infraction for anything, is a powerful negative force. What the pig says influences the Board more than anything else. Now my fate rests in the hands of cats like that. He might come in dead-drunk. So as long as they want to keep you, they can. The only way that you can escape from here is by crawling, groveling in there on your hands and knees, and licking the pigs' feet. No black leaves here by parole, walking out the front-door gate unless he has surrendered some of his face. And I mean none of them. There is no possibility of a guy getting around in here and not running into one of those guys and getting caught in an infraction. He's got to ass-kiss his way out of it or give up all hope. There is no chance of his avoiding having encounters with other cons. He's always going to get caught. It is impossible to go for two minutes without that kind of encounter. That's when the conflict does take place. If a conflict does take place and he doesn't get hurt too badly, then he's still got to contend with the pig. A key question with these joints, a central one among all the contradictions. You can't expect an idiot not to violate absolute power. You know, the cats in here totally run these little units they're in charge of. A bull is in charge of a wing. A sergeant is in charge of a unit. He runs the wing with his personality, you see. His personality—he puts his personal slant into the rulebook, the code book. If you object, then he'll show you right there in the book and interpret for you. Add to that the fact that most of these cats have psychopathic personalities."

"Well, it was like you suggested." I hesitate before going on for fear George may take offense and then, throwing caution to the wind, I plunge ahead. "The cons, their backgrounds, their problems—they are interchangeable with the guards. You could put the guards in cells and the convicts on the outside and you would be really hard pressed to find a difference."

"You wouldn't have any," George replied. "You know, a convict on the tier who is facing capital punishment, a case that is going through the courts right now, 4,500 and a couple of other little things. They could kill him, but they won't. They aren't mad at him. All they want is a showcase thing. Show that we don't just prosecute these niggers, we prosecute everybody. He will go to court and he will get a couple more years added onto his sentence and then that will be that. But still there is the possibility of him getting crossed and ending up on Death Row. I heard the same individual support capital punishment—man against himself. Talk about conditioning."

I nod my head, my chin almost touching my breastbone, and exclaim, "Wow!" and I feel an instant flash of shame for my childish naïveté. "You know," I add, "this prison is just like a replica of society. It is different, but it is the same."

"Just like a little city, a little town. The same exact way."

"This is a great place to learn about society, like the classroom."

"With one possible exception: things go down in here with the absence of sex that are kind of perverted, which add one more complication that you don't have on the streets."

"This is the problem of punks and homosexuality in prison. And enforced prostitution."

"The fights and stuff between convicts that go down behind that," George replies. "It creates a problem. You wouldn't have a certain element that exists in here out on the streets, an element in the social structure of the streets. It's a result of the psychological impact of going without sex. That cat walks along and another cat starts looking like a girl." With his shoulders George mimics a girl walking. From the look on his face I can almost feel him remembering a certain daydream. "Things like that, and they start fighting each other. You don't have that on the street."

"I bet some cats hallucinate, don't they?"

"Oh, man, this is not just every now and then, it's every day, all day long. Another factor is similar to what goes on outside. Cats get isolated in here and they need financial help and stuff like that. And one guy will have cigarettes and they don't have any, and they see another guy with things they don't have. It's something similar to extortion."

"That's like enforced prostitution."

"No, I'm talking about cats who don't have anything, and the cat who does have some stuff but who is weak. This other guy will prey on him and take his stuff. Pressure."

"Part of prostitution in prisons is people taking things from other people and paying off sexually. Right?" I am repeating something I have read in a book.

"Yeah, that is part of it, but that is just a minute part. The big part of the homosexual thing comes from one guy being stronger than the other guy. Guys will deny that, but it's the truth. Some guy will come in who is not familiar with these types of things or who has not grappled with problems like this and two or three guys set on him and threaten him, and when he sees knives, he sees guys getting killed, he don't want to get killed, so he submits. I imagine about one-fourth of the guys in San Quentin (there are about four thousand), about one-fourth of the population is in that bag, and they take it out to the street. The turnover in SQ, the population turnover, is about eighteen months. Of course you've got all your regulars, guys who stay around for six or seven years like I did. Now all these guys are not going out to the street, but to other joints, preparatory to release, you know. Nobody leaves these joints normal, man. Nobody. In some kind of way they leave perverted. And I'm not talking just about the sexual thing now. I'm talking about everybody."

I know George is talking about himself. There is a kind of soft compassion in his voice that comes from his recollection of his own past.

"You know, a guy in here, guys like the ones we were talking about a while ago, who have turned against the world. You know: 'Fuck the world,' things like that. What happens to a young innocent guy who comes into contact with guys like that? For one thing, he starts to look up to them because, as I said a while ago, these guys who tattooed this 'Fuck the world' thing across their forehead are the guys who are looked up to. They are usually the tough guys who walk around taking other guys' canteens. This little guy who just came in watches him and tries to emulate him. Pretty soon he incorporates those characteristics into himself." I wonder to myself if George went through this stage too. "Nobody leaves here healed, you dig? You know why they call it rehabilitation? You can't rehabilitate a guy in an environment like this. You're renouncing or contradicting everything that Western science has come up with. You know, man is a product of his environment."

"This is the insanity of capitalism, the insanity of an institution like this," I observe. "They are training people to destroy them."

"Then they hassle among themselves," George goes on. "If you stop to consider, convict and cop both come from the same class. What are we doing? What are we doing to each other? This guy manipulates you. This cat pulls the strings. But there is no way you can explain it to the guy sitting out there. He'd just sit there quoting rules, two hours of the Penal Code. So that problem has to be solved first. We need revolution, change of government. Then we sit down with the dialectical sessions and solve the other problems afterwards."

"If you keep it simple initially. I mean, when people are given real power, when they are allowed to be concerned about their real needs, and each other's needs, then we have a revolution."

"But you can't moralize over things like that because this cat with the blue suit is standing in your way. And he won't listen, so you've got to roll over him."

This is the whole difference between us. I want a nice humanistic revolution, and George supports the use of force. In George's situation, appeals to humanity and moral feeling are useless confessions of weakness. The conventions of my life are different. Tacit agreements never to acknowledge the primacy of power and force. I am paid for my silence.

The difference is even present in the ways we use our bodies. George, constantly in motion, like a generator emanating energy in an almost visible form, a scintillating yellowish light carving up space with every inch of his body, cutting it with gestures of his hands, pounding it with his head, rising up from his chair and almost levitating with the sheer displacement of force. It is as if he were taking the very space inside himself, absorbing, pulling in everything that surrounds him, almost visibly swelling with the intake of substance. Always alert, always wary, watchful, responding to every sound.

On the other hand, my body, when I sit, is limp, my hands rest wherever I put them and remain inert. As someone who leads an almost completely protected life, I have no need for my body. It is only a means of propelling my head from place to place. All my expressivity, my responsiveness, is concentrated in my face and my voice. I perceive the feelings of others, but I don't project my own feelings. Unlike George, I am not ready for action. Mostly I am caught up by the actions of others. Even though I know that our ways of being are simply the results of our different ways of life, I cannot help but be intimidated by his overwhelming vivacity.

Evasively, I reply to his statement about rolling over the man in blue by saying, "When the time comes." George, who is always seeking out the most active principle in any statement or situation, replies, "When we've worked out some method."

I ask how the prison deals with "troublesome inmates," and no sooner is the phrase out of my mouth than I want to take it back because, despite my tone of irony, it is still the vocabulary of his jailers.

"Any black who they can't beat or break down, they're going to kill him. You know, they made about twenty attempts to kill me. Most of them through the inmates. They proposition an inmate. They tell him to do himself some good. They promise that if he'll cooperate with them, he'll do himself some good. All he has to do is walk up and punch me. They got that thing going between the guard and the gun tower. He punches me, then drops to the ground and then the gun tower guy shoots me. Sometimes they will give an inmate fifty dollars. He'll cut your throat if he figures he can get away with it. The police give him carte blanche."

"Tell me about murders in prison, how common are they?" I ask the question, but murder is still just an abstract idea to me.

"When a guy gets pressed, pushed into circumstances where he can't see any relief, then he loses his hope automatically. When he sees things taking place all around him that make it obvious that there is nothing sacred, that a guy's life is not worth shit (that's the conclusion you come to when you see the way they handle the wounded and the dead), of course he starts losing his hold. Other guys get defensive. They overreact. And that's what causes fights. A lot of these guys are so degraded that they can be completely controlled by the prison authorities, who can force them to do anything they want. They don't even have to force them, all they have to do is indicate what they want done and then those cons will go and do it." Though George doesn't mention actual incidents, I can hear them in the background of his voice almost like a changing tableau.

"You have two different categories. You got the guy who feels that it's him against the world. He's not necessarily mean, he just feels it's him against the world and that he has to capitalize on anything that comes along because he has nothing. After an extended period in the joint, he's run out of relationships. You know, relationships from the street. He's got nothing, nothing coming in, nothing to remind him that the street is still there. He loses his hold. He knows he's got to do something for himself. He's desperate. They can use guys like that, see. They use bitter guys like that who have turned completely against the world and themselves. You can offer them anything. A carton of cigarettes is sometimes enough to get a guy killed. The pigs have ways of telling people what they want done without ever really telling them directly. They have signals.

"Then there are other cats who are just laying, who are just bending over backwards, breaking their necks to get along with the established power. They are trying to earn their way out of here any way they can. And they have that kind of personality where they like to please cats who carry guns. They want to stay on the good side of a cat who carries a gun.

"So you got two different categories. You got guys who are strong—no, they're not really strong"—he hesitates, trying to find the exact words to sum up his understanding—"but you've got this guy who is not weak and who is desperate. The cops relate to him on a man-to-man basis. The cop will come to him and start talking, like 'This is me and you, and not a pig-con relationship,' and then he'll say, 'I don't like that guy over there. He stepped on my toes and blah blah blah.' And he'll offer him something.

"One guy named Mack tried that approach. Now that guy is sick. He has a Hemingway complex. Tough guy, crew-cut, sleeves rolled up. He had his cap broken down the way the flyboys do. Listen"—he breaks up the word, drawing out the first syllable and then slamming out the second like a meat cleaver—"he quit the joint to go to Vietnam to work for the CIA. The joint wasn't tough enough for him. He approached about fifteen different guys in here. I'm talking about the guys who are the most vicious white cons in the state. He approached them with money to try to get them to deal with me. 'All you got to do, to do yourself some good, is get Jackson.' This guy Mack had another guy working with him who worked the gun rail. Mack would tell a con just to walk up and punch me and then hit the ground, you dig? If there was a fight, this would give the gun tower guard an excuse to shoot me."

"They broke up one fight here, didn't they?" I interrupt, referring to January 13, 1970, when the three black inmates were killed by a guard who was supposedly breaking up a fight.

"Oh, that's standard procedure. Believe me, I'm not going to let these cats defeat me. They are little idiots. They have certain little fixed procedures and they never deviate from them." George has studied them all so carefully. "They never deviate from them because that would call for some imagination and craftiness. They have those standard procedures, you see. I can allow for them because whenever I go out there on the yard, I'll only be there briefly and stay close to something I can jump under."

"Then you are constantly aware of the need to defend yourself?"

"Oh, you know, what really made me aware is the first guy that they propositioned. They didn't know that I knew the guy. He came and told me immediately afterwards that the pigs had just entered a stage where they are just going to try to get rid of me any way they can. The reason they wanted to get rid of me is that I'm a Marxist. And they were having a lot of trouble around the joint. It was really getting tight. Guys throwing Molotov cocktails. There were a lot of Muslims around the joint then. They weren't afraid of Muslims, but Muslims were potentially a threat. I was talking to these Muslims, trying to pull them out of their thing. And whenever incidents happened, I'd be right there because I grasped right from the beginning that if we did tilt with windmills, it would be better to tilt by tens." This is the theme he keeps coming back to again and again, the need to work together.

"The pigs put me right in the middle all the time. They singled me out lots of times as the guy who started the trouble, even when it wasn't true. When they said, 'Well, let's just get rid of this nigger,' you know." He laughs because even though they had all the power, they still couldn't do it. "They tried it a couple of times. They got a couple of guys to try it. The bullets were knocking plaster dust off the wall right near my head. Ah, man, it was pitiful and I just withdrew. It affected my mind quite a bit. I wouldn't let any white person get within arm's reach of me without being ready to defend myself. I'm watching a guy's knife hand even though I'm pretending not to but I'm watching it." I realize that one of the reasons he is always in motion is that he is always defending himself. "Whenever anybody gets around me, black or white, because there are blacks that they can use like that, I get ready to go into the defense-attack thing. They did try to use a black once. It was vicious, man! But I'm going to tell the truth. They got guns and I haven't got nothing and I'm still alive. But I'm still in the pen and they might kill me. My case is special. It is a very rare thing for someone in places like the Adjustment Center in Folsom or in the Adjustment Center in San Quentin, it's very rare for someone to get to be thirty years old and still be among the living. It's an accomplishment, man. And the fact that we lose so many times when the fight comes makes us react all the more harder, more viciously, because we remember the last time."

Listening to him, I realize how completely absorbed he is by the life of the prison. And I understand that it couldn't be any other way because it is the sum and substance of his daily life. It also occurs to me that no matter what he does and no matter how well he resists, the prison still owns him in a very profound way because it defines the totality of his experience, the cells, the walls, the clothing, the rhythm of washing and sleeping and eating. And so, without thinking, I blurt out, "They've got you then, haven't they? They can program your reactions."

"Of course. You know what I kick myself in the ass for?—and it might not be a good thing to record this—I kick myself in the ass for allowing these people to hold me. I should have long ago busted one of those walls out. I know how to do it. I'm locked up in a place right now where if I could get hold of certain materials, strong enough to bust open a wall . . . I know that once I walk out of here, once I bust out, it's not just the police against me then, it's all 200 million of them."

"Right! Right! So it's not cool to break out. There are other ways. There really are much better ways." I sense the hopelessness of his trying to escape, so I feel I have to persuade him not to try.

"That's what I was thinking of. But I might have been at fault. I haven't made up my mind yet. I might have been wrong in thinking."

"I think you were wrong, but I don't think you are wrong now. Other things are at work." I say it, but I don't really believe it. I just can't bear to fully acknowledge my sense of hopelessness to him or even to myself. "Yeah, but now there are people working. I'll tell you a lot is going to be done." But I really don't know what I mean. Perhaps that a lot of people, myself included, are going to put on a good show. And I think of John Thorne and Fay Stender— they are all that stand between George and the gas chamber.

"But I was wrong at that time. To sit around with those people holding me . . . !" I know he wants me to share his sense of the total absurdity of someone like himself allowing those fools to hold him prisoner. "The whole fabric right from beginning to end is wrong. The breach between what they profess and what they do. Even the little rulebook they throw at me every time I try to reason with them. They don't even stick to that. Unless it's in a confrontation with them. You know, it's against the rules for them to bring in narcotics. You've got convicts fighting over and killing themselves over dope. But it's here, right here. How does it get in? There is only one way it gets in. No, there are actually a couple of ways. The stuff that cats get in through the visiting room. That's just enough for them—one kiss. But the cats who deal and deal big, you know where they have to get that stuff. Thousands and thousands of dollars each week. There's more money around here than in many small towns in this country.

"I know I have an idea where it's going to end. Somebody is going to get hurt around this situation. People are going to be killed if this keeps going on. Aw, it's going to go on. There's no two ways about it. We have to face that eventuality. Like I say, certain people can't be reasoned with."

I sense that he is still trying to convince himself. "But," I say, "you've got to be cool. I mean, you have really got to be together, together enough so you can be cool. You got to be together to marshal the armed forces, our forces. Even cooler than you are right now. You got to get much cooler, much much cooler."

George's need for some kind of immediate action seems almost uncontrollable.

"We got to marshal our forces and then move on them. But we can't do it unless we find some way to protect ourselves first. You see the vicious circle. I've met some beautiful brothers, but the main reason for getting away from the younger dudes is that they were just going through this thing that I went through years ago, see. They were going through this thing of wanting to compete with me. I don't want to compete. If a guy tries to get me to compete with him, I want to get away from him because I don't want our relationship to degenerate to the point of fighting. I want to get with the cats who have gone through those changes already. Just so long as the cat has started going through the changes, I know where he is going to end up. He's going to end up in the Panthers. I know that's where he is going to end up. Just leave him alone to his own self. That's what we were talking about a while ago. You can't force things on people. I didn't pay too much attention to school or at least I didn't do as well as I could. The reason I didn't was that I didn't want nobody to force anything on me. I couldn't accept taking things from other people. I just couldn't accept taking things at somebody else's whim."

"You found your school, man. You did all right in your school."

"There were a lot of good times. You see, I don't have to worry about aging. I'll be twenty-eight sixty years from now if they don't kill me. I figure that by that time my problems will be over."

I suppose prison is like an eternal childhood because there is no way to grow up and nothing to grow up into.

"At one time you said you gave up on blacks altogether," I suggest, taking up his theme.

"They were too corrupt. And my position was I was going to leave this country, go anywhere, somewhere where people would fight. I wanted to go to Angola. You know, they started fighting there in the early sixties. It was my idea to go with Holden Roberto and fight in a revolutionary war, and then perhaps come back to this country. Leaving here was my politics . . . returning to my native country. Get myself together, get rid of the pains, the bad things, the way they destroyed my ego and so forth—the way that my ego was destroying me—and reorient myself into being human." His chest heaves like a bellows, and I know that he is deeply moved by his evocation of the damage that has been done to him and by his hopes of curing himself. "And then learn something about guerrilla warfare and come back. That was before I understood war on the family plan. I understand it completely since then. I figure that if I am going to fight or risk myself in any way, I believe that they should too. Their responsibility, their debt to history, is the same as mine. My mama, my woman, my sisters, should be able to accept the same responsibility of dying and all the rest that I accept. At the time, I didn't realize they were willing. I wasn't looking deep enough. There are certain undercurrents through all black people. You see, I didn't realize that till later about my mother, about my father, about my sister."

From what I had learned before from his letters and from what he has told me in the last two days, I know that this is wishful thinking and I can almost feel him projecting, imagining his own desires into the beings of the other members of his family. At the same time, I can also feel him shifting away, throwing his mind off to one side so that his reason will not be compelled to repudiate this notion which for the moment is so important to him. It is as if he has almost hypnotized himself.

"This madness, it's just laying to break, bust out to the surface. With the right provocation and the right direction you have a revolutionary potential that is monumental. The victims of fascism, the victims of capitalism, are lying to themselves now. All they have to do is stop lying. They can go down tonight in their beds and wake up tomorrow morning completely different people. That is when the trouble will start."

It is almost as if he is talking in the language of dreams. In the silence that follows, we both move around uncomfortably in our wooden chairs trying to find some nonexistent softness. So I won't be forced to respond to his utopian reverie, I change the subject almost too quickly, too abruptly.

"What happened in January 1967?"

"I guess that is a weapon used against me. Strike. Then again, maybe not. I almost got sucked into some foolishness. Oh, that was something else."

I can see him putting it together from the way he moves his head and the way he focuses his eyes as he reaches for his memory of the past.

"The police made a mistake—well, they didn't make a mistake, they did it on purpose. Why do I keep saying mistake?" He digs his words into himself so that he will not forget. "The police opened all the cells at the same time, see. So all the convicts come on the tier at the same time without gun cover, you see.* It was obviously a setup because the police will never let all convicts out at the same time without gun cover. 'Cause then there is no way to break up the fight except to come in here. Come in here and break it up with their hands. And with twenty convicts . . . you know what kind of fight that starts. Somebody would get killed. They opened up those cells and let all the convicts out at the same time. There was a white guy on the tier who was a righteous dude, a righteous comrade, you know. He is riding on the main line now, a little guy named Bucky. The blacks attacked this white dude. There were a couple of white dudes that needed attacking for racist attacks. They had stabbed a couple of brothers on the main line. Brothers jumped on them and beat them up real good. And I didn't say nothing. But when they started attacking this white dude, I stopped them. And I was trying to explain and I felt kind of funny about it, you know." He almost whispers. "I mean, I shouldn't have, but I did. But I told them not to bother that guy. And some of them resented me for doing it. You dig that? And I reacted to resentment. In my mind I react to resentment. So I talked to them about it. I told them about how this guy and I, we'd had some serious hard rapping, dialectics, you know. This was a beautiful thing, and I'm not going to let anybody hurt that guy."

---

* When the cell doors are opened, convicts are obliged to come out or face disciplinary action.

There is a gentle, almost loving protectiveness in his voice. "But do you dig what situation I'm in?"

"Absolutely. There is nothing more difficult."

"It is hard, man, because I had been in the joint by then for years and years, you see, and there is no question as to where my loyalty lies." It is almost as if he is renewing a pledge. "If there is any question in anybody's mind, in any black's mind, as to where my loyalty lies, there is something wrong with them. If he can't think at all, then he don't know anything about the jungle. Or he has been in the jug too long. So to question where my loyalty lies . . . but still, you know guys will ask the question." He breaks into gales of wild laughter. " 'Is George changing?' You dig? You don't smoke, eh?"

"Gave it up two years ago. Feels good, you know, really does feel good."

"I think there is something wrong with my throat. Anyone who smokes develops cancer of the throat."

"Well, not yet."

"I've been smoking since I was fifteen."

"I started when I was thirteen . . . smoked for twenty-five years."

"You don't look thirty-nine."

"Just started living a while ago."

"Hmmm." I can see him trying to find some way to think about the anomaly I represent to him.

"I just started living and getting my head in shape a while ago. I'm glad I feel young. I got a lot of life to get in." It isn't so much that I am throwing my future up to him, trying to hurt him with it. I only mention it to counterbalance the fatefulness of his own life. In comparison with the events of his life, mine are so tenuous and cerebral. I feel more comfortable suggesting I have a future because I don't believe he could ever understand my past.

"I'm not afraid of dying, really"—I hear a faint catch in his voice and I wince a little—"because I've never really seen any great value for me just to hang on at any cost. I've never had anything. I've never seen or witnessed or experienced anything so wonderful that I should submit." He speaks quietly and reflectively. What he says is simply a statement of fact.

"Of course," I say, "we can't get the wonderful things of life by submitting, because they are exactly what we lose by submitting."

"Like the respect of Angela Davis. You see, I want that woman to love me and respect me. And women like her. I want them to love me and respect me. I want them to believe in me. How could they believe in me if I kowtow?"

I know that it is not just because Angela is Angela, or because they are women, that he wants their respect. It is more that, instinctively, he realizes that they are the only ones who can judge the order of his accomplishments.

"Right."

"Vicious, man. Somebody has got to come up with some guts and with planning. I love Angela Davis. Love her. I hope she knows it." Because her knowing is the whole point, because that creates the tension of their relationship.

Just think what it means. Ten years in jail, seven years in solitary. No women at all. On trial for murder. At first no hope at all. Never very much hope. Endless dreams and fantasies of women. Fantasies of Angela in his cell at night. But then suddenly they have become real, or at any rate just as real as his will can ever make them.

"The last seven years, not the last seven, but out of the ten years I've been in the joint, several of them were spent in the lockup. We have no contact with . . . if you haven't been in these joints, I'll have to explain."

"Yes, please." I hear the expectancy and anticipation in my voice.

"In a place like I'm in right now, which is typical of all the other places like that in the other joints, they just lock up all day. The only guy on the tier is the bull, you dig? I'm going to try and stop using the word 'bull.' The only guy on the tier is the pig. The only time when we see a guy is maybe doing a shower bit. The only awareness you have of presences around you are voices. Now you know what type of voices—insane things, insane sounds, frustration sounds, asylum sounds, fear sounds, fear responses, fear reactions. I guess that's why they call it isolation. Now they have a special isolation, they have five or six special isolation units, in every one of these joints where you are closed in altogether. Where you can't hear any voices, any sounds. I'd like you to reconstruct in your mind, sometime when you're off by yourself, try to reconstruct what it would be like sitting in such a cell for two years. There is no presence around you except the ones you get by characters through books, because there's no presence around you, but madness, voices. No contact. You dig?

"They put me in a cell once, I stayed in a cell once for a year that had a lock welded on, a special lock welded on the door. And nobody in there. I'm strictly by myself, just me, except during certain periods. The only friend that I had was a book. I started talking in my sleep. I used to wake myself up and talk, you dig, because I'm reading a tale and I want to talk to the guy in the book. But he's not listening. I know he's not going to be listening, you know. No one was listening. So I walk a trench in my floor. Think. Do my push-ups. Do my exercises. But at night, when I go to sleep, I think there might be something to Freud's wish fulfillment. Hmmm. What do you think about that?"

"Yeah, I think so." I feel suddenly as if I am falling down, down, down, through endless space, plummeting.

"A little something, you know. When I'm asleep at night, I'm talking to these guys. I'm talking to myself. Seven years! It's almost like the street/joint situation. The guy who does two years in the joint, two months on the street, five years in the joint, two weeks on the street. I would do two or three months on the main line, and the rest of the time I was locked up. Most of the accusations were for things that I didn't do. Suspicion! They're anticipating. 'You mean you're getting ready to start trouble.' "

"Yeah, in one of those letters you say something about that. That's the most wild thing. They lock you up for your own good because they think you're going to do something."

"You know, they locked me up one time because of a letter my father sent. Yeah, he said I was bent on violent self-destruction. You know what? I told him in a visit that there was that one particular bull after me, you know, and he was propositioning a couple of guys to kill me. Now I told him if I heard just one more thing about this guy trying to kill me, I'm going to sneak into his office . . . you know what? I was just talking."

"Oh, sure."

"I was just talking, loose talk. You dig about that, loose talk. With somebody I got something in common with. When I got through talking, I was grinning, smiling, you dig? That's the way I thought he would take it. I told him that if the bull did one more thing, I'm going to sneak into his office and cut his throat. And my father went home and wrote a long letter to the institution and told them I needed psychiatric help and was bent on violent self-destruction. The bulls were passing the letter around, laughing at me. You dig? This is what they're saying to themselves, here's this guy who's talking all of this power to the people, people, power to the proletariat. And his father is a coward and is on our side. Vicious, isn't it?" Mordant, mordant laughter. "They were laughing about it all over the whole joint."

He closes his eyes and massages the back of his neck.

"The periods when I was out on the main line, the general population, every time I walked across the yard, every time I would come out of my cell for a trip to the library or kitchen (they would make me work in the kitchen), I'd have to be ready to parry an attack."

He pauses before going on. "What were we talking about a while ago? Leadership, the leaders, followers." He can't talk about his life any more.

"Yeah, I know. The white revolutionaries are now trying to do away with leadership. They're organized communally, and I'm afraid it's not going to work," I add. We both pull back from our feelings. There is only so much either of us can take.

"Yeah. We're herd animals. There's just no two ways about it. It's a thing from way back, thousands and thousands of years. You can't just deny it all of a sudden."

"Uh-huh. It's like the structure of the human family, I'm afraid, that creates a need for leaders. The early dependency of the child breeds the need for fathers, father figures."

"How do you see that in the 'brave new world' "—his voice sets the words apart in quotation marks—"the family structure?"

"I don't see families. I don't see a family structure. I see kids being treated like adults very early and as real people, not like—"

"And everybody being their mama."

I know he is really talking about his own mother's domination and his inability to deal with her. "Right," I answer.

"And every man being their papa." If no one has parents, then we both have solved our problems.

"Right, right," I repeat. "Yeah, and I don't see a man relating to one woman for years and years and years. I just don't see it."

"Man, I hate to say this, you know, because it might hurt a lot of people's feelings, you know, but I think a person should give full range to the thing he feels, the sexual thing, the sexual attraction. The guy should give full range to it. So should a woman. All the rest of the other stuff is just some stupid Victorian backward stuff from the Middle Ages."

"That's capitalistic sex."

"A possessive thing."

"Yeah, that's it."

"A possessive sex."

"Right," I said. For a few instants, it is almost as if our words are emitted in the short staccato rhythm of copulation.

"A person should give full range, full latitude, to those feelings of wanting to touch and feel and hold, legs and hands and mouths. Just give full range to it."

I am amazed at his words. When most people experience prolonged and intolerable pain, they try to cut off from everything around themselves that reaches out into the world. They don't allow any surprises or spontaneity. No feeling. Not only do they eliminate or suppress feeling in their lives, but they despise it and distrust it in others as well. This is the way I had been told it was in prison. No reaching out. No sense of self. Anything that arouses or tempts inmates to feel must be squashed or raped or murdered.

But George is different. The imminence of death seems to have made him want to live without any restraints. Ten years in prison haven't eliminated his feelings. They are all dammed up, just waiting to pour out.

"And it's healthy, because variety is an important thing. All right now, out of that situation every now and then there will grow a deep serious relationship. And then until something else comes in to change that, that deep serious sensitive relationship, it should carry on, but when it does change, why, of course it . . ."

"Well, marriage itself is often just another one of the cells that exist in this society, a prison cell in another form."

"Hmmm. Yeah. Another one of the ways we hurt each other, spoil each other."

"Yeah, right. And what people do in this country to stay together, the damage that they do to each other." I think of my own marriage, and the pain of my loss is still very raw.

"Oh, the psychological damage . . ."

"Wow! They kick the shit out of each other after a while. Because they had something that was probably real once, and then they're ossified and hate comes in—wow!" Now I am the one who is moved to silence.

"Do you know what? Are you going to be able to see me any more times?"

"I hope."

"Bring me that pamphlet that's called *Inter-fighting, Today's Woman*. I got some lady friends that I'm writing, some beautiful people who will try and develop into Marxist womanhood. Woman named Clara Colon wrote it."

"I've got to find me a revolutionary woman." All I mean is that I want a woman who will understand me. Someone who has been through enough, probably been hurt enough, so that she can understand the effects of my own pain.

"I've got a couple that want to be, writing me now. They're beautiful people and I love them, but . . ."

I mention the letters to "Z" that had been included in the manuscript I had just read. "She's a sweet little thing," George says. "Beautiful."

"Oh, yeah." She was the woman who had driven me down to John's office the day before.

"Aw, she's a sweet little thing, but she's mixed-up."

"That's okay. Being mixed-up at that age is really beautiful because you can see where it's going to go."

On the trip down to the prison I had thought almost continuously about making love to her. I had sat there beside her like a young boy wondering what she would do if I suddenly put my hand under her dress or rubbed my cheek against her breast.

"She can't understand that I can love Angela Davis and still love her at the same time. She can't understand it. She pretends like she does, but she doesn't." But it wasn't just Angela, and it couldn't be just Angela. There was Z and there was Fay. When there is no woman that you can really possess, you love all women and every woman. "Because she is making constant reference to it. Like in one letter she wrote me. She says that once she felt threatened by other women in her bourgeois days, but now 'I want all the sisters to love you the way I love you . . . and I want you to love all of them.' If she really felt that way, she wouldn't have articulated it."

We are talking about real women. George knows more about them than I do, and he has more consideration and tenderness for them.

"Not that way," I say, "not that way. Not all of the sisters, she's not really talking about all of the sisters."

"I want both of them to love me and I resent a third party, a state or society, entering and telling me that I can't love both these people the way I want to love them."

"In our society," I say, "Women are so conditioned that they cannot accept that. A man or a woman has no right to love more than one person."

"I've also tried to emphasize that because I know she's got a little boyfriend too. I figured that perhaps she didn't know that I knew. That might have been crude for me to mention it. You know, for me to say something like that might have been crude." And the way he says the word indicates how appalling and shameful that would be to him. "But I had to in order to help her or try and help her understand, and I can only write one page—you know, both sides. One sheet both sides, you know. It's hard to put abstract ideas in so short a space like that, you know. But to have her in love with some other guy, that's beautiful. You dig? It's the coefficient to life."

I get the feeling that he feels the women he knows have entrusted themselves to him and that he has an almost acute sense of responsibility.

"What it means is she's really alive."

"The coefficient to the life process, you know," he said.

"It bothers me when I find myself loving a lot of women, getting involved with a lot of women. I say, 'What the hell is the matter with you, man, are you crazy?' And then I think it over and I say, 'That's fine, that's really fine, that's good, that's the way it should be.' "

"I will confess that—well, we've just discussed that, giving full rein to the heart and to the mind, right?"

"Uh-huh."

"And then, sooner or later, the good relations start to manifest themselves. I'm almost positive there's just something that's attracted me to Angela. You know, I tried to get hold of her long before this case. The thing that attracted me to her was just a couple of statements she made in an interview that was printed in a small black tabloid in Illinois. And a couple of statements she made in the paper that were quoted in the interview. And then, too, the fact that she was beautiful."

"That helps."

"But I think that . . . I hope it doesn't cause any kind of ill will, bad feeling."

"How?"

"Power struggles. I'm talking about, you know, between Elizabeth* and Angela." From the way George's voice unfolds their names, I know that he regards them as the rarest and most perfect beings in the world, wondrous beyond all possibility of description. "Do you think there's a possibility between Angela and Elizabeth, could either one of them start resenting each other?"

I realize that part of him relishes the idea, because that would make their love for him even more real. How could he believe in any one person, how could he limit himself to any one person, because whenever he had counted on anyone in the past, they had always let him down?

"Sure. Almost certain."

"Do you think Elizabeth is serious?"

"Sure. I can't say, I can't say for sure. But I can say that from my knowledge of women, like if there is this situation, it's inevi-

* Z's real name.

table that there will be feelings between them. That's the way
things are set up out there."

"Here's what I'm asking. How well do you know Elizabeth?"

"Very little. I had dinner at Fay's house. Right? And she was at
the table. We talked for a while. And then we drove down from
Fay's house in the morning to San Jose, where I met John and then
came on down here. That's yesterday. So I think I spent like two
hours. So I don't know anything at all beyond that."

"Do you know what I've been suspecting all along? That she's
just trying to send me some cheer."

"Yeah. Well, I don't believe that. No, I don't believe that."

"I thought . . . I've been suspecting all along . . . give me
something to buoy, buoy me up." Because what he needed so
much was the real love of a woman.

"Well, I don't believe that."

The whole atmosphere of the room has changed in the last few
minutes. It seems suddenly very sultry and dense.

"You don't?" George's face becomes as tender and soft as an
adolescent's.

"I think you come across."

"We've met twice."

I refuse to hear his words. I brush them out of my head. "You
come across in your letters. I gave your letters to a girl back East,
and I could tell she was just powerfully attracted." I know now
what George meant when he talked about the deprivation of
women being the cruelest part of all.

"You mean her letters to me?"

"No, I gave your letters, all the letters that I have, your correspondence, to a girl back East. And she was fantastically attracted by these letters. And I could feel it and I was jealous."

George laughs. I am trying to make him feel good, but it is also
the truth.

"That's nice. But do you know what's been bothering me the
last few days, the last week or so, because I've been holding this
thing about Angela for a long time now? But the last week or so,
it's just slipped out on her. And I'm starting to think, since the
visitors don't understand those things, that I might be failing her,
you know."

"I think Elizabeth needs somebody to help her get her head together. She wants to. She really wants to. She wants direction." Trying to tell George how much she needs him.

"She shows it in her letters that she's trying to understand what I'm talking about—man-woman relationship. In a Marxist society, in a free society, free love. What's happening is the hippies took free love and degenerated it, you know, to a point where . . . I'm not talking about all of them, I'm talking about the ones that are in it just for the free sex thing."

"But that's good. I think there's nothing wrong with that."

"It's an intellectual thing to a hippie, to the hippie culture. It should be! You dig? But some of them don't bother with the intellectual thing, and those are the ones I'm talking about."

"You mean, they steal sex, they rip it off."

"They get in it for the sex thing. They didn't try it to learn the intellectual thing behind the freedom of sex. And the freedom of other types of thinking."

"I agree with you."

"This has been bothering me because Angela has been on my mind quite a lot. I think that maybe I might have failed, 'cause she doesn't understand. I mean, she's writing me letters. I'm not going to talk about it any more. The more I talk about it, the more I reveal a guilt feeling in myself, you know."

"Yes, it's a guilt feeling. You should work on that. How do you work on things? How do you work on problems like that?" Since I have been alone for so long too, my own feelings about sex and women are tangled and confused.

"First, I try not to do anything that I will feel guilty for or feel guilty about. That's been my whole life."

"Yeah, but when you do have a feeling of guilt, how do you work on it? How do you relate to the fact of guilt in the first place, the sensation of guilt? Do you accept it as a valid thing? I think you do."

"Some of the things I've done I feel are personal things. I try not to think about it, because I've taken things away from nice— please don't misunderstand—I've taken things away from people who had a lot in common with me." The sense of responsibility is heavy on him. "When the opportunity presented itself, I was thinking, 'Why, it's me against the world.'"

"In other words, you were in a predatory society." At this moment it is very important for me to help George forgive himself. Perhaps so I can forgive myself too.

"I like to think of myself as the type of guy who should have been above that." It's really his pride, not his conscience. "That's why I don't really condemn myself, because I wasn't above it. I know there's no real reason for me to ever think that I was and should have been."

I reply, "Guilt is another chain, another set of shackles, because it makes you relate to the past and not what's going on in the present. Trying to act on the basis of guilt closes you up, introverts you, right?"

"Yeah."

"I think you really expected something on June 12, 1969. Right?" Changing the subject. "The shortest letter that I have of yours reads, 'Mother: Final results. Denied one year. Go back to the Board next year.'"

"I want to talk about that. In December 1968 I had two years clean. I had been locked up after this fight with the police. They beat me up. My arms and legs and hands were swollen, and I'm mad. And I swore to myself right then, I wasn't going to fight any more until I could win. The day I took up the battle again, I was going to win. It didn't make any sense for me to put myself in a position to let this guy knock me crazy with a stick. I am just not going to fight until I can win. I'm just not going to do it. I will wait and get out of here. And then I will do my fighting. I swore this, you know. I made two years clean. Nothing. No confrontations whatsoever. I stopped putting out my position papers.*

"All right, they promised me in 1967, when I had one year clean, that if I brought one more year clean, they'd give me a date." For a year he was going to be a good con and do his own time; for one year he would just think of himself and not get mixed up in anyone else's trouble. For one year he would leave it to others to be defenders of the race. "In December 1967 they said,

---

* Essays he wrote and circulated throughout the prison.

'One more year clean and we'll give you a date.'* Now December 1968 came round and I go up. Now see, I told my father about this, about the promise they made. He wrote a bunch of letters. 'Well, since you are going to cut him loose because he's got two years of clean time now altogether, I just want you to know that we have a job waiting for him.' When I got in the Board room, they said, 'Now you know we didn't make you any promises. We don't do things like that. We don't promise nobody nothing.' So it's standard procedure. They'll tell a guy two years clean, and when he comes back, they tell him, 'We didn't promise you anything.' I didn't say anything. I didn't get mad. I figured he was trying to get me mad. I said I understand. So we talked, and I went back to the cell and waited for the results—you know, the results of the meeting. They denied me, but they said next year for sure. What they said is that 'We are going to transfer you to Soledad and you'll get a date for sure.' Because ordinarily they shoot you down for one year—they only shot me down six months. So I was scheduled to go back to the Board in June. And they said, 'Well, we can't let you go now, you're locked up. We don't let guys go to the street from lockup. Go to Soledad. Go to the main line. Don't get in any trouble and we will let you go.'

"So I came to Soledad, didn't have any trouble, you know, the first six months I'm here. No trouble at all. Of course I'm expecting a date, they promised me one then, you know, for sure. They're supposed to give it to me now, right? I go to the Board and they shoot me down again. I shouldn't have had any illusions because it was my ninth year in the joint. You see how weak people are—you know, with their illusions. Well, they shot me down again. That is not all of it though. The 1968 appearance—they told me in the Board room that I had a date. When I got back to the cell, I waited for the official results. I had told everybody on my way across the yard, 'I will be leaving pretty soon, I don't know for sure when, but when I get my results, I'll let you know where I'm going.' I got back to the cell and waited for the results. And when they came, that is when I got the explanation. 'Well, man, you are

* Under California's indeterminate sentence, a convict's term of sentence, "his date," is set only when he is about to be paroled.

locked up, we can't let you go from lockup. We'll send you to Soledad for six months on main line, and if you do those six months, we'll let you go.' So, in other words, while I was on the Board, while I was sitting in the room, they promised me things. They actually did promise me. I told my folks I was getting ready to come home. I wrote them both long letters. I told them, 'It won't be long.' They all came up to see me. Everybody was happy. Two days later I get the official results. Denied. Now maybe a naïve person would just figure it was an accident, a happenstance, that maybe they would have some justification for conducting the affair that way. But I know they conducted the affair in a calculated way to make me mad. They think I'm some crazy maniac who will do something maniacal or ridiculous. Then they'd have justification to repress me some way with a bullet or with a club. You can ask my father about that, I told him all about it. I told him just what they told me. Can you imagine how I felt? Can you imagine how I felt June the last year? I went to the Board and I was shot down again for a whole year. That's when—"

"No, I can't understand."

"That's right. It's an existential impossibility."

We are both silent. I can hear our breathing and the agitated rattling of George's chains.

"That's when Huey Newton sent word that he was going to send Fay Stender. In the last year, Huey started a correspondence with Fay. At the opening of this year, I hadn't seen her yet and I guess Huey had asked her to see what she could do. We made arrangements for a couple of meetings, but she was busy, you know. But the opening of this year when this case went down, she came right up to see me. January 16. If she had come earlier, the Board appearance yesterday could have been my last official crawl." His last words are almost a sob. "These ten years went by pretty fast." These words are said as if they were his own epitaph. "When it's gone, it goes by fast. I hope the next ten don't go this fast." Again he laughs in a way that is so much like tears. "Let it slow down."

I remember that there are only a small handful of letters between his last Board appearance and the murder for which he has been indicted. In most of the letters, it is almost as if he is deliberately making a legacy. One letter to his brother stood out in my memory:

November 27

They called me up to classification last week. Said they were considering sending me back to San Quentin. They're supposed to need the space here for something, and I wasn't doing well enough. They said that if I improved a great deal, it is possible that in four or five years I might be considered for Chino—the prison for honor inmates.[*]

In five years he would be thirty-three years old. From that letter on, I don't think he ever expected to get out of prison alive. He must have known he would never be able to do "good time" again. He had made the mistake of believing in the prison authorities. He would never trust them again.

"Did they send you a message, a notification, after yesterday's appearance?"

"No. They asked me to sign something. I told them to stick it up their ass. Might have been a confession or something. I'm very careful about what I put my name on now. They're getting awful vicious around here." He looks down at himself self-consciously, and his body is still and inert. "You see how I'm dressed, don't you? They don't usually make us dress this way."

"I like it when you react to the whole world's rejection of you as a tribute to your character."

He laughs again. "I told you how the Parole Board tried to call me up again. I don't care how this thing turns out. I'll never go up there again. In all the days of my life, they'll never see me again."

"In one of your letters you mention a woman lawyer could get you a parole if you gave her a thousand dollars. Did anything come of that?"

"Somebody gave me her name. I didn't know anything about her or her qualifications, but one of the brothers told me, 'Man, you been in the joint too long, you need a lawyer, a lawyer who could work behind the scenes for you, talk to some people. If you pay her, something like that, she can perhaps do some good at your next Board.' "

[*] *Soledad Brother.*

"Did anything ever come of that?"

"No. She was never contacted." There was another long silence. "They never contacted her." By "they" I knew he meant his mother and his father.

"It is kind of ironic the last twenty-eight years to end up like this. I will be a better guy because of this last one though.* It has been pretty clear to me right from the beginning. Even before this incident it was pretty clear to me. I had read Marx and Lenin. I had the big picture in my mind right away, and I read the guer- rilla books. (The only fiction I have ever read was a war story.) Since this case has been going on, however, the way it has pro- ceeded with the coalition between institution, DA, judge and jury, it has become even clearer to me. You know they have got this country locked up." George sighs, but some of the tension is beginning to lift.

"Tell me a little bit about the frame-up."

"All right. After several unsuccessful attempts to get rid of me up at San Quentin, my folks put pressure on the authorities. They wrote long letters to them saying, 'We know you are trying to kill our son.' You know, my father got mad at the end there. Even talked to a couple of friends he had. He calls them friends. They're not really friends of his, you know. That was a slip of the tongue. He talked to one or two people that he knew in the politi- cal arena. And they were investigating my case, why were they holding me so long. So a little pressure hit San Quentin, that is why they transferred me down here. This being the type of joint it is, I thought, well, they sent me to Soledad now because they couldn't succeed up there. They will have a clearer shot at me in Soledad. They're going to get rid of me in Soledad."

"Get rid of me"—the words reverberate in my head. "I'm really interested in how prison officials manipulate cons. Like how they get them to turn against each other and give evidence, bear false witness against fellow cons."

"That is what I am leading up to. Soledad is known all over as the most racist type of joint. This is the area where police can beat guys to death, and get away with it because of the coalition

* The indictment for the murder of the guard.

with the DA and things like that. Here in Soledad the police have the strongest control over the convicts. This joint is so tight because you got this one long hall running down through the entire prison. The pigs can see everything that goes on all the time. They got the inmates in a state of complete submission and panic. They are really terrorized, and that terror brings out all the weakness in some people, all the weakness. And uppermost in their minds is getting away from here. Getting away alive and everything else. They will sacrifice self-respect, the truth. The fact that they are destroying someone else doesn't even enter into the equation. You got people here who stand around and wait for incidents so they can give information, earn a star, get a point behind their names. It was the same with this situation here.

"I don't think anybody really knows what happened in that wing that night except the participants. Because I imagine that anyone who would go to kill a pig in a joint like this with so many rats and weak type people would do it in dead secret. They would be well organized. But the situation was so opportune, they had guys lined up outside the captain's office to give information. All the captain's got to do is lead the questions and reconstruct it for them. Listen, think of it this way. In the grand jury testimony and in the statements that our lawyers have from the witnesses, the only thing that any one of them is sure of, the only thing that all of them correlate on—listen, this is not just coincidental—the only thing they are certain of are the three guys involved. All the other testimony is wildly contradictory."

"In the testimony that I read yesterday one guy has you like this [arm around neck] around the guard. The other witness has you punching the guard in the face. An absolute contradiction. And how anybody could confuse you with Fleeta! It's fantastic! You don't look alike, man. There is no way of mistaking the two of you."

"But you didn't read it close. If you had read it close, you would have read that somebody has got me holding this guy with my right arm. He's over here, but still he can't see my face. I'm supposed to be holding this cat with my right arm. Now listen, man, he didn't see my face until later on when I dropped the guy and I'm supposed to be beating on him."

The words just slipped out: "He didn't see my face until later on when I dropped the guy." He hears himself—his face pulls back for just an instant and he sees in my face that I have heard him, heard the same words he had heard and understood what they meant. He goes on without stopping or even drawing a breath.

"It's only one thing that all of the guys are certain about—the three guys who are supposed to have done it. It's deliberate. They showed these guys pictures and said, 'These are the guys who did it.'"

I pretend not to have heard him, but I know he has seen it in my eyes. I have to believe that he wanted to tell me, or at least some part of him did. Or perhaps it was just because he had told me so many things, opened himself up so completely, that it just came out with all the rest. Or perhaps he realized that I would understand.

"It's what you call canned testimony," I suggest.

"Look, if they can get away with stuff like that, it's the last of my rights. It's gone. They're going to kill me and that's the last right I got, the right to live."

"I don't think they are going to succeed this time. I really get that feeling, you know. Talking to Fay and to John. Those people are just not going to give up. They are not going to give up at all."

"Those are beautiful people. There's no two ways about it, I love them. You know, for a cat who has never had any help, never had any assistance . . . I consider myself a cat that has been neglected all of his life, I consider myself a hardened conditioned cat, you know, who doesn't give a damn—I mean, they kill me, so what?—you know? I tried anyway. And when I do die, I still have all my face intact. But you know how I feel about a person who will step in and put his arms around me. Oh, it's wonderful. Do you know how I feel? You don't know. You don't know. You couldn't know." And his eyes soften and become moist.

He is still a doomed man, but now that he has a new life, he wants to make the most of it while it lasts. He has literally stepped from the death house into a dream world, and it seems as if all his wildest dreams can come true, all except the one that could really make all the others worthwhile, the dream of freedom.

"I guess I only know a little bit."

"You see, I knew that people like that existed, but where the hell were they? Man, now this is the time, the time when I need them most, and they show. That's what counts, it's the last battle you got to win, you dig? For a cat who has never had nothing, he can't be practical, he got to leap. The cat who has never had any kind of sympathy, who has been neglected from the womb to the tomb, when somebody comes along, man, and puts his arms around you, then you can harmonize. It affects that guy, it's like what I was telling you about before—the cadre, the heart of the revolution, it's going to come from here, from places like this. Take a cat who is sitting up in Folsom right now, in 'The Pit.' That's as low as you can go. What's going to be his reaction to somebody who comes along and pushes a hole in the wall and says, 'Come on out—come on, man, don't stay on here'? This guy is going to listen to what I am going to say. All right, this guy thinks he will never get out of here. He feels like he will never get out of here. Police have made him feel this way. Just imagine his gratitude when someone helps him escape."

Then because the feeling is too much for him, he changes the subject by asking if my tape recorder belongs to Fay.

"No, it's my machine. I was going to use Fay's machine, but since I was going down to Los Angeles tomorrow, I thought I'd get one of my own."

With a look, he reaches over and places his hand on my tape recorder. "Do you mind if I turn this thing off for a while?" I shake my head. And for a few minutes, we sit there in silence. Then he moves his chair closer to mine and almost whispers in my ear.

"You know those other two guys didn't have anything to do with that incident. I didn't need them. They would have only gotten in the way." He leans back and then comes closer again. "If it looks like the trial is going bad, that's what I am going to say. Nobody else is going to hang for me."

His eyes catch mine and tell me to trust him to do the right thing. I half-close my eyes and nod my head. He sighs. Then he gets up from his chair and walks hobble-legged in a circle around the room. Then he sits down again. After a few moments of silence, he reaches over and clicks on my tape machine with a look as if to say, "Is there really anything else to talk about now?"

I am the first to break our silence.

"Did you know there is supposed to be a rally tomorrow? I hope I can go. Do you get to hear much about stuff like that, about what's going on in terms of developing support?"

"Oh, yeah. I had a wonderful woman writing named Joan Hammer."

"Oh, I know Joan. Sure, I know Joan. I just met her for the first time this morning."

"She's a wonderful woman. There should be a world full of women like that, we'd have no problem." It is as if he is tasting something sweet and fresh like a peach.

"I'm going to have to play this for her because I'll see her when I go back there."

He laughs with delight at the idea of establishing contact this way. "If we had a world full of people like Joan, then I wouldn't have any problems. You wouldn't have any problems."

"Right."

"She is a wonderful woman. You know what I mean. You can sense it right away. Just reading the stuff she writes, she is a woman that every woman would like to be. But she wants to be my mama, you know, and I can't stand that."

"Someday there'll be no mamas."

"No, she's nice about it. She came up to see me."

"She'd like to come up more, but she can't." When she had heard I was coming, she asked me to explain this to George.

"No, they won't let her. I mean, she came up to see me and I just saw this big natural beautiful woman. I just grabbed her and squeezed her like a lunatic. It was a natural thing to do, right? All right, we're sitting and talking and I wanted to hold her hand."

"Right."

"Now she stroked me across my face like you would do your son."

"How about that?" I shrug my shoulders.

"But you know, maternalistic. But she wrote me, she wrote me a letter and said that all women should be all men's mothers and sisters and lovers. That's a beautiful sentiment, isn't it? Mothers, sisters, lovers. Mothers and comrades and lovers. She's my eyes and my ears. She keeps me informed. Life on a treadmill. You know, it's very difficult for a guy who you know hasn't experienced this thing to understand."

"I don't know how anyone can understand it—imagination, empathy, identification, you know. But you don't get it, you don't get it. . . ."

"You can't."

"You get some, but you don't get it."

"Now, you know, like I have been trying to express, I believe in people's government. I believe in people. I believe in Marx and Lenin and Nkrumah. I believe in Sékou Touré and Mao Tse-tung. I believe in Castro."

It is like the prayer I used to say before going to bed when I was a child.

Without warning a guard breaks into the room. "You'll have to terminate this now."

A sudden chill comes over me. "Do we have any more time?"

"No, sir."

"Shit."

"What time is it?" George asks.

"Two-fifteen. Right?"

"Do we have pickets outside or something? Is somebody picketing this joint?" George had been told that a group was going to picket the prison. But it actually didn't happen until the next day.

We embrace. I feel his rib cage giving just a little bit under the pressure of my arms, and I see the look of surprise on his face. We give each other the Black Power handshake and the clenched fists. George leaves with the guard. I feel as if he is being torn out of my arms.

As he leaves the room, the guard tells me, "I'll have to leave you here, Mr. Armstrong, until I can get an escort for you. It won't be long."

I am left in that drab empty room that reminds me so much of a conference room in my old high school. My hands move mechanically and put my belongings together. I put all the empty candy wrappers and the two empty cigarette packets in the waste-basket. I empty the ashtray and wait. I am numb all over.

Finally the guard returns and leads me out through the gun-metal-gray corridors and down the stairs, through the five electrically operated doors and the barbed-wire fence into the parking lot.

The car is almost boiling-hot from the sun. I fumble open the door and fall onto the scorching-hot seat. I want to cry, I want the release of tears, tears of rage. I can't move. I don't know if I will ever see George again. My impotent rage at those walls and those chains, all those years that he has spent inside, completely immobilizes me, and I sit there feeling blanched and lifeless, with all the empty cars around me like dead insects.

George killed that guard. I heard it from his own lips. So there was no way out for him; he was doomed. They would convict him and they would gas him to death. Sitting there, I think back to all his deep sighs, and they seem like omens of his asphyxiation. George knew it too. "They are going to take away my last right, the right to take in air and push it out again." That was why he breathed more deeply than anyone I have ever known; unconsciously taking in such great quantities of air to store it up against the day when there would be none.

He had done it. That was why he worried about his father suddenly going berserk in the streets. Because he knew how it could be.

I think of Bucky, the white inmate whom George had protected from his black comrades. "We had some serious hard rapping, dialectics, you know. This was a beautiful thing."

I remember his cryptic remark: "At one time I just felt there was no possibility of any white person ever liking me." And the little white boy whom George approached on his first day in school, and felt his hair and said, " 'What the fuck is wrong with you?' I didn't say it like that, but you know. I did that a couple of times, and later . . . somebody found me with the back of my head split open." And I think back to the grand jury testimony:

"Jackson had his arm around his throat and this other black was punching him in the face." And the guard and Bucky and the little white boy all come together in my mind. And the guard could have been any one of them. The guard could even have been me. I think back to that moment when I had been afraid. Had it all been just my imagination or just for an instant had I reminded George of the man he had killed?

I realize that we have all come too late for George, that Fay, Angela and the book and all the rest are just pretend; the reality is the pain that his smiles barely manage to conceal. The reality is the aching and pressure behind his eyes which never stop.

The Family

"Women just don't suffer the mental mortification of defeat and emasculation that we men do. Lester has lived with it for many years trying to rationalize it, justify it, pretend that it does not exist, but it has affected him very deeply."

—Soledad Brother

June 20, 1970

It is there in the air between them, an old unsettled argument, a piece of family history that freezes their eyes whenever they meet. I don't know them. I just met the girl the night before. I'm sitting here waiting for George's father to arrive. Later his mother is supposed to come. The girl is a member of the Soledad Brothers Defense Committee. Her parents are old-line left-wingers and they have put their house at my disposal. And I get the sense that there are many things and people who pass unquestioned in and out of their lives and that their home is accustomed to sheltering people who don't want to talk about themselves. They know about George and that I have been to see him the day before, but they don't show any curiosity. When I volunteer any information, they shrink away from it as if I might be telling them something that they had no right to hear. Everything about them seems deliberately washed out as if they had removed all identifying marks from themselves, as if even their fingerprints had been removed. As we sit around the breakfast table, the tension between the girl and her parents becomes more and more shrill. I have a sinking feeling that soon they will run out of trivialities and start screaming at each other. And I am acutely conscious that at any minute George's father will arrive.

An old heartbroken black man was the way George had described him to me. I had wanted to visit him and his wife in their own home—to see where George had lived, perhaps even to go into his room because I am sure that his mother has left it just the way it was before he was sent away to prison. The night before

105

I had dreamed about sitting in his chair and suffusing myself with a sense of George's past. But they would only agree to visit me here, and not even together but separately. And something about their voices told me that their marriage was breaking up and that they had come to the point where it was intolerably painful for them even to be in the same room together.

At last the doorbell rings and I go to answer it. There at the door is a slim, elegantly dressed black man. I look and look again. He is George, but George stripped of all his muscle. George with his sensitivity and delicacy completely uncovered.

"You must be Greg. I'm Lester." He hesitates and then adds, "George's father." His tone indicates that he finds it painful to identify himself this way. He looks more like he should be George's younger brother than his father. As he crosses the room, it is almost like seeing George again because even their bodies move with the same fluid grace.

The girl and her parents slip out of the house almost invisibly and Lester and I are left alone.

As we begin to talk, his look warns me not to go too far, not to trespass where I am not wanted. It is the same look I have seen on so many black faces, a look that always seems to say, "Don't mess with me, Whitey, or you'll get more than you bargained for." And yet the menace in his eyes is completely contradicted by the quiet unassumingness of his dress. It is as if he were trying to distract people from the deeper truth of his eyes. I look into them and I can almost see what he is thinking: That I don't really care about him and that I never will. That I'm only trying to get something out of him. That I won't care how much I hurt him or how much I have to humiliate him to get what I want. That I will never be his friend because I already care about his son.

"What a fantastic tragedy that something like this should happen to George," I begin.

"And that it should happen to someone like myself. I am one of a thousand. I mean, I am one of a thousand that might be subjected to conditions like these. Why me?" he replies.

At first I don't understand what he means. Then I realize that he has been forced to identify himself as the father of an accused murderer. And that he imagines that all the stigma of George's supposed crime also adheres to him, that he is a marked man.

After a long silence, he looks up at me and takes a deep breath and purses his lips. Then looking away at the wall, he asks me almost inaudibly if I have talked about the murder of the guard with George.

"We talked about it," I reply.

There is another long silence. Lester continues to breathe heavily. He leans forward and this time, staring right into my eyes, he asks me if I think George murdered the guard. And just for one instant, I want to slap him in the face with the truth, just the way he had beaten George when he was a child, the way my own father had beaten me. But I know what I have to say.

"There is no question about your son's innocence."

For an instant, Lester's eyes open wide. Then he sinks back into his chair with obvious relief. His body goes limp. He looks around the room and smiles as if to reassure all the invisible presences that everything is really all right.

For what seems a long time, he just sits there beaming. When he looks back at me, there is no more distrust in his eyes. Words begin to pour from his mouth.

He had always thought that George was getting what he deserved. George didn't know how to carry himself. He was always getting into trouble. What could Lester have done? What could anyone have done for George? Lester hadn't even bothered to get a lawyer for his son. What good would it have done? George would have just gotten into new trouble.

"I thought that the charges they were leveling against him were deserving. That shows you how naïve I was." No indignation yet. No outrage. He is still trying out the idea of George's innocence.

I can almost see the track of his thoughts. If the authorities are wrong about the murder, maybe they were wrong about everything else too. But the idea of his son's innocence is still too new to him and he can't hold on to it for long. He has defined most of his adult life on the conviction of his son's guilt. Perhaps I am only lying to him. How could George possibly be innocent? George, who never hid his feelings. George, who never had any respect for authority, who challenged everything, who never stopped fighting. And yet here are all these people suddenly telling him that his son is a great man and a great writer, telling him that his son has been a victim of injustice all his life. It is such a new and startling idea that Lester needs time to think about it. It couldn't be true and yet . . .

It would be a whole new role for Lester to be the father of an important man. He wants to believe it. And yet it means that everything he has done for the past ten years has been wrong. That his whole way of life—everything he has been up to—is now suddenly open to question. For over a decade, he has done everything possible to dissociate himself from his son. And now his son has made him an important man. Can he begin to live through his son? Does he dare? George has never given him anything he ever wanted before. Never given him anything a son should give his father. Why should it suddenly be so different now? How could everything change so suddenly and in such a completely unexpected way?

The suspicious look returns to his face. Someone has told him that George is a born leader. He wants to know what that means. I explain that George is a leader because he is admired and trusted by the other inmates. "They look up to him because of his intelligence and strength. That is why the prison is trying to get rid of him on this murder charge. They feel that George knows too much, and that makes him dangerous to them."

Lester flinches. "What they should do is change their whole rehabilitation system. Then they wouldn't have these problems."

"I don't know about that. But I feel that they really want to eliminate George. That is what we are seeing now."

"Why not send him home then?" he asks, stumbling into more emotion than he had expected. His voice catches. He turns his head away. It has been so long since he has allowed himself to feel anything about his son.

"Because they don't do things like that. They have him there and they are going to control or destroy him. One way or the other."

"And if they destroy him, then they can use it as an example for future prison operation." He sighs deeply.

"Absolutely!"

"Is this helping their rehabilitation, is this helping black rehabilitation?"

"No, not a bit."

"And they don't care, do they?" He fights back his tears. He
shakes his head to clear away the pain. I realize that he doesn't
believe for an instant that George is ever coming home. "They
just want him to come out a broken man. That's all they want,
to make broken men. Every man I have seen come out of there is
a broken man. I don't want George to come out that way, believe
me."

He turns away and fights to recover his composure. The last
thing he wants is to break down in front of me.

In a sudden rush of compassion I tell him how much he
reminds me of George.

"Well, don't quote what I'm about to tell you." And he looks
at me suspiciously.

"I won't quote anything that you—"

"If you think it is wise, if you think that it will help him. Or if
it will clear up anything about him." As if I were some kind of
special judge. "Perhaps it will clear up some of the things that are
cloudy right now. I hope it will anyway." From his look it is clear
that he believes he is going to reveal something truly extraordinary. But then he falls silent. I wait for him to speak and the
silence is excruciating. I wait and wait, and finally he is forced
to go on: "But things will get a lot better. They will."

"I think you were going to tell me something and then you
decided not to? You were going to tell me that you were like your
son in a lot of ways too. I think you were going to explain that."

But he has decided not to tell me now. "There is a lot more
that I can tell you, but I can't tell you now. About our future.
That is, if he can get out of this thing. I can't tell you now. We
have already planned what we intend to do. Not to overthrow the
government as most people would think, or do something that
. . . it is a very unusual move that we intend to make if he can
get himself out of this thing."

I don't know what he was going to say, but to myself I guess
that it must have been something like *George and I are more alike*

than anyone will ever know. I simply have held in my anger all
my life. I have never let anyone see that side of myself.

He pauses and then goes on. "George's mind was so muddled
earlier in his life. I am surprised the way he turned out. Hopefully
we don't take this away from him." He pauses again and goes on in
a quavering, almost whispering voice. "Take his life away from
him. They're not going to do it."

For a while we just sit and stare at each other. Then we get up
from our chairs at the same moment because we both know the
conversation is over. I walk out with him to his weather-beaten
car. As he drives off, I remember one of George's letters about his
father:

I love his brother, my father, and when I use the word "love" I am
not making an attempt at rhetoric. I am attempting to express a reful-
gent, unrestrained emanation from the deepest, most durable region of
my soul, an unshakable thing that I have never questioned.

He stayed with us, worked sixteen hours a day, after which he
would eat, bathe, and sleep—period. He never owned more than two
pairs of shoes in his life and in the time I was living with him never
more than one suit, never took a drink, never went to a nightclub,
expressed no feelings about such things, and never once reminded any
one of us, or so it seemed, never expected any notice of the fact that
he was giving to us all of the life force and activity that the monster-
machine had left to him. The part that the machine seized, that death
of the spirit visited upon him by a world that he never influenced, was
mourned by us, and most certainly by me, but none ever made a real
effort to give him solace. How do you console a man who is unap-
proachable?*

It is still early afternoon when I turn back toward the house.
Now I see it for the first time. Last night I had arrived from San
Francisco in darkness. A squashed rose-colored stucco building
like a dwarf's mansion. Small rubberoid grass lawn. Wild profusion
of poinsettias and tiger lilies. In the blinding sunlight, it almost
seems to be laughing back at me.

I start back into it, half-hoping that I have locked myself out.
Why do I have to care? What is there about me—what kind of

* *Soledad Brother.*

gaping hole is there in my sense of myself—that makes me want
to put myself through all this? Now I have to wait for George's
mother, the woman who had "attempted to press, hide, push,
capture" him in her womb. Once he had written that he wouldn't
be in prison if "she hadn't been reading life through rose-colored
glasses." And I wonder why my heart is beating so fast and why
my face feels so hot and flushed.

It is after nine when Georgia finally arrives. "So you are Greg.
I've been wanting to meet you. That's Angela and Jonathan
behind me."

She has the kind of weariness that results from years of waiting
up every night for someone who never comes home. Her dark eyes
glitter feverishly. She is slightly stooped, as if from a great weight
carried too long. With her head bent forward and her chin resting
on her chest, she gives the impression of someone who is braced
for a final crushing blow.

Angela and Jonathan are expected somewhere else, but they
seem to want to stay and hear about George. At least they make
no motion to leave. Georgia and I sit apart in one corner of the
room, and she begins to tell me about her son's childhood. I ask her
where they lived and her eyes flash.

"I don't call it the ghetto. I just call it a place where poor
people live."

While she is talking, Jonathan moves nervously around the
room, getting up and then sitting down again beside Angela—
talking in loud stage whispers as if to say that it could be of no
interest to anyone what his mother says. I realize that he is performing for Angela, trying to convince her that he is completely
independent of his mother. But it is in vain because everything
he does only reinforces the sense of his dependence.

Georgia begins to describe the Catholic school where she sent
George. I interrupt almost pugnaciously.

"Did you know that George hated Catholic school?" Trying to
show Angela that it is really George I care about and not his
mother, playing up to her.

Georgia glares at me with sudden anger. "No, he didn't. He

says he did, but he didn't. That is an opinion that he has formed since he grew up."

"Didn't he try to stay home from school?"

Her eyes flash at me for trying to refute her. "No! You don't know, you're not his mother."

Jonathan has moved closer to us. "Can I say something?" From his tone of voice he seems to expect his mother to tell him to be quiet.

"Say it," she replies in that exasperated tone mothers have when their children interrupt.

"All right. George rejected the Catholics. He rejected religion altogether because he found out that it has no value. It's just a crutch." This is the moment he has been waiting for, the opportunity to protect his brother from his mother's distortions. He speaks his brother's name with something close to awe.

Georgia glares at him and then turns back to me. She explains how she used to make all George's clothes. He was the only child from the block who went to school dressed in a shirt and a tie. Sometimes he would roll in the dirt and jump off streetcars and fight and so his clothes would get soiled and torn. But she would stay up at night mending and washing. "If I took a notion, I'd get up and wash at twelve o'clock at night and hang the clothes out in the yard."

She taught all her children proper table manners, the importance of chewing with their mouths closed and which fork to use, because those things influence the way people think of you.

Listening to her talk, I realize that she must have been a powerful dreamer. I can almost hear her saying to herself over and over again, *This is the way it should be. This is the way it has to be. My children will be perfect. No one will ever find anything wrong with them. They will be so perfect that no one will ever reject them because they are black.*

This was particularly true of George, her first-born son. George the choirboy whom they always put up in the front row, who memorized things he heard on the radio when he was only two years old, who snuggled up in her skirts to read. George said that she wanted to trap him in her womb, but I think it was really just her girlhood dreams of how a boy should be.

I ask her about the first time George was arrested for stealing a purse and she explodes at me.

"George won't tell you the truth about this. He didn't steal the purse. It was the other guy who did it. George will swear to this day that he was the guilty one, but you see I know better."

Whenever George was arrested, she would go down to the station house, but the police would not let her see her son until they were ready to let him go. George would never admit to her that the police had beaten him, but she would see that his eyes were red from crying.

And though I hear her words, and find myself moved by them, I'm really only half-listening. My eyes are on Jonathan and Angela, who are whispering to each other in the opposite corner of the room. I want to find some way to become a part of their conversation, an excuse to move over to the couch where they are sitting and feel their bodies close to mine and sense their presence enveloping me.

With half an ear I hear Georgia telling me, "I can't get drunk and I get this twitching in my neck all the time now. There's not much I can do except get up and say a few dumb words at some rally." Her voice pulls at me, but Jonathan and Angela seem to be getting ready to leave. My mind is racing. What can I say to keep them here? Gesturing with my hand to Georgia, I get up and go over to them. Smiling at Angela, I ask her if she will write something for me about the case. Will I be able to see her again? Is she going to the Defense Committee party on Sunday? Can she bring me her letters from George? Will she ever be able to spend some time with me? She nods her head at everything I say.

As she and Jonathan move toward the door, Georgia reminds Angela almost waspishly not to forget to bring cigarettes when she comes back. Angela smiles and leaves the room. Jonathan comes over to his mother. "Remember what you promised George, Mama."

"I remember," she replies sheepishly, lowering her eyes.

"That's right. It's very important to George," I add.

"How do you know what we're talking about?" Georgia looks up at me reproachfully. I explain that George had asked me to talk to her about being nice to Angela. She shakes her head and sighs. Angela comes back into the room to collect Jonathan. I sit and watch until their young excited voices are cut off by the closing of the door behind them. I am left alone with George's mother.

"I remember one day when his father found him in the house reading. He accused him of 'sitting up in your mother's dresses.' He made him go out in the alley and play ball with the boys. My husband seemed to think that if George loved me too much, if he hung around me too much, it wasn't good for him. He'd be a sissy or something like that. In other words, he was jealous. He was always jealous of me and George." She catches me with her gentle eyes and this time she won't let me go.

"You want the truth, don't you? I'm going to give you the truth. I've been longing to give it to somebody for a long time."

She could never forgive her husband what he had done to George. He never took any notice of his accomplishments at school. Once she had convinced a parole officer to put in a good word for George, but Lester had intervened and spoiled everything. When George has escaped from a reformatory, it was his father who turned him in. Once Lester had even written a letter to the Parole Board, asking that George be kept in prison when they were actually considering letting him go. And everything he had done to George was intended to hurt her.

Sitting there beside her, watching her dark, almost liquid eyes, I know that she is really telling me about herself and the tragedy of her marriage. Because George is herself, the self that she wanted to be. And even as I am thinking these words, she tells me about how she used to be a tomboy and that her name would have been George if she had been born a boy. And I know that she has suffered everything that has been done to George exactly as if it had been done to her. As she talks, her face is glistening and moist. Rilke wrote of people who use up all their faces and are left finally with no face at all. Georgia's face is completely naked now, as if it had just been born. The memory of so much pain seems to have washed away all the intervening years.

I tell her that it isn't just George and his father, that it is all fathers and sons. "Terrible things happen between fathers and sons. Terrible things."

Our heads slump for a moment. Then Georgia goes on. Her pain is so sharp as she remembers that it seems as if her flesh is about to bleed. She doesn't want to blame her husband. She knows that he has had to support her and their children and that he has had to work sixteen hours a day giving all his life force to the death-machine, as George once called it, but still there should have been something left over for her, for her womanhood.

"He thinks because he's hiding behind those long hours, he has served his purpose in life. I would say to him, 'Why don't you talk to the kids more? Why don't you try to know them? If George has done anything wrong, you just have to talk to him.' Instead of talking to him, he'd beat him up. You know, you just can't go to a person and start beating him up before he knows what you're going to beat him up about."

Coughing, she lights a cigarette. "I'll probably quit when they finally decide that my son's not an animal and that he is a human being and that he has a brain and an intellect and that just because he is black doesn't mean that he has to be expelled from the human race."

I close my eyes and breathe deeply. My head is swimming. I look up at her and she catches me again with her eyes.

"You know what? I'd just like for my husband to go up there once, put his arms around George, hug him and tell him, 'I understand, I understand.' I want that as bad as I want him to get out of that place. Do you know that? Just once in his life, just go there and hug that guy and tell him, 'I understand how you suffered.' If he'd do that, I could almost stand up and die happy. But do you know what? He is not going to do it, ever. And just once, if he could come to me—he doesn't have to say he loves me—all he has to do is come to me and say he understands.

"You know that they are going to kill George, don't you?" Heaving the words up from her chest. "They have medicines and things now that they put in people's food. You know, once they electrocuted a man in New York who was innocent. Afterwards they found out who committed the crime. Someone asked them about it and all they could say was 'Well, you know, mistakes are made. Nobody's perfect.' That's what they said, but somebody was already dead and buried." And her dark eyes burn into mine for the last time.

June 21

Before going back to New York I attend a meeting of the Soledad Brothers Defense Committee. Georgia brings her family album. She doesn't relax her grip on it from the moment she enters the house. With her two daughters flanking her, she sits on the stairs leading to the second floor turning the pages. Her daughters constantly exclaim with surprise. I hunker on the floor in front of her. When she wants me to see something, she pivots the book ever so slightly in her lap, and I swing around as much as I can.

As I watch her sitting there turning the pages, it occurs to me that it must be like having George sitting in her lap again. The expression on her face reminds me of the look that young girls have when they play at being mothers. As she goes on, a faint mistiness comes into her eyes and her voice takes on the quality of fond recollection. I can see her thinking, "Why did it ever have to change? Why couldn't it have been this way always?" Fixed, immutable, like photos in a family album. It is the same look I see her give Jonathan. Shy, as if she felt that she didn't really deserve so much happiness. Wary because she seems to feel that if she takes too much notice it will wash away like a daydream.

George in the family album. As a young boy, he is bright-eyed and smart-alecky, one of those charming, infuriating know-it-alls who are as seductive and lovable as they are irritating. Too much life, too much brightness for the world. Then when adolescence comes, he begins to change. About the time he first gets sent to reform school his eyes begin to darken and his face becomes brooding. Just before he is sent to prison, his spindly body, the proverbial fencepost, has become heavily muscled and monolithic, faintly grotesque and deformed. He has begun to prepare himself for his lifelong ordeal.

Back in New York

June 21, 1970

Back in New York, I play sections of the tapes I made with George for some people in my office. Heads slump. No one looks at anyone else, all eyes focus on the floor. Bodies go limp. The air becomes still and heavy. People come and go. It is too much to take. Too oppressive. The glass and aluminum buildings of New York aren't made for so much reality. Nothing to absorb or deflect it. It all passes directly into us.

No work is done on those first two days that I am back in the city. It seems as if the tapes never stop playing. Is there a part of me that hasn't heard them a hundred times? Is there any pain left to be leeched from them? You'd think I would have sucked the very words off the tape and left it blank.

June 23

It is official now! The site of the trial has been moved to San Francisco. The Brothers will be transferred to San Quentin Prison at the end of this month.

June 25, 1970

DEAR GEORGE,

I have been sick ever since I left San Jose for New York late Sunday night. The way I've felt has a lot to do with what went on between us and what went on later with your mother and father. The truth is that I left a lot of myself with you in prison. Part of this feeling is simply missing you, missing our intensity and our friendship. The other part is much deeper and has a morbid, maiming quality which disturbs me. I identify myself with you. I see my life somehow connected with yours. . . .

I don't think I've ever told you how proud I am to be your editor. Wait till you see the reviews.

Your brother and comrade,

GREG

117

June 27, 1970

DEAR GREG,

The man who has never received a kind message, a gesture, and who has never held anything of value, material or otherwise, if he is healthy, or I should say remains healthy (my persuasion presupposes original innocence), he never becomes so practical as to expect more of the same—nothing. Less but never nothing.

And if he is still healthy of mind, he knows he can't be practical, he can't afford practicality. His have-nothing status, the absence of the all-important controls, predisposes him to impracticality, he can never relax, he is or becomes the desperate man. And desperate men do desperate things, take desperate positions; when revolution comes, he is the first to join it. If it doesn't come, he makes it.

But the significant feature of the desperate man reveals itself when he meets other desperate men, directly or vicariously; and he experiences his first kindness, someone to strain with him, to strain to see him as he strains to see himself, someone to understand, someone to accept the regard, the love that desperation forces into hiding.

This significant feature in the desperate men, and women, people, redeems them, redeems the revolution, alters the sanguine coloring of war, and gives revolution its love motive.

Men who have never received and have had little occasion to express the love theme of original goodness respond in a very significant manner to that first *real, spontaneous, gratuitous* kindness. Those feelings that find no expression in desperate times store themselves up in great abundance, ripen, strengthen, and strain the walls of their repository to the utmost; where the kindred spirit touches this wall it crumbles—no one responds to kindness, no one is more sensitive to it than the desperate man.

I'm trying to say thanks.

Power to the People—

COMRADE GEORGE*

June 28

This month there have been articles on the Soledad case in both *Hard Times* and *Ramparts*.

July 2

I find myself listening over and over again to the tapes I made with George. It is almost as if I expect those fateful words to

---

* *Soledad Brother.*

have disappeared. As if I had only imagined them. I can't help thinking that another person might listen and hear nothing at all, or hear those words with an entirely different meaning.

July 5

I've decided to let my son hear the incriminating tape. He is the only person I can really trust. I start the machine and there is George's disembodied voice against the background of the machine's dull whirring, like the sound of an ancient fan in an old hotel. Time passes and it all seems so unreal. And it does seem as if I have imagined it, as if the point has actually passed where I had remembered those words, and that nothing is there, and then suddenly I hear those words again. A swift puff of air, sardonic, accusing, reproachful. "Now listen, man, he didn't see my face until later on when I dropped the guy." And I watch my son's face. There is no change in his expression. I play the tape again, and this time he hears the words too. The fact that we have heard them together finally makes them incontrovertibly real. I think again of how George must have felt at the moment when those words "fell out of his mouth." Did he actually say them? Did I hear them? Was it all perhaps just a dream? Would he suddenly wake up in his cell alone with the beautiful sense of relief you have when you realize that something terrible that happened occurred only in a dream? But it wasn't a dream and he knew it was real. Did he wonder what I would do? Would I stop work on the book? Would I withdraw my support? Would I tell other people? Go to the authorities? Because there were those words on tape. Could he risk destroying them? Turning back the machine and obliterating them. What if I hadn't actually heard them or what if I hadn't understood their significance? Then destroying them would be like proving his guilt all over again. And at the same time, he would be showing me that he didn't trust me. In that instant between that final word and the next word, he had to make his decision. And everything was there in that one short look, in that moment of raising his eyes and looking into mine.

July 9

Fay has rented the second floor of a house in S.F. as a central office for the Defense Committee and as a place for defense workers to stay. Her original idea was that everyone associated with the case would live under the same roof. But the case has grown so fast that no single house could hold everybody now.

July 11

As I sit in the waiting room of Grand Central Station, the girl I am with suddenly screams out, "Look what they are doing to that man." I look up and two policemen are pulling a man across the station floor by his hair and the back of his shirt, beating him at the same time. We rush over. By the time we reach them, one of the police has dragged the man behind a barrier and out of sight back where the trains come in. The other policeman, a sergeant with an oily grinning face and a huge pendulous belly, stands at the barrier to keep us back. My eyes focus on his belly, and the shiny blue fabric which is smoothed over the distended flesh, as if it were the skin of a balloon. Several other people have come up to the barrier with us. I scream at the cop to stop beating the man. He has no right whatsoever. It didn't matter what the man was doing. They have no right to beat him. My temper is flaring and I am on the verge of going out of control.

One of the men beside me tells the sergeant that he doesn't agree with my kind (I am badly dressed and my long hair is disheveled), he is a conservative and supports the police. But he saw what happened, and it was wrong. The sergeant never stops smiling. "It's all right, folks. Just go on about your business. It's all over now. We just had to take him in." And his leering face seems like a concatenation of all the callous cynical brutality in the world. He is glad we have seen him. Part of him thrills to our recognition of his brutality.

I keep screaming at him. I feel my face going red with rage. The girl holds me tight. The other people go back. I allow her to pull me away. Several other police cross the floor of the station and go beyond the barrier back where they have taken the man. The leering sergeant follows them. I shake myself loose from the girl and follow them behind the barrier. There is no one there. Half darkness. The lighted tracks are off to one side. Bins and shadows and steel pillars.

An employee of the railroad passes by, and I ask him if he has seen where the police have gone. He points to a door. I go over and stand a few feet away and I hear the sound of scuffling. Two policemen come out and see me standing there. They turn around and go back in. A few seconds later a police captain comes out of the room and walks toward me smiling. I tell him what I have seen and he explains to me that it is all right. The man who was being beaten was a policeman. I tell the sergeant that it shouldn't make any difference. He is still a man and even policemen have rights. His benign smile suddenly disappears. It is replaced by a look of implacable hatred. *They are going to take care of it. And if I don't want to get taken in, I had better leave.*

I still stand there shouting. He reaches out and touches me. I recoil. I want the sergeant's badge number so I can make a complaint against him. The officer's mood changes abruptly once more. Smiling in complicity, he asks me to trust him. "I'm going to make a complaint myself," he says. Once more I ask for the badge number. His smile turns to white-hot anger. "I told you I was going to take care of it myself. Are you trying to call me a liar?"

I realize that if I say one more word I will be beaten up on the spot. Still seething, I walk back to the main waiting room. The girl's train is just about to come and I walk her to the main track. Then I walk back past the room and stand there for a while trying to hear some sign that they are still there. But all I can hear are the muted sounds of the station. So I start walking home. I begin to think about killing the sergeant, about buying a gun and waiting for him to leave work and then killing him. In my mind, I can see the bullets tearing apart the smooth expanse of his belly. I run the scene over and over again in my mind, trying to make it seem more real. And it seems to me as if I might actually do it. It is obvious that the sergeant should be killed just like that guard in Soledad. I wonder about how I could get a gun. My imagining of the event becomes so real that I am almost overcome with dread and foreboding.

July 13

Coming home I pass Grand Central again. Why shouldn't I kill the sergant? Doesn't he deserve to die? If I really cared, if I were a real man, I would do something.

July 17

Today I went to a political meeting. S. was there with whom I lived a few months before. Once I would have sat in silence and merely listened. But today I began talking violently and vociferously. I could feel S.'s beautiful dark brown eyes darting back and forth at me with surprise and anger. After the meeting was over she cringed away from me. I had become frightening to her. I had become frightening even to myself.

July 18

A girl told me today that she didn't want to become involved in the case. She has been asked to work with the Defense Committee. But she doesn't want to get to know the accused men, because there is a chance that someday she will have to sit helplessly by while they are gassed to death.

July 19

With Judy and her black boyfriend and two Black Panthers in her apartment.

The conversation turns to why whites become involved with blacks. One of the Panthers looks around the room at the paintings on the wall. Each of them depicts black men and women in a form of abject suffering. The largest is a study of thousands of grieving blacks massed in postures of dejection. He asks if she knows why she had chosen them. Judy suddenly becomes very wary. She starts to explain, but nothing she says makes any sense and she knows it. She incriminates herself deeper and deeper with each word.

Finally in despair of finding any acceptable explanation, she gives up. "I just like them."

With a sneer, the Panther provides another explanation: "Why, it makes you feel just like the mistress of the plantation."

And he is probably right up to a point. But there is something else, too, that I don't think he could understand. Her feelings about blacks make it possible for her to grieve for a part of herself that she couldn't grieve about directly. I think it's this way with most of us.

July 23

I put myself to sleep last night imagining that I was invading Soledad by helicopter to free George and the other two men by force.

I see the helicopter dropping onto the roof, blades slashing the sky. I hear the sounds of scurrying feet on the concrete in the darkness. I try to imagine a machine gun in my hands shaking my whole body. I see the tracks of the bullets lighting up the sky. In my dreaming, everything has a semblance of reality, except for the three men. I can never actually visualize them during the escape. Three shadowy figures who are simply taken somewhere— who have no life of their own. Who never talk or move without direction.

July 24

I couldn't get to sleep for a long time last night. Lying in a pool of my sweat, playing the same scene over and over again in my head. The first part was just like the night before. The helicopter, the guns flashing in the darkness. But last night, instead of taking them to a cabin in the woods, I imagined taking them out to a boat off the coast.

July 25

D. has started to walk home with me after work. We have gotten in the habit of staying late. Whenever we see a policeman, I shout, "Off the pig," and hurry on.

July 29

Lately I have been imagining that someone is going to break into my apartment and kill me. My bedroom has begun to seem like a coffin. I've taken to resting my bicycle against the door at night, so if someone breaks in, I will be sure to hear the bike falling and have a better chance to defend myself.

August 2

In my fantasies of rescuing George and the Brothers, I always stay behind. I never go with them and we never speak.

August 3

Last night I tried not to think about George, but it was no use. It has become like a piece of song that I can't get out of my head even though I despise it.

August 7

Friday night. Pacing the streets. Back and forth. Searching for something. Back to my apartment. Through the lobby past a slightly drunken girl who momentarily stirs me with desire. Her helplessness like a strong whiff of ether. A momentary swooning like someone turning out the lights. Into bed. Can't sleep. Why do I have to be alone? Out of the apartment building again into the streets. Up Third Avenue past the singles bars. Men and women in brightly colored clothes spilling out of the bars onto the sidewalks and the streets like petals falling. Very aware of walking close to them. Burning myself with their nearness. Trying to tire myself out. Finally, I buy a newspaper. Still in the street, I open it. There on the front page is a story about some blacks who have invaded a courthouse in California just a few hours before and kidnaped a judge. They are all dead now. Shot by the police. A judge is dead. Others are dead too. Bodies and blood everywhere. In my mind, I see a courthouse like an impregnable citadel, dead bodies of the invaders piled up around it like cordwood. Then I see the words "Soledad Brothers" and my heart beats faster. "Before they left the courtroom, the man who brought the guns into the courtroom shouted, 'Free the Soledad Brothers by 12:30.'" Then I see Jonathan's name. And in one instant I realize everything, and it seems as if I had known it already the minute I picked up the paper and saw the headline. But I refuse to believe what I know and I put it out of my head. I say to myself, it can't be Jonathan. It must be a mistake. If it was really Jonathan, they would have identified him as George's brother. Jonathan was too young. A reporter had probably gotten confused and included his name just because of the connection with the Soledad Brothers.

It is like one of those stories I think I read and then when I look for it again it is gone. And yet I know this time it is true and that it won't disappear.

Why are all the people still in the streets around me? Don't they realize that something extraordinary has happened?

Back in my apartment I sit looking blankly into space. The phone rings. It is the woman in whose house I had stayed in San Jose before seeing George the second time.

"Have you heard what happened?" I hear the tears in her voice. "It seems pretty certain that it was Jonathan. It has been announced on the radio."

Part of my mind tries to see his dead body. Immediately I wipe the image away. I feel my own body deadening. I remember a suit my mother had given me when I was eleven that had belonged to a boy who had died. She had forced me to wear it one day and I had gone outside and cut myself and torn the suit to ribbons. I feel as if someone is trying to force me to put on Jonathan's death just the way my mother had forced me to wear that suit. Just for an instant, feel as if George is killing us all. I see myself among that growing pile of bodies.

I can't stay in my room. The sense of Jonathan's death is so strong in it. The streets are almost empty now. I think I see a body in an alley, but I look again and it is a pile of garbage.

George alone in his cell. How will that small space contain all his grief and rage?

I find a later edition of the paper. There is no doubt at all now. A photograph! Jonathan in a short raincoat, standing, rifles in each hand. A look of stunned amazement on his face like someone who has crossed halfway on a tightrope only to realize that he can go no farther and that there is no way back.

And yet somehow there is an aura of theatricality about him, as if what he is doing is simply a performance and not an irrevocable act. No doubt he had imagined what he was going to do many times, closing his eyes and watching himself in imagination performing the same actions that he was actually performing now in real life. Because there was nothing natural or flowing about what he was doing. It all had to be willed and calculated. I detect a kind of bewilderment in his face as if he is wondering whether what he is doing is actually real or if it is still just another fantasy.

The newspaper quotes him as saying to a photographer, "Take

our pictures. We are the revolutionaries." *Take our pictures so we can see ourselves and so the whole world can see us and we will be more real and more tangible to ourselves.* How awesome his power must have seemed to him. Controlling the motions and lives of all those people. So outrageous and unbelievable. And to be taken so seriously by everyone. At some point he must have worried for just an instant what he would have done if no one had taken him seriously. If someone had just reached over and taken his guns and told him to go home. I wonder if, when he was in the midst of all that action, he thought about himself as himself or if he thought about himself as George.

There is one photograph of the police pulling his dead body from the van with a rope. According to the text they were afraid of the dynamite he had been carrying. Before this was over, Georgia had said, there would be blood in the streets. But she hadn't known then that it would be her son's. And I could remember her saying to me when I pointed out to her that most young blacks get in trouble with the law: "It won't happen to him." And giving him a look of smoldering reproach as if he wouldn't dare because of what she would do to him.

I feel myself being pulled by that rope. What would I have done if Jonathan had asked me to come along with him? I would have told him it wasn't a good plan. And I would have suggested he wait until we could devise a better one. Inwardly I would have hoped that there never would be any other plan. Or if there was one, that I would find a way not to be a part of it, because I don't want to die and be pulled along the street.

I am afraid of my own desperation. I realize how vulnerable I am to obsessions because of my emptiness. It seems to me then that I am in terrible jeopardy because any idea that enters my head will find nothing to oppose it and I will be driven against my will to almost any desperate act.

I start crying in the street. I am glad when my tears come because they make me aware that I am still alive and that I can still feel. And I want to feel more than anything else. And my tears somehow release me and put Jonathan's death outside of me.

I remember being with Jonathan that weekend in San Jose. I

remember him telling me almost resentfully about how he wished he could have spent as much time alone with his brother as I had. I could remember the adoration in his voice, and the awe with which he surrounded his brother's name. And he had seemed to want to stay close to me as if being near me made him closer to his brother. I also got the sense just for an instant that he felt I might have usurped his own special position with his brother.

At one point in the afternoon, a basketball game had started. I had suggested to Jonathan that we join them. As we had walked onto the court and begun to move the ball, I had heard a woman's voice behind me. "Look, Jonathan's playing basketball. I've never seen him do anything like that before."

Later that afternoon, Angela and Jonathan and I had gone over to George's lawyer's office to photostat some of George's letters for the book, and while Angela read them over and copied them, Jonathan and I had wandered around the large office, going into the icebox, taking soda and cheese, moving restlessly from room to room, talking about George and his book. I had a sense of him searching for something to do, not knowing where to turn or how to go on. And I had a sense that he couldn't keep still because everything seemed so trivial in comparison to the problem that had begun to obsess him. George was in jail. They were going to kill George. He knew it. His mother knew it. Was there anything else that mattered? And we all were just standing around talking.

As we were getting ready to leave, Jonathan had asked me when I was going back to New York. I told him that I was going back that night. His eyes lowered slightly and clouded. "I'd really like to go to New York. What does it cost one way?" I had told him, and he said he didn't know how he could get that much money. I had told him I would loan it to him, but I didn't have that much cash. He wandered off in another direction and those were the last words I ever said to him.

In some of the photographs of the courthouse raid, he is completely still. The photos of the others give off a sense of fluster and hysteria, but Jonathan has an almost eerie calm about him, as if he had passed over altogether into another realm of being.

August 9
Back to the office on Monday.

A black girl who works on the same floor is waiting for me. Her eyes are glittering and she rocks back and forth. "What a great thing he did. Everybody is talking about it. At last somebody did something. Killing a judge. Oh, Gregory, it's just too beautiful."

I can't look at her. Doesn't she realize that a young boy has died and what that means—the grief of his mother and father, his brother and his sisters and the grief of his friends?

It is the same all day. It seems as if every black I know calls to tell me the same thing. *What a heroic thing Jonathan had done. What a great man he was.* They are all glowing with pride. They have an entirely different sense of life from mine. They don't grieve for Jonathan's unlived life; he didn't have one because he was black. To them, Jonathan had saved himself by the manner of his death. Because they were black, they saw long life not as I did, as the means to greater accomplishment, but only as a prolongation of defeat and pain. In their eyes, Jonathan had saved himself from all of that. His death was a deliverance. By dying that way he had won for himself far more than he ever could have by continuing to live.

And all that day, something George told me repeats itself again and again in my head: "Don't ask him about his age. He's only a youngster and . . . he is sensitive about being sixteen."

San Quentin

"I have a young courageous brother whom I love more than
I love myself, but I have given him up to the revolution. I accept
the possibility of his eventual death as I accept the possibility of my
own. Some moment of weakness, a slip, a mistake, since we are the
men who can make none, will bring the blow that kills."

—*Soledad Brother*

August 10, 1970

Angela has disappeared. The police claim that Jonathan used
her guns at Marin. She is being accused of complicity in murder
and kidnaping. The DA claims that some of the guns have already
been traced to her.

August 11

Coming into San Francisco from the airport at twilight is like
entering El Greco's Toledo. Silver-hued sky. Black clouds tearing
overhead. Sudden shafts of sunlight. My taxi stops at a three-story
frame house on a deserted street. The door is open, so I start up the
stairs. Suddenly I am in a room filled with people. Everyone on
tiptoes straining toward another room, chins in the air so they can
see over the heads of the people in front of them. I turn in the
direction of all the faces. Georgia, her daughter Penny and John
Thorne are standing with their backs against a row of windows,
storm clouds racing over the tops of the buildings across the street
behind them. The table in front of them is littered with tape
recorders and microphones like sleeping lizards. Georgia's face
seems almost charred by grief. There is a hush in the room. The
only sound is the straining of people to get closer. Then Georgia
starts to speak.

"After Soledad, all he would talk about was George. All he

129

would think about was George. . . . Jonathan felt George was going to be killed by the courts if he wasn't killed in prison.

"I think that the so-called justice in this country is the cause of my son being dead today. I don't know if you went to any of the hearings in Salinas or not, but just to go to one of those hearings and sit there, even if you weren't concerned with the people who were being tried, would just tear you apart."

It is just the same voice that I'd heard two months before. But it is scorched like her face and her eyes. Looking at her, I can't imagine where she can possibly get the energy even to form her words and push them out from herself. It is as if she is heaving up her very bones. And there is just a hint of reproach in her voice. As if to say, "Why do you have to put me through all this since you already know what I am saying? How many more times will you have to put me through this before you are satisfied?"

"He would go around to the courts in L.A. and watch the way they would treat people. He said that there wasn't any justice in court. He said that when people go to court everybody thinks they're guilty, they don't even have a chance to defend themselves. After he went to court once he came home and he told me: 'The judge just sits there and says no to everything. He doesn't even stop to think before he says no.' A lot of times when we'd be at the hearings he'd get up and go out and he'd be crying. It got to the point where he didn't want to eat very much—and he really loved to eat. One night in June he said, 'Mama, if I die, I want you to know that I died the way I wanted to die.'"

She pauses. Her eyes are wet.

"If I had known what was on his mind, I would probably have gone and helped him. I wouldn't have let any of my children do anything without my help if I could help them.

"My son was a good person. He saw what they were doing to his brother and he knew they were trying to kill him. The black man doesn't get justice in the courts. I'm a black American and I want the same justice a white man gets. I think Jonathan did what every other black man or white man who cared about his country would do. If you can't get justice one way, you take it another."

She has no more words. She has given everything. There is a

long silence. Then the reporters' questions begin to lash the air. "Do you know where Angela Davis is? Are you in contact with her?" "How do you feel now with one son about to go to trial for his life and your other son just killed trying to save him?"

Georgia's mouth drops open. Involuntarily she winces back toward the windows. A voice from the center of the room screams out that the press conference is over. The TV lights go off. The table in front of Georgia is cleared away. John, Penny and Georgia stand there quivering and shaking their heads. The room begins to clear. It is almost as if people are running for shelter from a sudden rain. Before I even know what is happening, it is empty, and Georgia, stooped and bent, clutching her large pocketbook against her chest as if to make sure that nothing else is taken from her, moves with her daughter and three young black men in a phalanx toward the door. When she sees me, she looks up. "Oh, hi, Greg. I hoped you would be here." One of the men holds Penny. She has fallen against him. Her body is thrashing in his arms.

I follow them as they make their way down the stairs. It is totally dark now. Out on the street, Penny throws herself into an adjoining hallway, huddling against a door and shuddering convulsively like someone with a high fever. The men speak to her very softly as they help her into a car and depart into the blackness.

August 12

I am locked inside one of the small coffin-shaped rooms usually reserved for the visits of San Quentin's condemned men, sitting at a table that divides the room, staring at the door through which George must enter. The foot of the door is screened and after a few minutes I see black shoes walking by in the corridor. Then I hear the sound of handcuffs being removed. The door opens and George enters tentatively, looking back almost gratefully at the guard who had brought him in. Probably the guard has said something to him about Jonathan because George thanks him. Then turning to me, he looks up with surprise and then looks away. "It's good to see you again, man."

Everything about him is hushed. His eyes glitter. He has that look of gaunt, feverish tenderness that always seems to follow in the wake of grief and exhaustion. He is young, almost like a boy. His hair is damp, as if he has just come out of the water. He tries to show me how glad he is to see me, but his face can't hold his smile. I see it forming and then slipping away. We stand silently.

Then George sinks heavily into the chair and with a sudden exhalation of breath like a sigh blurts out, "So they finally got my little brother." There is something questioning in his voice, almost as if he hopes I might tell him that it isn't really true. "I won't let anybody say anything against that boy. He was a beautiful brother and he thought it was going to work. Some fools are talking about him killing himself." He says the words like spitting out rotten meat, as if they are totally repulsive to him. His face contracts momentarily in pain. I realize that he is warning me so I won't say the wrong things.

"Nobody back there has gone to sleep since it happened." Gesturing with his head in the direction from which he has come. "We've all stayed up listening to the news reports on the radio. Everybody is really together now. It's never been this way before." He shakes his head in disbelief. "I really loved that boy." Long silence. I feel on the verge of tears. I don't even trust my voice to speak.

Finally George shakes himself out of his grief. "What have you got there?" he asks. I have brought the manuscript of his book. I ask him if he wants to work on it. "Oh, man, I really need something to take my mind off things. Let me see what you've got. You know, I've never seen this before."

He takes the manuscript from me and holds it for an instant, almost as if it were a living thing squirming in his hands to get free. Without loosening his grip on it, he begins to leaf through the pages, stopping sometimes to read. "Oh, I remember this"—smiling, getting lost in his words.

He looks up at me apologetically. "Does this give you much trouble? Do you have to spend a lot of time fixing it up? You know I'm no writer, I never thought about myself as one."

I suggest that now he might want to write a new dedication for the book, something about his brother. George looks up at me with appreciation. He is almost overly gracious, the way people are when they are trying to live with intense pain. One part of his mind is totally with me, the other part seems never to stop thinking and feeling about his brother.

"Did they shoot him up very bad? He didn't mean to hurt anyone. It was going to be a nonviolent action." His eyes dart around the room. He bends over close to me and whispers, "You know I sent him in there." He looks around the room once more, rubs his face and settles himself in his chair.

He looks over at me to gauge my reaction, as if waiting for me to tell him that he shouldn't have done it. But I only nod my head.

"I sent him in there," he repeats. "To think after all that I've been through, he was the one to do it. I haven't shed a tear because I am so proud." I know that in George's world a long life has no meaning. Only spectacular action lives on. Jonathan has made himself immortal.

"They were heading straight for the airport. That's why they used the yellow van. They wanted everyone to know just where they were. They needed those hostages to be alive so they could trade them for our freedom."

I ask him about a rumor I had heard that someone else had been supposed to go in with Jonathan. George presses me for the name. "Oh, no! You got it all wrong. There were supposed to be eleven others going in with him. When he found out they weren't going, I tried to persuade him not to go, but he went anyway. Angela had nothing to do with it. It was just a mistake that he used her guns. He never thought he would be caught.

"Did you read the things he said? 'Okay, gentlemen, hands up. We are taking over.' Oh, that's just so beautiful." George throws his head back and roars with laughter. "And do you know what really got me? Those railroad flares that he wrapped up to look like dynamite. The man-child with a Chinese AK-47. That's just too much." I feel the waves of pain battering his aching head as he laughs again. "They'll remember that boy. They'll never stop regretting it. I'll see to that." I can't even look at George as he says the words.

He bends over and whispers, "Did they find the Volkswagen yet?" I pull back and look at him with surprise. How could I know anything about a Volkswagen? I don't know anything at all about what happened or any of the circumstances. I realize with a sinking feeling that the world outside his cell is completely unreal to him.

"Have your parents been to see you?"

"They came on Sunday. Fay came too, and she really helped them to understand. I don't know what I would have done without her."

The door behind him is suddenly forced open. "I'm sorry, Mr. Armstrong. We can only give you two more minutes." And as if anticipating an argument, the guard adds, "We have other people who need this room."

George rises up to protest and then falls back into himself.

"You coming back tomorrow?" *He really needs me to come.*

I give him the pages I want him to work on. "I'll try to get here early so we can have the whole day to work."

"Okay, man. I'll have a lot of stuff for you. I plan to work all night. I can't sleep. This will give me something to do."

He hesitates before turning toward the guard, and I can almost see him gathering his strength together for the return trip to his cell, pushing away his feelings, flexing them out with his muscles. The door opens. Again we embrace and exchange clenched fists. He disappears. I can hear a metallic crunch as his chains are replaced.

I just want to run out of there. I have to do something to deal with my mounting hysteria. Without even knowing why, I find myself driving into San Rafael to the Hall of Justice, where it all happened.

A few hundred yards along the highway. Down the main street of San Rafael, which is indistinguishable from any other small city. The routines of everyday life have already been restored. *George is probably already back in his cell now. How long will he be able to force himself to stay alive? How long will it be before he is forced to provoke the final battle?* Mounds of sand and scrubby trees. Sweeping curves. Then there it is, like Xanadu: Frank Lloyd Wright's Hall of Justice. Totally unexpected in this naked, half-barren countryside.

I park my car. I ask myself: *Why am I doing this? Some things should be forbidden. I don't have to see everything. I don't need any more grief.* I almost want to be prevented from entering.

Finally I get out and walk toward the entrance. No feeling. No faces that I know. No bleeding bodies or shattered glass. Up the elevator. People with briefcases and scared eyes. Attorneys. Clients. Defendants. Clerks. I walk down the long hall. Olive light through the tinted windows. The courtroom where it happened is roped off, but I can still see in. More like the board room of a big company than a courtroom. Large plush chairs. Gently sloping floor. Curved maple panels. Down in the elevator again. Out into the street. Still no feeling. It is as though I were anesthetized. The need for feeling is smothering me. I have to get it out. It is as if my bones were contracting inside and crushing me.

I see two policemen and walk over to them. Arrogant, sun-burned faces. Black boots up to their kneecaps. I ask them about what happened. They point to a spot where the van stood. Then to the place where they took out the hostages. They point to two black splotches in the street just a few feet away from where we are standing.

"That's his blood. They tried to get it up, but it's baked in. Guess it'll never come out." A problem for the street cleaners now.

"You see those two mounds of dirt over there? That's where the guards shot him."

They smile at me. I catch their eyes with mine and coolly announce that Jonathan was my friend and that what he did was just the beginning. Then I turn away, half-expecting to be shot, or to feel their hands suddenly around my neck. Inwardly shivering with terror, but alive again and free inside myself.

That night, Inez Williams, Fleeta Drumgo's mother, and I are alone in the house where the press conference had been held the night before. When I go into Inez's room to say good night, she is stretched out stiff as a board on the bed, arms held rigidly at her side. Her eyes are wide open and staring at the ceiling with something in them like stark terror. Her body is absolutely rigid as I sit down on the corner of her bed to say good night. We plan to get up early to go out to the prison together. As I leave the room, I am about to close the door when she suddenly almost screams, "You don't have to close the door. Just leave it open."

August 13

Inez and I start out for San Quentin. The sun splashes off the trees and the street. The air is charged and buoyant. It is one of those transfiguring days that seem to come only after a heavy storm. My body feels light and miraculously alive again.

I complain to the man at the desk about the brevity of my previous day's visit with George. I demand that I be accorded full visiting hours. There is a series of calls back and forth to the warden. "We'll have to take you back into the Adjustment Center. We can't provide one of the condemned men's rooms for an extended visit."

I nod my assent and try to conceal my amazement and delight. I am actually going to be taken inside the prison, back into the cells. I take a deep breath. Perhaps I am going to visit with George in his own cell.

"It'll be a while until we can get an escort, so you'd better sit and wait."

I sit down beside Inez, but it is almost as if I am not sitting because my expectation is so great. I am almost praying that they won't change their minds and put me back in one of those small rooms where I was the day before.

I hear my name. I look up and a young guard is standing beside me. "Mr. Armstrong, are you ready to go back now?"

I follow him out of the room and through a side entrance in the main wall. I sign my name in what seems to be an ancient logbook, and then my escort leads me through an electrically opened door into a courtyard and along a curving concrete walk. A profusion of flowers. Pools of reflecting water. It is like being inside the courtyard of an old Spanish church.

My escort leads me to a small three-story building almost in the center of the courtyard. Then through another electronically operated door. Another logbook to sign. Everything is quiet. My escort leads me along a corridor. Off to my left, sunk down about a foot beneath the level of the floor, are two rows of cells like one of the wings in a zoo. But I don't hear anything or see any flicker of motion. At the end of the corridor, I am taken up a small flight of stairs to a large room with a table and chairs, separated from

another, smaller room by a partition of metal and glass. I realize
with a sinking feeling that I am not going to be taken to George's
cell.

"We'll be bringing Jackson in in just a second." The guard
leaves and I hear the door locking behind him. Off to my left and
down the flight of stairs I can see another row of cells. An inmate,
his skin glistening with perspiration, comes up to the bars on the
side away from me and two guards approach him from the other
side.

He has just finished exercising. His chest is heaving. He passes
his clothing piece by piece almost tantalizingly through the bars
to the guards. When he is completely naked, he clasps his hands
behind his neck and pulls his elbows back parallel with his body,
offering the guards the sight of his hairy armpits. Then he thrusts
his open mouth forward, pursing his lips. Smiling, he lifts his
testicles to demonstrate that there is nothing hidden underneath.
Then he turns his back to them and squats with an antic wiggle
in a deep knee bend so that anything concealed up his anus will
be squeezed out. He turns and faces the guards again, still smiling.
They unlock the door and he comes through, almost mincing.
They hand him back his clothing. The three of them stand there
smiling and talking—the guards like policemen at a school crossing
talking to a sexy adolescent girl. I realize that everything the
prisoner has done—his demeaning ritual of coquettishness—has
been done solely to insulate himself from the experience of unbearable shame.

I stand back off to one side and away from the door so that he
won't see me watching him. I imagine how painful it would be for
him to be seen by other eyes, and how much he would hate it if
he saw me at the door. A window is open and I can hear the sounds
of men passing outside. When I look out, I can see them bringing
in a cart of food.

Standing in the waiting room, I notice that my whole mood
has changed. My breathing has become heavier. I am tapping my
foot and shaking my head, walking restlessly around the room. I
hear a key in the lock and I look up. George and a guard are at
the door.

We put our arms around each other and smile. George stands back and admires me with mock awe. "So you managed to get them to take you back here. Pretty good."

Even though I know I have done nothing special to get here, I still feel a sense of pride. I ask him if he has done much writing.

"Man, I been working straight through ever since I saw you yesterday. I haven't had a minute's sleep." He pulls a large sheaf of papers out of the file of legal documents that he has brought with him to conceal his writing. "Now, let's see. How shall we work this? Do you want to just take this stuff out with you or what?"

I tell him that I'll take it out, but just in case of trouble, I'd like him to read what he has written into my tape recorder.

George starts walking around the room, enjoying the sense of space. I can see him stretching himself out like someone regaining his full size after having spent the night in the back seat of a car, blowing out his chest and loosening his arms and legs.

"Okay, shall we get to work? Here is the dedication I wrote last night." He reads the first words quickly: "To the man-child. Tall, evil, graceful, bright-eyed, black man-child, Jonathan Peter Jackson"—the next words come slowly and widely separated—"who lived on August 7, 1970." He almost gulps the words back and then corrects himself—"who died"—and then he goes on. But I have heard him and he has heard himself. "Who lived." It is what he really means to say, it is what he really feels. But he has to change it because who else could understand? Even George isn't ready yet for that kind of truth. ". . . Courage in one hand, assault rifle in the other . . . my"—his voice catches on the next three words—"brother, comrade, friend, the true revolutionary . . . the black Communist guerrilla in the highest state of development. He died on the trigger, scourge of the unrighteous, soldier of the people." His voice is slightly menacing and staccato, like a series of sharp fast blows. "To this terrible man-child"—his voice softens—"and his wonderful mother, Georgia Bea; to Angela Y. Davis, my tender experience"—he says this word with hesitation and remorse—"I dedicate this collection of letters. To the destruction of their enemies"—and he concludes with a sudden surge of emotion—"I dedicate my life." Hushed, trying to sink the meaning of the words into every part of himself. A moment of silence. Then a sudden word of command: "Replay." We rewind the tape and listen to his words again. I feel the strength that has come back to him with his reading. It seems to me that he has transformed himself, at least for the moment, with his vow.

I ask him whether he brought out the manuscript that he had been working on in Soledad. He whispers that he sent it out before he left. He tries to tell me the name of the person he sent it to, but he stutters and repeats himself. A horror-stricken look passes over his face as he realizes that his control over his mind is slipping away. Then he finds the name and repeats it twice to reassure himself.

Looking over his pile of papers to cover his embarrassment, I remark on how much he has done. "I couldn't do all I wanted to. Preoccupied with this other thing, I keep seeing the black man-child with that machine gun in his hand, eyebrows raised." He lights a cigarette. "Are you going to the funeral?" I nod. Long silence.

"I'm going to see to it that my brother didn't die for nothing. There is no way in the world they can stop me. I'm going to make sure of that. That's for sure." It is the same voice he used to read the dedication, the public voice of vows and pledges, the voice of survivors who try to mesmerize themselves into fidelity to the dead.

We are silent for a moment. He shifts himself in his seat.

"Huey Newton is going to give the funeral address on Saturday."

"For my brother's funeral?"

"Right."

"I heard something about a church. St. Augustine church."

"Yeah, it's going to be in a church. Huey is going to give the—"

"Are they going to have a priest and all?" Suspicious.

"Oh, I don't think so."

"I hope not."

"It's going to be a revolutionary service."

"Good. They're just using the church because it's large and they can get lots of people in there?" Reassured.

"Right."

"I don't guess the authorities would let them take a dead body anywhere else except a church. You know how bad my brother was hurt? Was he shot up, shot to pieces, or what?" The same question he had asked me the day before. I can almost see the image of his brother's body that must haunt his mind.

"I don't think he was shot up."

"Oh, I loved that boy."

As I hear those words again, I feel as if I have been suddenly hit on the back of my neck. My legs become weak and rubbery.

George sits there rubbing a pencil heavily back and forth on a piece of paper until there is a solid black square in the center.

"In the back of my mind, I've always thought about the possibility of escape. In the group we talked about escape. I even got a couple of beefs, right there in '65, for having escape paraphernalia in the cell." He laughs. "They moved me from the cell I was in to one that was tighter security. You'll find that in the record. I learned all about locks. Picking pressure locks by the shims and so forth. So I had all the paraphernalia in the cell getting ready to go. And then a brother got caught on his way to my cell with some stuff. I didn't know that he'd gotten caught, so when they ran in on me, I didn't have the stuff stashed away."

A long silence to absorb the memory of his disappointment. Escape was all he had dreamed about for so many years. Why had he stayed? He knew how to do it. He knew the weak spots in their defenses. What was wrong with him? It was just that there was nowhere for him to go. What would he have done? There didn't seem to be any way out, no matter what he did. So his brother had died.

"And they caught me too."

Prisoners outside the window are beginning to talk very loudly back and forth. "Will that affect your tape recorder?" I shake my head negatively. I don't want anything to interrupt him, nor do I want him to show himself at the open window for fear someone may think he is trying to escape and shoot him. Too many people have already died.

"I saw somebody being skin-searched down there as I was waiting for you."

"That's really demeaning."

"The guy was smiling and talking to them while they were proceeding to fuck him over."

"I don't smile myself. If they have nothing to say, I don't listen. You know that I'm living in a state of total war with these fools. I want to make it impossible for them to ever organize along these lines again. So I'm not going to let them maneuver me into a position where they can just shoot me."

"Rip you off like some shit?" My voice is deep and throaty.

"I'm not going to limit myself to taking out two or three or four or five of them. That's what I'm saying. I could walk right out of here right now and dispatch all of them right out there in the hall. But then it would be all over—" hushed—"because they would close the tier off and bring in the rifles. I'd be limiting myself to one or two cats who really are intermediate."

"What you would be doing if you did that, you'd be—"

"It would be suicide. I thought about it the other day, though. Right here in my room, my cell."

"What you would be doing is losing faith in your ability to do something bigger than that. You'd be defining yourself in the act. If there was the only way you could define yourself, well, then, that's cool." As if I could dissuade him once and for all.

"If it comes to that, yes. If it comes to that . . . ."

"It eliminates the possibility of other ways that are more significant. You have to think about the other ways."

"I try. People underestimate my ability to be realistic. But I try."

"You don't have to be realistic to the point of eating so much shit that when the time for action comes you've got nothing left to act with; that kind of realism is deadly."

"That is the realism of my father."

"There is another kind of realism. It pertains to your strength."

"The kind Ho Chi Minh practiced. He negotiated and smiled and bowed to give Giap time to organize his men out there in the hills, and one day all of a sudden he just stopped smiling." He laughs. "Do you know that when people call me or call a person like myself a fanatic, when they use the word, the term 'fanaticism,' they're getting pretty close to understanding?" That is what he wants to be, not a person, but a pure, unremitting, irresistible force. "It's going to be a beautiful war. We will build a whole new culture during the war itself. Culture will help us after the war to understand where we're going and how to get there. We'll have to build a viable revolutionary culture, a thing to live with during the war. I got things in my head concerning that. A lot of things. I am working on them. I've started already.

"Has anybody heard from"—he hesitates—"Angela?" Whispering confidentially, he adds a guttural gagging laugh, almost like a fist in his throat.

"I don't know." I stutter and fumble. George shouldn't be asking me such things. It's too dangerous. "I would be very unlikely to hear if anyone had. I don't go after information like that and if it comes my way I hold on to it."

"She's got a couple of pieces that I'm working on."

"I want some of that in the book."

"John Thorne has copies of some of them. The real lascivious parts, I'd leave them out." He smiles like someone sucking on a sweet candy.

George starts to pace back and forth across the room.

"You must do a lot of walking."

"In the cell? Back and forth, I do."

"You are pacing around here like a caged animal," I remark, wincing after I hear my words.

"My cell's about, perhaps, one-fifth the size of this room. Maybe smaller."

"How many hours a week do you get out? Do they let you out at all?" Off in the distance, I hear cell doors opening and closing.

"Well, maybe about twice we get an hour out in front of the cells. There's nothing can be done about that." His voice fades down almost to a whisper. "You know, since that incident that happened at Marin all of us have been awake."

"I went over and checked out the Hall of Justice in Marin County yesterday."

"What does it look like?"

"Like a mandarin palace. It attempts to disguise its raw power with the architect's skill. It is really a huge imposing edifice."

"My little brother went in and invaded it." With awe in his voice.

"I went up in the elevators and followed his route."

"Man! I really loved that boy!" His voice almost bringing Jonathan back into the room.

"Blood is still on the street drying. I talked to one of the pigs outside and he said the blood was cooked forever into the macadam." I can't seem to get it into my head that it is really George's brother's blood, and that I have no right to tell him such things.

"They couldn't get it up." His voice is almost inaudible. "Was there much blood?"

"Yeah, in the streets."

"That was the first real battle of the war. They made a terrible mistake there. They should have let that boy through. That was a terrible mistake."

"I got the pig to tell me all about it and then I told him that they were my brothers and I walked away." George laughs appreciatively.

"They shouldn't have hurt that boy, though. He wouldn't hurt nobody. They should have let him through. They made a terrible mistake shooting that boy." The only way he can talk about it at all is as a kind of tactical error that has been committed by those who killed his brother. "Ah, man, they'll never stop hearing those shots. A beautiful boy"—laughing tearfully—"working on a shoestring. Do you know what was really significant about that?" He is almost totally inaudible. "The highway flare wrapped up to look like dynamite." He is almost breaking up with laughter and tears and pride. "That little cat. He had nothing to fight with but his heart. I love that boy. I'll never hear nothing derogatory about him." Referring to the people who had called his action suicidal. "He was working on a shoestring."

The sounds of men's voices and cells opening and closing enter the room.

"Working alone," I said, "that's what's fantastic, working alone."

"Man, there'll never be anyone like that in this country again. There'll never be another cat like that."

"I doubt it! He's made a lot of men look very sick. He showed up a whole generation of men with that one act. He showed them what can be done and what they never did."

"Taking your goddamn courage in your hand." George clenches both his fists and shuts his eyes. "When John Clutchette heard about it, he fell all over himself. When he heard something like 'We want the Soledad Brothers freed by twelve-thirty,' why, he just fell out all over himself. A total commitment. That's what everybody was waiting for. Everybody's wondering, well, will this guy go all the way? As soon as you show them, then they'll be with you all the way. Any reservations they have, they'll just fall away." He pounds his hands on the table. "I got belief! I got hope! We will make it. John has been awake ever since, catches every newscast." He clears his throat. "Really awake. I mean physically awake for six days." His voice underlines the words. "We've all been awake, catch every newscast, and I can't reiterate any of the beautiful things he said, but the things he said were significant because he had been so cynical, aloof. So reserved. He's just let himself go." George taps on the table. "Every time he passes by my cell, his eyes are wide and red and moist. I get two clenched fists and a big grin. We are really together. Like one, all of us." This is the ideal. "All of us. The secret army is forming right here, behind these walls."

"I knew about that even before I met you. I knew it just had to be happening."

"Some of us are out now. A couple of cats from the old general staff. What were those cats saying over there in that court? 'We are the revolutionaries.' It's very significant. You know about that. The guy who is going to fight the hardest is the guy who feels the most pressure. Nobody, nobody feels more victimized.

" 'Take all the pictures you want. You're seeing the real revolutionaries.' " He laughs raucously. "We are coming out of here before long. We are going to need some direction. We know how we are going to fight, but we want to coordinate ourselves with the political thing. We actually want to put ourselves under their control and command. We don't want any reservations. Let us have the job. We want to work. We want to work for the people and for the political party.

"Man, I love that boy." Long silence. "I loved all three of them. James's* mother took him, took his body South to bury him in Los Angeles?" I nod. "Where are they going to bury"—he almost can't bring himself to say his brother's name—"Jonathan?"

"Mount Vernon."

"They're going to take him back to Illinois?" Disbelieving.

"That's what I heard."

"What is the purpose of that?"

"I'm not sure."

"My mother must want him to be with her mother."

"I'll find out for sure tonight."

"Boy, what a beautiful boy." Hushed.

"The physical remains are not where it's at." Trying to reassure him.

"I know, I'm talking about his mind, about the whole thing, the whole man." Thinking about the symbolic function of Jonathan's grave.

"I know the guy who pulled the trigger"—confidentially—"I know the guy who shot him, who pulled the trigger. He also killed my own comrade right here in prison." Wild laughter. "I hope they got enough sense to keep that guy away." Talking through his laughter. "You see, if they had any sense, they could destroy me right there." It seems like a strange way of putting it. But I guess that he only wants a pretext to fantasize about killing his brother's assassin.

A cell door slams shut. The sound of keys clattering.

"Did you give Z my love?" He had asked me to tell her the day before.

"I was working on the manuscript yesterday and she was organizing at a desk right beside me."

Someone is tapping on bars outside the room.

"She's a sweet little thing with a big smile. They might throw a bomb in that house, any time now." He laughs bitterly. Everyone he loves is dying.

"Do you want to put this in?" I show him a section of a letter in which he accuses his father of cowardice.

---

* James McClain, one of the two convicts killed at Marin.

"That's up to you. It doesn't matter. It seems a little wordy, you know."

"Yeah, that is true." I am getting very tired.

"I wish you would go through all this and take things out in those places where I'm being too sarcastic or wordy."

"Okay, tell me what this letter means. I can't make head or tail of it."

"That must have been to my father. July 15."

"But you say something about 'Eddy.' So it has to be to somebody else. Did somebody get two letters mixed up?"

"Let me read the whole thing. Oh, yeah." He has a sudden illumination. "I got a memory. You know what this was? This was a letter intended for this guy named Eddy. Part of it was supposed to go to my father, and part of it was supposed to be passed on to Eddy."

"I wonder if that letter ever got to Eddy."

"Lester was supposed to give it to him."

"But he never did! I wouldn't have a copy of it if he did, right?"

"No, I guess not! Maybe Eddy came and read it, but most likely Lester didn't even give it to him." He reads from the letter: "'Well, Pop, I'll be going.'" Pause, as he begins to remember. Explaining to me: "I'm talking to Eddy, I'm telling him that I'm going outside on the seventh of August. County Court, that is, to testify for a friend. This cat had a retrial on August 7. 'So I'll get a glimpse of the world at large, if you can call San Rafael the world at large.'" His voice shakes as he reads.

"Are you suggesting that he be there?"

"Of course." We both realize the significance of the date at almost the same instant. It is three years later on the same day in August that Jonathan tried to rescue three of George's comrades from the same courthouse.

We are both silent for a long time, and I know we are both thinking about almost the same thing. George is searching his mind, trying to find out if this date was involved in any way in his planning of Jonathan's action. I see that it disturbs him because his unawareness of this element throws everything momentarily into doubt. He suddenly suspects that what he had thought of simply as a military operation had its roots in deeply hidden parts of his own mind. He almost looks as if he is beginning to hallucinate. Watching him I realize that George is very afraid of losing his sanity.

"Was he there?" I break the silence.

"No." Hopeless for an instant, his voice like a body falling in bottomless space. "He never read the letter, that's why he wasn't there." He taps on the table. "This whole thing was to go to Eddy and I was expecting a rescue." I make gagging sounds myself, mimicking the pain I feel coming so strongly from George. "We'd already blueprinted it for him, all he had to do."

"The letter," I stutter, "never got to him." I whistle.

"Let me look at that thing there—the manuscript—the last part, the letter to Fay. I don't think you have all the letters. How much is stuff I've written recently? Oh, man. They've just given you everything without any regard for private stuff." Smiling as if he didn't really care.

"How do you feel about that?"

"Well, I'll let you use your discretion."

He goes on reading. He notices that something has been cut out and he breaks out into gales of laughter. "I know just why Fay cut that out." Delighted because he is able to understand her so well. "Are any of my generalizations about history inaccurate?"

"I'd be the last one to know."

He picks up a letter and shows it to me. "Do you know what this means?"

April 4, 1970

DEAR FAY,

For very obvious reasons it pains me to dwell on the past. As an individual, and as the male of our order I have only the proud flesh of very recent years to hold up as proof that I did not die in the sickbed in which I lay for so long. I've taken my lesson from the past and attempted to close it off.

I've drunk deeply from the cisterns of gall, swam against the current in Blood Alley, Urban Fascist Amerika, experienced the nose rub in shit, armed myself with a monumental hatred, and tried to forget and pretend. A standard black male defense mechanism.

It hasn't worked. It may just be me, but I suspect that it's part of the pitiful black condition that the really bad moments record themselves so clearly and permanently in the mind, while the brief flashes of gratification are lost immediately, nightmare overhanging darkly.

My recall is nearly perfect, time has faded nothing. I recall the very first kidnap, I've lived through the passage, died on the passage, lain in the unmarked, shallow graves of the millions who fertilized the Amerikan soil with their corpses; cotton and corn growing out of my chest, "unto the third and fourth generation," the tenth, the hundredth. My mind ranges back and forth through the uncounted generations, and I feel all that they ever felt, but double.*

"The first time you were put in jail?"

George shakes his head.

I sigh with disappointment. It is so important for me to show him that I understand everything. "There is probably a lot I don't understand." I feel as if I have failed him by not knowing.

"'My recall is nearly perfect,'" he reads from the letter. "I figured that no one would understand that anyway." He goes on reading: "'I recall the very first kidnap'—that meant the one about four or five hundred years ago. 'I've lived through the passage.'"

"Purely poetic. You are speaking in the voice of all black men."

"'I've lived through the passage, died on the passage.' I want to tell you, I felt it all even when I was reading about it in history. Sometimes it was just too much for me. Back and forth. I couldn't handle it.

"'It pains me to dwell on the past. As an individual, and as the male of our order I have only the proud flesh.' Do you people know what proud flesh is? Do you know what it is? If you don't know that word, you lose the whole meaning."

"Proud flesh is yourself completely intact?"

George shakes his head. "No, it's a medical term. Proud flesh is a medical term that means, that describes a certain thing, that abnormal growth of flesh that sometimes forms around a healing wound. See, the whole meaning of this passage is that the male of our order, the black male, has only the proud flesh of recent years to hold up as proof that he didn't die in the sickbed that he has lain in for so long. Proud flesh is an abnormal growth of flesh that

* *Soledad Brother.*

sometimes forms around a healing wound. It's very little and very
insignificant. It holds up all right."

"Scar tissue is the strongest tissue of all."

"It won't break a second time! Not as easy."

There is a long silence. I guess I do understand now. What he
has said explains so much. He doesn't regard himself as just an
individual. He has taken it upon himself to represent all black men
with his own life. Sitting there in the silence, I remember some
lines from a letter he had written to me:

I don't recognize uniqueness, not as it's applied to individualism,
because it is too tightly tied into decadent capitalistic culture. Rather,
I've strained to see the invisible thing cutting across the artificial bar-
ricades which have been erected to an older section of our brains, back
to the mind of the primitive commune that exists in all blacks.*

This is his scar tissue, his proud flesh. He has been forced by
all the things that have been done to him—by all his wounds—to
regard himself not simply as George, but as the embodiment of the
essence of the black male. His life as himself has been condemned
by society and prison.

Seeing how he watches me when he talks about this sense of
himself, I realize how close it must have brought him at times to
insanity, or at least to the sense that he might be going insane. It
is almost a magical conception of himself, the kind of deep fantasy
that can't be discussed without the very walls seeming to bend
and quiver like beams of light, something so deep and so basic to
his whole conception of himself that it can never be discussed
without seeming to jeopardize his entire being. I wonder if sometimes he isn't afraid of passing over completely into this fantasy
and losing all contact with himself as an individual.

Sitting there, I also realize that, despite everything he does, his
old self must still be there inside him. Never very far away. Waiting to betray him, twitching and quivering with night sweat,
tremors, wet dreams, hallucinations.

While I have been thinking, George has been rummaging
through the manuscript. We have lost all track of time. George
finally breaks the silence. "You have complete latitude in things

* *Soledad Brother.*

that seem too trite. You know, to make any kind of changes you want. I don't care. We need money for the Defense Fund. That's the point. Not too much in me that hasn't been said a million times. Does everybody make mistakes like I make here?" he asks very shyly.

"Sure, how could you avoid it?"

"Hey, they took a part out of here. Here is where it's supposed to go." The "they" he refers to this time is me, and I am catching my breath, getting ready to tell him, very apprehensive about how he will react.

"Right," I said.

"I don't want anyone cutting me up like that." Suddenly he is angrier than I have ever seen him before.

"That's me trying to improve you."

"Was that you?" His voice expresses his astonishment.

"Yeah. God save you from your helpers."

"I'll give you absolute discretion on this stuff. You don't smoke, huh? When did you quit?"

"One year ago."

"You'll be in the best of health when Armageddon gets here."

I wince, because this sounds so much like a dig. The guards have come back to the door.

"Is there anything else you want to include?" The guards are fussing at the door. Our time is almost up. We start putting together our stuff. I ask George if he wants the writing pads I brought with me, but he shakes his head. I have taken all his writing and mixed it up in the pile of manuscript I brought in with me.

Noting the pencils I am packing up, George remarks, "I can take the pencils."

"Hmmm. Pens? Can you have pens?"

"I can't have pens in my cell." He takes the pencils. "Are they looking? I'll take this out real smooth."

The guard opens the door and enters. Before he can speak, George asks, "It's time for me to go?"

The guard nods and addresses me: "It will be a few minutes here. Give you time to get cleaned up and get your stuff together and get you out."

I stuff all the papers on the desk into my envelope. Then I embrace George. He pulls back almost imperceptibly as he has almost every other time we have embraced. I know that it is not that George doesn't want to have contact, because our hugging is a mutual thing. It is more as if he is pulling away from a kind of intimacy which threatens him just for the slightest instant. We exchange clenched fists and intone, "Power to the People." The guard follows George out of the room.

I sit down at the table and listen to the voices of the inmates passing outside in the yard. I have the same sense of heaviness that I have had every other time I have had to leave George behind. I am not even aware of walking or moving when I finally exit with the guard. I can hardly even see where I am going because so much of me is still back in that room with George. I get about halfway along the corridor to the door when I hear my name, "Greg," said softly. I look around and at first I don't see anyone but guards. And then I see him. My face falls. I almost say out loud, "Oh, my God, what are you doing in there?"

George is standing looking sheepish and abashed inside a small half-cylindrical holding cell which is just barely large enough to contain him. I know he doesn't want me to see him that way, but I know also that he is too proud to hide from me or simply to let me discover him by chance. We are both embarrassed, and there is nothing to say except that I will see him tomorrow and to shake hands once more through the bars and say, "Power to the People."

I walk along the corridor with my escort beside me, almost totally oblivious of my surroundings. I half-notice a black convict standing absolutely rigid against the wall. He has made himself almost completely inanimate, as if he intended never to move again. I see him and then put him out of my mind, because he so obviously doesn't want to be seen. I know it is Fleeta, and still I don't recognize him. I walk closer to be sure that it is really him and that my eyes aren't fooling me.

As I draw closer, almost without moving his lips, Fleeta speaks. "Don't you say hello to old friends, Greg?"

We take each other's hands and I reach over awkwardly and try to embrace him. Without even really moving his lips (they say this is a technique you develop in prison) he says to me, "I want to see you, Greg." The only thing about him that moves is his eyes. I tell him that I will try my best. And because I want him to know that I care and that I am truly on his side, as I walk away from him I look back and shout, "Power to the People." George, still standing in his cage, hears me and shouts back. I turn and give him the clenched fist as I leave the building.

That night Inez and I go to visit George's mother. She is staying with her daughter at the Berkeley Community Center, which is actually a branch office of the Black Panther Party.

We knock at the front door and a peephole opens. We identify ourselves. The peephole closes. After a few minutes, the inner door opens, and then the outer door, and then we enter. Sandbags are packed against the front windows. I see Georgia, and we fall into each other's arms. Her body is as hard as stone, yet so tense that she is actually quivering in my arms.

"It's been a long time since anyone hugged me. It feels really good." Then she turns to the others and says, "You know Greg is for real. He really means what he says. He is one of the few."

Then she turns back to me. "You see, I told you what sort of things they can do, and you didn't believe me." I tell her that I have seen George, and she replies, "They'll kill him too! Just wait and see."

I feel myself shutting my eyes and reeling slightly, remembering where I have left George. We go inside to another room. Penny is there and we all sit down. There is another woman, and two men who walk constantly back and forth. One of the men is doing the dishes. Georgia teases him gently and a touch of sultriness comes into her voice.

When the phone rings, Penny starts to answer it and Georgia says, "If that's Huey, tell him there won't be any funeral unless he comes up with that money." But it is the undertaker, and Penny speaks angrily into the phone. With a look of irritation and weariness, Georgia gets up. "You don't get anything right." She takes the phone away from her daughter.

"Look, isn't there any other plane before that? I've never heard of such a thing. You are sure that is the only plane? It just can't be. I'm going to call some other airline." Turning to me, she explains, "He says the only plane to St. Louis is at twelve, and it doesn't get there until six in the morning. Penny, call some other airline."

She comes back to the couch, and a little boy in diapers and a tee-shirt comes into the room, half-crawling and half-walking, heading straight for Georgia with a melting grin on his face. When she picks him up, he squirms all over her lap with pleasure. Georgia turns to me. "They call him Jonathan." The baby coos in her arms. After a few minutes, one of the men comes in and takes the baby from her. "He's just so cute," Georgia says, and she smiles the way someone does when they sit back in their chair after something particularly delightful has happened. The child is liquid sunshine, warm, peeking and coy.

After a few minutes, he walks and crawls back into the room and heads straight for Georgia again. The man returns and takes the baby. "You just get upstairs and stay there." Georgia turns to me and, with the man still in the room, says, "They're so mean to him." Without hesitation, the man replies, "We're going to make a tough little nigger out of him." Georgia looks down at the floor.

I show Georgia the dedication to the book. She glances at it and hands it back to me without a word but with just the slightest hint of scorn. Later she says, "He thinks just because he calls me a revolutionary mama, that everything will be all right." She accepts it the way she accepts George, with a kind of grudging fatalism.

When all the others except Inez leave, Georgia begins to tell me about Jonathan. She wants an autopsy made because people who have seen the body say the wounds aren't substantial enough to have caused his death. Georgia herself believes that they strangled him to death in the truck. None of the lawyers will listen to her or help her. She has gone down to the police station to get his clothes and they won't give them to her because they say they are evidence. The lawyers give her all kinds of assurances, but she knows they are just trying to brush her off. She doesn't know where to turn. I tell her I will talk to Fay, and Georgia gives me a look of burning distrust. I don't think she wants to share her son with any other woman in any way. And Georgia has always held it against me that I still see Fay and sometimes stay at her house when I am in San Francisco.

We are silent for a while, and then Georgia and Inez begin to talk about the lawyers. There is no money left. No one can say where it all has gone. The case is coming up for trial soon and there is no money left to pay for the defense. As Georgia describes the situation, her voice is not bitter or resentful, just utterly exhausted. Everything she says about Jonathan still being alive and the money for the defense being gone starts running together in my mind. I can see the photos of them dragging Jonathan's body from the van with a rope. Did the police strangle him before or after they pulled him out? Georgia has examined her son's dead body in the morgue, moving his limbs to see the wounds. No evidence could ever convince her that he had not been murdered in cold blood. And what could have happened to the money? Could someone really have stolen it?

It gets later and later, and finally I have to leave, feeling that if I don't leave, if I don't get out of that house immediately, there will be nothing left of my world.

I motion to Inez that we must leave. We get into the car and start the drive back to San Francisco. My eyes are bad at best. But the lights from cars blind me even more than usual. Neither of us knows the way back, and we go back and forth through the unfamiliar streets. The more lost I get, the faster I drive. Down one-way streets the wrong way, making sweeping U-turns in almost total darkness. Neither of us speaking, both of us on the verge of hysteria. Inez because she is joined to Fleeta's life just the way Georgia's life was joined to Jonathan. For an instant it is almost as if I am sharing Inez's mind. I can almost hear her unspoken thoughts. "What about my son? Will it happen to him too? Someday will I have to take his mutilated body in my arms too?"

I am near hysteria too, because everything seems so hopeless. We will never find our way. We will all be murdered, clubbed to death, strangled, dragged through the streets. Georgia's voice still drones in our ears.

It is like drowning in a hurricane sea. Pitched back and forth, swamped and pushed under again and again with Georgia's voice ringing in our ears, and mutilated bodies pitching back and forth all around us. Finally, miraculously, the sea just gives us up and puts us back on shore and we find the place where we are going to spend the night.

Later, back in my room I find myself thinking about something else Georgia had said:

"I bought two graves in Mount Vernon, side by side. One for Jonathan and one for George."

I ask myself how she could possibly do such an awful thing, but I know she realizes how unendurable the pain of George's death would be. So she has had to start preparing herself long before. It isn't that she doesn't expect him to live, it is just that she can't allow herself the luxury of even believing in the possibility of his survival. The worst thing has always happened. Why shouldn't the worst of all things happen now? The only way to survive disaster is to accept it. She tells me because I am his friend. She wants me to start living with his death too, because she wants me to share her pain. The pain is part of caring about George and caring about her.

It seems right that she should stay in a house with sandbags and barred doors. How can she go home to her house in Pasadena when Jonathan isn't there? It had been almost impossible without George. Without Jonathan, the emptiness, that vacuum, would be beyond endurance.

I don't think I ever heard a word of hope from her. Just as some people can survive only with an illusion of hope, Georgia can exist only with a certainty of hopelessness. Most blacks have been forced to teach themselves that there is no salvation in the world. And for me to be a real friend to Georgia, I will have to learn too. The first time we had been together, she had told me that they would try to kill George. "They put things in their food and no one ever knows." She had told me about the two convicts who were supposed to have escaped from Soledad, but a couple of months later, their bodies were found buried in the farmland outside the prison walls.

I think of her as if she had no hope, and yet I know that isn't true. Like everyone who has been disillusioned, who is capable of being disillusioned, she has more illusions than anyone. And she still keeps having them, they keep springing up inside her no matter what she does, and that is why she has to school herself so ruthlessly in despair, because, in spite of everything, she still believes. Anyone who is really without hope is simply cynical and unfeeling, and Georgia still feels so much. That is why she is really being very kind and loving when she tries to disillusion me.

When Georgia talks about how George trusts people too much, I think she is really talking about herself. And that is also why she is hardly ever consistent with people—why she loves and hates them almost in the same breath—because her natural impulse is to trust them so completely and yet, wherever she goes, they always turn on her or disappoint her. The only way she can protect herself from disillusionment is to reject them before they have a chance to disappoint her. All this was part of why she told me about the second grave with such a strange pride, because by buying it she had managed, at least for the moment, to conquer her greatest fear. She had managed to accept the worst life has to offer her.

August 14

The next day I drive out to the prison again. Instead of being taken into one of the condemned men's visiting rooms, I am led into a glass-enclosed room just off the main visiting room. After a while, they bring George in. He is taller than I have seen him. His whole body is swollen and quivering with rage.

"The pigs took my envelope with everything I was working on. I'm not going to let them get away with it. They can't do that. It's my legal material." He slams open the door to the little room, and surges out into the general waiting room. "Get that desk sergeant up here," and he moves to the door which leads into the visitors' waiting room. I get ahead of him and gesture for the man at the desk, who is already moving toward us. "Don't you know who you are dealing with?" George's whole body shakes, nodding back and forth almost as if he were going into a trance. "Where is the material you took from me? I need it for this legal interview."

"It's up at the desk and I'm going to hold it until your lawyer comes. That's not legal material, that's a manuscript." This is a guard who won the Congressional Medal of Honor in World War II. His face is like a school of small fish moving hysterically away from danger.

"Don't you know who you are talking to?" George says. "I could take you out right here and now."

The guard flinches. "You mean like you did to that other guard you killed?"

His words stop George momentarily in his tracks. He turns, and I follow him back into the small room. "These fools can't be allowed to get away with that sort of thing."

After a while, John Thorne, whom we have been expecting, is led into the room. George tells him what has happened, and John leaves to negotiate with the warden. When he comes back, he tells us that he has worked out a deal with the warden to pick up the papers when he leaves the prison. He has personally seen to it that the envelope they are in is sealed. Then John leaves again to bring in some reporters and a cameraman who have been waiting to interview George. We all crowd together in the small room.

That afternoon I go back to the prison to see Fleeta as I had promised. For the first few seconds after he is brought in by the guard he rustles back and forth in his chair like a boxer waiting for the bell. His eyes dart back and forth like the eyes of a deer. His first words cut into me. "Speaking as a Soledad Brother, I really appreciate all that you have been doing for us, Greg. I have been doing a lot of righteous studying and really getting myself together." As if to say, "Your trust in me is not misplaced. I am someone you can depend on."

I try to respond. But he doesn't really want to hear. I can almost feel him shaking off my words. He didn't ask me to come for a conversation. There are some things that he has to tell someone. Things he has been thinking about. He wants to be able to talk without interruption. I know that he is repeating things that he has said over and over to himself in his cell, I realize that the reason he wants to see me is because he wants to hear himself saying these things aloud so he can hear if they sound right. If they are as real out here with me as they are back in his cell.

Suddenly his eyes flash up at me for an instant and look down again. "I want you to tell my mother something." It is an order, not a request. "I don't want to be buried in a suit. I never owned a suit in all my life."

I nod my head.

Our time is over even before we have had a chance to begin to talk. But I realize that we are both relieved that our visit is over so quickly because, after the weight of what Fleeta has said, there is really nothing else left to say.

Later, when I see Inez, she is very suspicious of me. When I am with her, I can almost see her cocking her ear for any racial slurs or innuendoes that I might let drop. On the one hand, I sense in her an enormous need to accept me, and yet just because that need has been disappointed so often by others, she forces herself to be utterly cynical. And it seems to me that because I am white, I am trusted both more and less. She wants to trust me more, but because she has been hurt so many times she can't trust me at all.

The term "for real" appears a lot in her speech. It is set off from everything else by long hesitations and said with a deep throatiness which suggests that the most important thing in her life is to discover a bedrock of reality where she can finally rest in peace.

When she begins to suspect that "There's something fucky going on," all her senses begin to quiver, as if she feels herself trapped in a corner and is getting ready to fight her way out with every weapon at her disposal.

It is not just Inez; I have sensed something similar in all the other blacks I have known. It is as if they feel that as a white man I possess the power to deliver them from the pain and stigma of their blackness. As if I had the power to deliver some special dispensation that would finally cleanse them. It makes me feel ashamed. I realize that it is because whites have held power over blacks for so long that it is almost inevitable that blacks should look to whites more than to other blacks for a judgment about the quality of their lives, and that judgment from a white would be more significant than one that came from a fellow black. It is what George meant when he said: "At one time I just felt there was no possibility of any white person ever liking me." This is solely because power creates moral authority. This remains true even though, for blacks, the power of whites has been used only to degrade and humiliate them. I feel it with George and all the others I see and I know. Yet I don't want to acknowledge it, probably because I don't want to accept what it signifies about the nature of morality and power.

The newspapers today are full of quotes about Jonathan:

Lester Jackson: "He was strong. He listened to nobody. Put yourself in his shoes. His brother had been in prison for ten years. What effect would it have on you?"

One of his teachers: "His obsession which determined his view of this country was the plight of his imprisoned brother whom he could not really have known."

The principal of his high school: "I was very fond of him; everything I knew about him was positive. He played basketball on the Jr. Varsity and had an I.Q. of 117. He was a smart kid."

A classmate: "He seemed to think that the whole thing was very urgent. He'd go to hearings and he'd come back and seem very depressed and uptight."

A fellow editor of the high school underground newspaper, *Iskra:* "He wanted a socialist society—a society of mutual brotherhood that would be a fulfillment of the American dream as seen by Jefferson."

Jonathan himself: "People have said that I am obsessed with my brother's case and with the movement in general. A person that was close to me once said that my life was too wrapped in my brother's case and that I wasn't cheerful enough for her. It's true I don't laugh very much any more. I have but one question to ask all you people and people that think like you: What would you do if it was your brother?"

It is still afternoon when I arrive back at Soledad House. Some friends are there and also some people I don't know. They ask me if they can hear some of the new tapes I made with George. I turn on the machine. When we finish listening, I turn off the machine and take the tapes into my room and hide them.

Later I go out to dinner with some friends. Afterward they

start passing around joints. I get very stoned. When I leave, I can hardly find my car. When I start to drive, the car feels like a great balloon hovering over the street. And no matter how I press the accelerator, the car seems only to undulate imperceptibly. As in a dream, I finally find myself back at the house. Two strangers answer the door and they won't let me in until my identity is checked with people upstairs. When I am finally admitted, dozens of people are milling around looking dazed and saying things I can't quite seem to understand. Only little by little does it become clear to me that there has been a police raid on the house. People keep asking me if anything is missing, but I don't even know where to find the room in which I am staying. It is somewhere in that milling crowd, but their bodies conceal it like swirling clouds. Three or four people begin to talk to me all at once.

The bell rang and when we opened the door they just burst right in, dozens and dozens of them with shotguns and machine guns and there were so many of them that they kept hitting each other with their guns. . . . And they kept saying things like "If you make a move we don't like, it will be the last move you ever make." . . . Some people who could see out the window said they had blocked off the street. There were pigs with submachine guns stationed on all the rooftops surrounding the building. . . . While they herded us together in the front room, they went through the house and we could hear the sound of wood breaking as they tore the cabinets off the wall in the kitchen. . . . All we could think of was Fred Hampton and Mark Clark and what happened in Chicago. We thought we were all going to be killed. They kept us here for twenty minutes and more of them kept coming in all the time. . . . We saw them leaving with things. They took boxes of papers and some things we couldn't see and they put them in pouches. And when they finally left, they took Fania* with them.

After listening to the account of what has happened, I stumble into my room and look in the laundry bags, where I have hidden my tapes. They are gone. I dump the contents of the bags on the floor and in my narcotic stupor sift through them again and again. Then I look everywhere else in the room. When I finally convince

---

* Fania is Angela Davis's sister, who had come to San Francisco for Jonathan's funeral.

myself that they aren't in the room, I go out and start telling people what has happened. Everyone gets excited and starts talking about the missing tapes. It is as if the whole event suddenly becomes real again. I am offering them tangible proof of what they are already beginning to doubt because it has all been so fantastic.

After a while, some reporters arrive and they want to know about what has been taken from me and who I am. But I am so stoned and suspicious that I can only shake my head and try to disappear into the crowd. While the reporters are still there, the lawyers arrive and start taking statements from people.

One of the lawyers whispers to me that the police have found a gun underneath the mattress in my room. They have been told that it is mine because I am the only one with a clean police record in the whole house. While they are talking, I go in and lie down on a bed, listening to them. Then I get up and go inside and sit with them for a while again. Then I go back to lie down on my bed. At about midnight, the lawyers and reporters depart, and almost everyone else seems to depart with them. Some men that I don't know stay behind. Someone has appointed them to remain as security, and since I am already in the house they automatically defer to me as "the man of the house."

A little while later, members of various radical groups begin arriving from all over the state for the funeral. They have been told they can spend the night at the house. The door on the street floor is equipped with a buzzer, but we agree that, for security, someone will go down and examine each caller before he can be admitted. I don't know anyone at all, so I simply let everyone in. Soon there are dozens of strange people sleeping everywhere, and finally I fall asleep myself as dawn is breaking.

When I check my car in the morning, I discover that someone has broken into the trunk. The manuscript that I have been working on with George, which had been in a manila envelope, is spread out as if someone had taken it and thrown it into the trunk from a distance of several yards.

August 15

When we arrive, there are only a few isolated clusters of people gathered around the entrance of the small frame church.

The space around it is empty and desolate. I stand off to one side, hoping more people will come, lost in my thoughts.

Suddenly there are people as far as the eye can see. The streets shimmer with them. They squat on rooftops and perch in trees. Photographers are everywhere. The sun sparkles off their camera lenses. As the crowd continues to grow, I am pushed farther and farther back into a wall of shrubbery until I am almost completely enveloped by leaves and branches. Everyone is craning and expectant. The doors of the church open and there is a general surge toward the entrance. I move with it, but it is no use and I am quickly thrown back into the shrubbery.

Suddenly everyone around me is on tiptoe and craning their heads to the left. I turn with all the others and see the cars of the funeral procession slowly inching their way through the crowd. The sun is flashing golden waves off their polished metal surfaces. Clenched fists are thrown into the air. People begin to chant, "Long live Jonathan Jackson! . . . Power to the People!"

Finally the two hearses reach almost to the door. Leather-jacketed Panthers clear a corridor for the coffins. The chanting has become an almost deafening roar. Thousands of clenched fists are raised in the air. William Christmas's* coffin is in the first hearse. It fans out from the side of the hearse on a hydraulic platform. Six Panthers carry it through the corridor of people and up the stairs into the church. Jonathan's coffin, draped in a white silk flag with a black panther emblazoned in the middle, comes next. The families of the two slain men follow the coffins into the church. Georgia, head lowered, back bent. Lester, weary and somber. As the people see them, they redouble the volume of their chanting.

From inside the church, a woman's deep voice, dirgelike against the background of an old upright piano, soars out over the noise of the crowd. My eyes moisten, but I hold back my tears. A loudspeaker broadcasts the proceedings from inside the church into the street. A Panther leader reads some letters of tribute and regret. Huey Newton gives a short speech. The deep-voiced woman sings again, and then the two coffins emerge into the daylight. The crowd is silent. It is all over so quickly, like life itself.

---

* One of the other two convicts who were killed during the shootout outside the Marin Courthouse.

The funeral procession departs, inching its way once more through the crowd. Everyone begins to leave, walking slowly, shamefacedly away from the church. Only a few people linger. Soon the streets are nearly deserted, the way they were when I first arrived. As I walk away, I get a feeling like one I used to experience coming home from high school football games. It isn't just that I am moving away from a place where there were crowds of people. It is the memory of the forlornness of being utterly alone.

August 16

The next morning I go out to the prison to visit George for the last time before my return to New York. When I finally get to see him, he smiles at me with a kind of eerie complicity. Lester has been to see him the day before. "He told me about the second grave." He waits for me to tell him what I know. Only after he realizes that I am not going to volunteer any new information does he go on. "It's for her, you know. She bought it for herself." I guess that is what Lester has told him. George hasn't guessed the truth: that it is really for him.

Passing Time

"None who leave here are normal. If I leave here alive, I'll leave nothing behind. They'll never count me among the broken men, but I can't say that I am normal either. I've been hungry too long. I've gotten angry too often. I've been lied to and insulted too many times. They've pushed me over the line from which there can be no retreat. I *know* that they will not be satisfied until they've pushed me out of this existence altogether."

—*Soledad Brother*

August 20, 1970

George says he is feeling a little better. He saw my head and shoulders and clenched fist in that crowd at the funeral a few days ago in a photo and for some reason it snapped him out of the gloom into which all the events of what he calls the end game had thrown him.

The preface for the book has come in from Jean Genêt. He calls it "a striking poem of love and combat."

August 21

The lawyers went into court today about the raid. My tapes have been returned. The police claim to not even have listened to them. As far as I know they are still holding on to that mysterious gun.

August 25

I have just spent the best part of two days trailing after Fay. She is amazing. The case is her whole life. She doesn't seem to care about anything else. No small talk. No diversions of any kind. Just a constant stream of meetings, hearings, phone calls to other lawyers, interviews with reporters.

165

She literally can't keep still. She seems to be afraid of silence or the absence of frenzy. Long-fingered, long-armed, always moving, always coming at you, always reaching for you.

August 27

George's book is going to be published in England. His agent has just concluded a deal with Jonathan Cape and Penguin Books. It is also being published in France by Gallimard. George may be in prison, but it seems likely that soon his book will be known all over the world.

October 5

Jonathan Jackson is going to be a father. Before he died he was friendly with a woman who was associated with the Defense Committee. Now she is pregnant with his child.

October 14

At Fay's house the day before the publication party for George's book, which is to be held outside San Quentin.

It is about six o'clock in the morning, and I am puttering around the kitchen, still not adjusted to San Francisco time. The phone rings. An utterly bleak voice begins to speak. I know instantly that it is Georgia. She just starts talking as if she knew I would be the one to answer. She starts complaining about the book, which she has just finished reading for the first time. I feel the stark despair in her voice. "Those people who put the book together ruined everything." I tell her that I am completely responsible. But she goes right on talking about "those people."

I don't understand what she is trying to say and I feel bewildered and frightened. I knew the book would hurt her, that the reality of seeing George's bitter and painful letters to her in actual print would be shattering. But I sense that this isn't what she is talking about. She has seen everything before. Certainly she has seen all the letters George wrote to her. Yet she is complaining that no one has shown her the book before it went to press. I tell her that I thought she had already known what would be in it, that nothing has been added that wasn't in George's own words. She replies that the whole thing is just another example of white people ripping off black people. The book which she had looked forward to so much has turned out to be one of the bitterest disappointments of her life. I have been responsible for destroying one of her fondest dreams.

Yet what have I done that is so awful? What terrible error has escaped me? Really frightened, I ask her again to tell me what bothers her. She answers, "The arrangement. The way it was put together." I feel a great sense of relief. I didn't make any mistakes. She is referring to the long autobiographical letter that I had put in front of all the other letters. It must be the statements George made about her trying to keep him in her womb that have disturbed her so. I tell her how sorry I am, but that there is nothing I can do now. She replies that there is something she can do. She can get on the radio and say that the book is all lies put out by white people. I am terrified that she will actually do it. I tell her that I am going to see George in just a few hours and I will tell him what she intends to do. She hangs up the phone without another word.

I am there at the prison even before the gates open. The minute I am brought into the visiting room I announce to George that his mother is threatening to go on the radio to repudiate the book. First he is stunned. Then he becomes enraged. She has always done things like this to him since he was a child. He won't let her get away with it this time.

When his rage abates, he becomes thoughtful. First he asks if she can do anything to stop the book. I reassure him that there is nothing. I tell him, however, that she can do emormous damage to the book by bringing its authenticity into question. He thinks for a while and then he tells me to call her and say that if she ever does anything, and repeats the word *anything*, to damage the book he will never speak to her again. He is satisfied that this threat will stop her.

I call Georgia from a phone booth right outside the visiting room. I repeat George's words. She replies that George doesn't even know what he is talking about. He has been hit on the head too many times. It's all a pack of lies. All those lies he told about himself. I explain that he has the right even to lie about himself if he wants to. She responds that some people have to be protected against themselves. That George has always tried to make himself the guilty one.

With these words, I finally realize what has devastated her. It has nothing to do with her or with George's feelings about her. It has to do with George's innocence. In one letter to me, he had bragged about being a criminal: "I've been a thief and a brigand all my life." This is what has crushed her. I had ruined everything by including that letter and putting it right up front. Because her son is innocent. He has always taken the blame for what others have done. He has always trusted other people and allowed himself to be led. His innocence is the most precious thing in the world to her. If I hadn't included his autobiography and some of the other, more recent letters, there would have been no question about his innocence.

The book she had dreamed about was the book that would vindicate her son. The bleakness that I had heard in her voice was utter dread. It was as if she felt that now that he had confessed in print, there would be no way to save him. It was almost as if she felt he had passed a death sentence on himself. She had thought the book would save him, and now she was just as sure that it would kill him.

October 15

THE SOLEDAD BROTHERS DEFENSE COMMITTEE
INVITES YOU TO A PUBLICATION PARTY FOR
SOLEDAD BROTHER
AT THE GATES OF SAN QUENTIN,
OCTOBER 15, 1970, AT 1:00 P.M.

I have to give a speech. It is unavoidable. Everyone expects it. It is my ordeal and I have to go through with it. But I am terrified. I go with the other members of the Defense Committee to buy the champagne and ice. But I am so lost in my fear that it is as if I am walking in a dream. Suddenly I feel a tremendous blow and blood begins to spurt from my forehead. In my unconsciousness, I have walked into a door. After I manage to staunch the wound, we all drive out in separate cars to San Quentin with our refreshments hidden away in the trunks. There is some concern that the prison may have learned about the party and closed off the road leading to the prison. But there is no blockade and we drive in and park on both sides of the road outside the post office. I am still slightly stunned by the blow. I sit in my car with the door half open, trying to decide what I will say. Finally, I write out my speech because I know I will be too frightened to remember it.

For a while it seems as if no one else is coming. Then a few people begin to appear. Then they seem to come by the dozens. The deserted road is suddenly like a field of flowers in a strong breeze. People in colorful clothes milling back and forth. We get the champagne and cookies out of the car and people begin to eat and drink. The inevitable moment gets closer and closer. Soon Fay gestures for me to get up on the staircase of the post office, which is our podium. All the faces of the crowd seem to sway in front of me. I feel a silly grin on my face. I try to get it off, but it sticks like glue. It makes me feel ridiculous. I hope somehow that something will happen and I won't have to give my speech, that the guards will come bursting through the gates and sweep us all away down the road.

Finally I hear my name and I know I have to speak. For an instant, I stand there with my silly smile on my face. Just as I am about to try to open my mouth, someone in the front of the crowd shouts up at me, "Why are you smiling? Do you think there is something funny going on here? Do you think there is something funny about people going to the gas chamber?"

The smile leaves my face and I want to run and hide. In a voice that is barely audible even to myself, I explain that I am nervous because I am not used to speaking in public. There is a long silence. I stand there thinking that I will have to go insane because there is no other way. Finally I begin to read my speech. My voice is strange to me. As I listen to it, it reminds me of bits of torn and crumpled paper. I try to make it louder and stronger:

This is a victory celebration. The publication of *Soledad Brother: The Prison Letters of George Jackson* is a victory over San Quentin, over Soledad Prison, over the entire California prison system which ten years ago set out to silence George Jackson.

Inside the California prison system, George is known as a teacher.

His subject is truth, the truth about the prison system in America and the truth about the society which created it. Prison authorities hate only one thing more than the truth, and that is the inmate who dares to tell it. They have tried to break George Jackson. They have kept him in solitary confinement for over seven of the last ten years. He told me that there have been over twenty attempts on his life set up by the prison officials. The publication of this book is absolute proof that they have failed to silence him.

This book is a victory for George, but it is also a victory for every inmate in the California prison system because it expresses the truth about how they live. The question for us here today is what we do with this truth now that we know it.

When George Jackson entered prison ten years ago for stealing seventy dollars from a gas station, he wrote in a prison questionnaire that he wanted to be a writer. But I don't think he regards himself as a writer any more. He thinks of himself more as a medium, a voice for all oppressed people, white, brown and black. What he writes is literature, but also something more. He writes for justice, brotherhood and finally revolution. What kind of man is he? What would he be like if he were actually here with us today as he should be? When I first met him in Soledad, I was apprehensive and uncertain. I had never been in a prison before, I had never met a man accused of murder. George recognized my nervousness, and even though he was the one who was shackled and chained, he set . . .

Suddenly I can't go on. I know I am about to break out in tears. So I stop and close my eyes for an instant. I try to think of something else than the experience I am about to describe. Slowly I recover enough composure to continue.

George recognized my nervousness, and even though he was the one who was shackled and in chains, he set me at my ease. He forgave my ignorance and proceeded to teach me things about life I had never known before. Somehow in his solitary cell, he had become warmer, more human, more sensually alive than anyone I have ever known on the outside.

When I was with him yesterday, I gave him a copy of his book. It was taken away by the guards within an hour.

If he is convicted, George Jackson faces a mandatory death sentence. When I saw him, he told me, "They've taken away every right I have except one, and now they're about to take away that one too, the right to take in air and push it out again."

We are here to celebrate with George and to demonstrate our concern. What does that mean? George is a strong man, but he still needs the concern of people just because he is a man. When we were talking about the people who were becoming involved in his defense, he said, "You don't know what it means for a cat who has been neglected all his life to have people just come up and put their arms around him. You just can't know what that means." There are a lot of neglected cats in this country, and we'd all better start opening up our arms.

My voice breaks on the last words, and I end with an inaudible sigh of relief, expecting to hear a short outburst of perfunctory applause which would allow me to disappear back into myself. Instead, there is just a long and heavy silence. Not a sound anywhere.

Then a voice speaks out sharply, the same voice that had spoken out before: "What are you going to do with all the profits from the book when you go back to your fancy New York office?"

I catch my breath once more and answer him that I have nothing to do with profits and that the royalties from the book are going to George's defense. And that if he wants to do something about profits he will have to change the whole system.

Then in a moment of demagogic inspiration I go on. "You know right now George is supposed to be standing in one of the visitors' rooms where he can see the gates. Let's go over there and tell him that we are here."

I walk away from the podium, leading the way. Others follow. Standing with my face to the bars of the gate, I begin a series of chants: "Free all prisoners! . . . Free the Soledad Brothers!"

Soon people are chanting automatically, and I withdraw into the crowd. Fay sees me and comes close to me with her eyes glittering. "Is that the first speech you ever gave?" I can see that the words are delicious in her mouth. But it doesn't matter because it is a beautiful day and the sun is shining and I have survived.

October 16

The San Francisco *Chronicle* runs an account of the celebration, entitled "Radical Chic at San Quentin." My speech is described as emotional. The reporter quotes my statement that George's book is a "victory over the entire California prison system." Beside the article there is a photograph of a girl, described in a caption as "Linda from Larkspur," with a bottle of champagne raised over her head, the wine pouring down her open mouth.

George is happier than I have ever seen him. He is radiant. He heard about the party on TV. He has seen the article in the *Chronicle*. "That Linda. You know, the one who was drinking the champagne. What about her? Did you get to meet her?" I shake my head. "What's the matter, comrade?" George asks, half-nudging me in the ribs. "You aren't taking care of business."

The first reviews and advertising for George's book!

". . . In one of the finest pieces of black writing ever to be printed, he summarizes 300 years of rage for untold millions of blacks, alive and dead . . . this is the most important single volume from a black since *The Autobiography of Malcolm X*."
—*New York Times Book Review*
(Julius Lester)

"Probably nothing so artless has been published by a black American— or anything as close to the bone . . . these letters are the raw stuff, ragged and bleeding, or proudly refusing to bleed . . . [they] show us something of the process of becoming a man under such circumstances, and of becoming black."
—*Look* Magazine
(Peter S. Prescott)

"The personal passages express a whole new dimension of the black dilemma which has not until now been articulated. Jackson picks up where Cleaver left off. . . . Where Cleaver throws you back on yourself because you're not black, not oppressed—and that has its value— Jackson draws you in through your shared humanity—and that, I think, has a far greater value. Cleaver gives you no time to breathe, drives you to the wall. Jackson breathes you in.

"His range is extraordinary; hard-wrought sentences of anger, long unfolding sentences, short dense ones; the anxiety, the bewilderment, the knotty struggle with self, and the sad, reflective moments where everything else is suspended, when the long years of suffering flood back upon him, swamping his forward motion."

—*The Washington Monthly*
(SUZANNAH LESSARD)

"I have just finished the last page, read the last 'George' and turned sadly to the dedication and re-read it, sick at heart, depressed, yet somehow terribly rewarded by this touching and powerful 'story by letters.' . . . It makes no difference whether one 'sympathizes' with the Soledad Brothers or not—this book is one that should be read by every white American adult so that he or she gets a clearer picture of just what 'black' thought is."

—Palo Alto, California, *Times*
(ANNE ALEXANDER)

"A very remarkable book . . . His letters are the story of his self-discovery, self-education, and self-mastery in a prison cell 5 feet by 8 feet. At first they are the stumblingly articulate letters of a boy to his parents, touchingly gentle and patient as his mental world develops far beyond their comprehension. Prison makes him a poet and a revolutionary. Miraculously he refuses to be brutalized by a system almost unbelievably brutal."

—*Manchester Guardian Weekly* (London)
(PETER JENKINS)

October 18
The air is heavy and still. Fay and I and some of the members of the Soledad Defense Committee are sitting around Fay's house talking desultorily when a call comes for Fay. She almost drops the phone.

"Angela has been arrested in New York."

A reporter has just seen a teletype and wants a statement. Suddenly it is as if the house is transformed into pure energy.

"What shall we tell the press?"

"Shall we have a united committee?"

More phone calls.

"No, we are not handling Angela's defense. She will have her own lawyers."

Reports to all of us who are listening.

"There is a rumor that Charlie Garry is going to New York."

A reporter calls with confirmation of the arrest: Angela was caught in a Howard Johnson motel on Ninth Avenue in New York City with a man named Poindexter.

"No! I don't want to give an interview. Call John Thorne. He was representing her in a case."

Later Fay's husband, Marvin, comes home and we all help to prepare dinner. The table is set with crystal glasses, linen table-cloths and silver that hasn't been used since the Stenders' wedding day. It's the most festive evening I have ever spent at Fay's house. I get drunk. My lips are too heavy to open. I don't understand people at all. It's not that I think I am particularly good, or better than the rest of the people there. I have a great deal of respect for Fay and her husband. But the news of Angela's capture makes me too despondent to participate in this curious celebration.

I remember the afternoon I had spent with her in John Thorne's office and the completely unexpected softness that there was about her. I remember the way her shirt pulled away from her blue jeans as she reached across the pile of George's letters on the floor and the gentle curve of her hips and her waist that was momentarily revealed.

I sit there at the table thinking that there must be something I don't know about, because I believe that all the people at the table are better than I am in some way that eludes me. They know how to be with each other. I don't know how to get along with anyone. They know how to control their emotions. I don't. In spite of myself, I am convinced that there must be some kind of higher logic to their celebration. I ask Fay about it later on in the evening. She tells me that they all are trying hard not to be affected by what happened.

As she talks, I have a sudden flash of insight. Of course they don't want to admit how they feel, but in spite of themselves they can't help revealing it. They are all glad in a way that Angela has been captured. I am even glad in a way myself. It is exciting. I can feel the blood pounding in my veins. We all feel important because we know her and so we are involved. But at the same time I know that none of us would feel this way if we really stopped to think what imprisonment could mean to Angela, who is still just a young girl, but the drama of the occasion doesn't lend itself to empathy. And I think Fay and the others on the Defense Committee have a very special reason not to be despondent.

Angela is like Georgia in many ways. They claim she was a disruptive force on the Defense Committee. I'm sure that it is true. I'm sure that she made it very difficult for Fay to exercise control. Her blackness gave her a moral authority that made her impossible to deal with. And she was George's woman, George's black woman. "My tongue through the gap in her teeth."

She must have made it very hard for liberal white ladies to function in all their grandeur.

October 19

"So they finally got Angela," George remarks, almost in passing, when I go to see him the next day, just the way he had brought up his brother's death. "You know, the Communist Party has decided to forgive her." I don't follow up on his remark and we drift on to something else. Finally he comes to what really concerns him. "That guy she was with. He was just taking care of her while she was trying to get out of the country. I don't think there was anything between them." It is more of a question than a statement. He is not talking to me so much as he is trying to reassure himself.

October 20

Lester has told George the truth about the second grave. "You know, she really bought it for me. I never realized she could grow so fast. I guess I've always underestimated her." He is proud of his mother, the same way he was proud of her after Jonathan was killed. It is what he has always been trying to explain to his mother. *Now look, Mama, don't expect anything of me. I'm a doomed man. I'm not white. Their world isn't mine. I don't want to pretend any more. Mama, I'm black and I'm doomed, and I've got to make it in my own way, on my own terms.* Buying the grave is like finally cutting George loose. Letting him go. It is a way of saying that all she expects from him now is his death. And so George rejoices. I suppose he feels that now he can be free of her at last.

October 21
The effects of Angela's arrest go so deep. George told me that one of the guards insulted Fay when she came to visit him yesterday. The next time it happens, he is going to attack them regardless of the consequences. He has to assert his power. He has to show Fay how much he is willing to risk for her. There was no way he could save Angela and he has to save someone.

"You wanted me to give you a history of my life in prison, right? It starts in February 1961. These are rough dates. I'm going by the months. I couldn't possibly remember the whole thing. I entered Chino reception center from the Los Angeles County Jail in May 1961. I was sent to Soledad to do my time. One year to life." He sighs and his voice catches. "Second degree robbery.

"I got angry in March 1962. A brother was stabbed in a bad race incident. The pig disarmed all the blacks. They let it be known that the blacks who walked in the hall would be searched while they would let the whites pass." George sets off the key words with special emphasis. "That, of course, disarms us because if you are caught with a weapon, it's a new beef altogether. The whites carried weapons without fear of being caught. When a brother was stabbed as a result, James Carr and I moved to punish the assailants. The pigs tried to intervene, so we attacked them instead"—matter-of-factly, as if what they had done was as natural as breathing. "They came out in force, shot at us from second-tier windows. They broke out the window, then they could control the hallway. They fired gas. Then they ran in in force, chained us, and sent us to San Quentin." He purses his lips and his brow wrinkles as he remembers.

"April 1962 was spent in San Quentin's isolation. At the time, it was right across from Death Row, sixth floor, at the north block. We did our thirty days in the hole and we transferred about May of 1962. James Carr and I were sent to Tracy and placed in the Adjustment Center there. James Carr and I, we did quite a bit of time together. Wrote many a page in the book of life in the joint, trying to stay together and keep the brothers alive." He uses the same hushed voice that always characterizes his commitment to his comrades.

"October and November, I can't remember exactly. I know I did about five, five and a half months in the Adjustment Center and they let me go," he said with surprise. "They sent James over to another lockup that they called 'Segregation,' and put me on the main line. Later on he went home." But George didn't get to go home with his friend.

"October 1962. I was sent to general population there in Tracy. I spent about one week on the main line, general population. Then came the incident of the TV room. They'd established this un-written law, or unwritten rule, or custom, that the blacks had to sit in the back. But I've described that incident to you before.

"It was about November of '62. A fight went down. No one helped me at the time. None of the brothers anyway. It turned out all right. They locked me up and let the white guys go. But the write-up was so egregious, so outrageous, that I think they lifted it out of my jacket altogether. It was written by an officer who was right there in the TV room when it happened." He still can't believe the hypocrisy of it. "They read the beef off to me when I went to the kangaroo disciplinary court. The officer said that he thought I showed symptoms of insanity, but if you look at the thing in the whole context, that becomes absurd. We weren't supposed to be relegated to the last row. It doesn't show insanity at all"—he fumbles the words as if he still isn't quite sure—"that I wanted to sit, you know, where seats were available.

"December 1962. It wasn't too far after this incident. They locked me up and transferred me back to San Quentin. I was locked up for a week, two weeks, and then released to the general prison population. It was a terrible situation at that time. It was wintertime. It was raining. They would force the blacks to stand out"—he spits the word out—"right under the weather. They have a shed which offered some of the inmates protection, but it's not large enough to hold all of them so the blacks were forced out into the yard. I took that shit for about a year. I did well in a manner of speaking.

"That's what they call well, when you take shit like that. There were a thousand other things too. I did well the first year and I was moved from close custody and put on north block. At the time, it was a regular housing facility. Now it is considered an honor block. But the brothers were being misused, abused, assaulted and murdered. So I had to organize a little defense group. Alexy, James Carr, myself, Red, D.D. and Howard. Together we formed the old general staff. We did all right with organizing. Fended off the fools, pigs and incompetents.

"In February 1964, I was locked up for paramilitary activity. I think I stayed locked up for four months. But there was nothing they could pin on me, nothing. I don't remember exactly what it was. It was associated with the group. Either I was caught with some money or something like that. I handled the finances of the group for a while. Then later on when they put me in the hospital and I handled that end—"

"You mean the pigs put you in the hospital?"

"Yup! I accepted the job because it was clean and because we needed somebody in the hospital. You know, a serious injury means death, so you had to have somebody to watch them.

"While I was working in the hospital, I performed the function of, let's say, an MTA.* I learned quite a bit about handling wounds, stitches and"—he laughs remembering how he had put something over on the pigs—"dispensing of pain killers and so forth. They put me in the psych ward. I helped the cats that came up there. Sometimes some of the brothers, not many of them, came up to get a little relief from the lockup cell. They'd play nuts, come up to the psych ward. They'd give me the keys, you

* Medical Technical Assistant.

know? So I could get in and out of the psych patients' cells. I'd let them out in the evenings. They put me on the graveyard shift to keep me away from everybody. I'd let them out of the cell block to see TV.

"That was a beautiful affair," he laughs. "That was November of '64. I think I stayed locked up then about five months. During this period, this '64 period, I lost the little job that I had in the kitchen." He says the word "kitchen" as if it had a vast hidden significance. "The period I was just talking about then came a little later on. That was in 1965, or was it '64? But the '64 period I had a job in the kitchen, a good job. So an incident went down in there. One of Hitler's Helpers, one of the Nazi clique, went wild in there."

"Were they already calling themselves Hitler's Helpers then?"

"I think they've been doing that for a long time. They work quite a bit with the police. Most of that type will not, but there are certain ones who will play along. Fun and games. But one of them went wild in the kitchen there and they piped some brother, hit him in the head with a pipe. Called a couple of others derogatory names and so forth. But this guy that did this later got assaulted with the end of a sword, with the tactical edge of the sword." The catch in his voice tells me who had committed the assault. "They never caught anybody. You know it was so efficient that they couldn't put down anyone. They locked up Mexicans, white guys"—laughing. "Finally they let them go and kicked me out of the kitchen. But let's move on.

"March or April of 1965, I got arrested," he whispers. "You know, I got busted on the yard for assault with a deadly weapon. I was living in the east block at the time. Living on the fifth tier and that's where the assault went down. So of course they busted me." He says "me" with the feeling that they always tried to make him responsible for everything. "I pleaded not guilty, but they locked me up fifteen months."

"If anything happens anywhere in the jail, I guess you're going to be the first one they look for?"

"That's the way it was, starting in 1964. It didn't matter. They don't care where I was at. If it happened in the east block and I was living in the south block, they're going to lock me up for complicity. I was supposed to have assaulted a Mexican. The way the write-up reads is that he took something from some member of the group. I was supposed to have retaliated against him. They had a couple of people say they saw me do such things, but you know, they can get people to say anything. They didn't have enough evidence to prosecute, so they just locked me up for fifteen months. All right. That was the year of the Watts riot. I was locked up when it was going on.

"The next year, 1966, I got out of lockup. I was placed in the general population. That's when they put me to work in the hospital. And that's when I was trying to organize some kind of medical routine to defend and help the brothers that got hurt in the yard.

"I stayed out and did well that whole year. I had one fight with a black. It was a real nasty incident. I think we were arguing about Vietnam. He called them gooks or something like that, one of those names, you know, that they call." He sits back and sucks on a piece of candy while he ruminates. "It grew from one thing to another. He wasn't in the group or anything, but he was living on the fringe of the group. He was a friend of one of the cats that was with us. We had bad feelings. We had an argument, I think it was concerning some money he owed to the group or something like that. Several things went down. Then all of a sudden, one day he just hit me. I turned my head to him to walk away and he attacked me right here"—pointing to a spot on his neck—"a very tender point there. I don't think he knew what he was doing"— laughing at the irony—"but he hit a real sensitive point. And my legs buckled and just instinctively before I went down I hit him in the groin." Very proud of his instinctive reaction. "He was a mac man.* So you see I was hurting and he was hurting too. And the brothers ran in and broke us up. But I thought about it a while and I got mad and I went back. And I got to thinking in the back of my head that I'm going to hurt this guy because I'm that mad about things he's said, things he's done, personal attacks and so forth. So I went back and attacked him with the edge of the sword, but they pulled me off of him again. Police locked me up. He turned out to be a rat and started snitching on me. You know,

* A pimp or ladies' man.

scared of them. The police locked me up and left him on the main line." He laughs because the police had gotten it wrong since he was the one who was retaliating. "The brothers made him go to the police and tell them that it wasn't anything serious. And so they let me go. I think I was about a month, a month locked up, and he finally got me out, you know? Went and told them that it wasn't that much and you shouldn't lock the guy up and blah, blah, blah, you know? And it turned out he's cooperated with them before, and so they let me go."

The guard is sitting outside the window looking back and forth, his head bobbing in and out of sight. He yawns like a bull elephant. George pauses and then whispers in my ear, "They're discussing us out there now." I look up. Two guards are looking in and moving their lips. "They mentioned my name," he adds. I realize that even though George seems to be concentrating completely on what we are saying, he is always completely aware of everything that is going on around him.

October 22

My first visit with George in the main visiting room. A guard in the upper left-hand corner is perched on a high chair like a Dickensian clerk, his head moving almost mechanically back and forth as he scrutinizes the room. Rows of tables and benches. Inmates on one side, visitors on the other, necks bent, faces almost touching.

With other convicts in the room, George is a different person. Like a politician at a meeting with his constituents. Long looks. Solemn nods. Raisings of eyebrows. Discreet clenchings of fists and raisings of arms. Occasional whispered conversations with convicts entering and leaving the room. Somehow he manages in spite of everything else to keep up his conversation with me.

"You know that thing you sent me"—referring to part of a book I was writing on the Soledad Brothers and the meaning of the revolution in prison—"man, let me tell you, you really understood. I don't know how you did it."

George smiles encouragingly. I raise my hand above my waist and clench my fist and George does the same, and for an instant it seems as if everyone else in the room disappears and we are alone together.

"I've read in economics very extensively, you know. The purer forms of economics, Mills and Henry George. I read all of *Wealth of Nations.* I read *Progress and Poverty* fifteen times. He made some beautiful points, but his conclusions were all messed up. But he made some beautiful points, and his descriptions of how capitalism robs the worker methodically of his part, his share in the improvements, in the arts of civilization, how workers are passed over, robbed . . . he explained this beautifully. Remember with the barrels?"

But I don't remember. "Did you ever read Swift?"

"No! I read Descartes and all of the so-called great European thinkers. Spinoza, John Stuart Mill. I got into Malthus and all those fools. Adam Smith and *The Wealth of Nations.* I got into Marx and all the other comrades." He is hushed. "You know"—he breathes heavily and hesitates—"the thing that really put me onto Communism was the feeling, my sense of the fear response it created in the people in this country that I hated."

"They told you where to go. If they were afraid of it, there had to be something in it."

"Of course, there had to be something happening, you know. I'm going to tell you just exactly when it started. After Castro completed the Cuban revolution—Castro and Che and Camillo completed the Cuban revolution. It was big news in '63. And they were really shook up. Delighted the hell out of me. Of course, I knew all about what they said about Communism prior to that, but I started investigating. That was about the same time that George Lewis gave me this book, *The Communist Manifesto,* and after that I waded through . . . struggled through . . . *Anti-Duehring.* But I think the thing that really put us on, put me on, is the thing that it shakes these cats up so. I just concluded that anything that they were against, I was for it.

"I don't consider myself a writer. Writing is a tool. You know where I got my long sentences from, though? I read a book called *The Red and the Black.*"

"Oh, Stendhal. You read Stendhal. Wild."

"*The Red and the Black.* The first psychological novel. The girl was impressed with this little cat who was trying to make his way up, because he wrote long letters. He wrote long letters that had long sentences. I said to myself that must be what I want"—laughing. "I started using commas instead of periods."

I realize how important it is for him to bring people under his spell. Like Angela. "*I had to make her love me.*" The letters he refers to in Stendhal were copied by the hero, Julien Sorel, from someone else's letters for the purpose of seduction. Not because he loved the woman he was trying to seduce, but to impress another woman with his conquest.

"They hung Julien." He pauses, realizing that he has been imitating the prose style of someone who was executed. He breaks off and reflects for a moment on the irony and coincidence. "For just attempting to murder a woman. Strange, those French folks." He breathes heavily. "I read all of—what's that cat's name?—he wrote *The Lion Skin, Scaramouche.*"

"*The Lion Skin?* Oh, yeah, Rafael Sabatini."

"Sabatini. I dug it. The one part that I really liked out of all of them is the line that goes like this: 'Once there was a man who did sell the lion skin while the beast lived and was killed while hunting him.' " Stretching out the words to prolong the pleasure of saying them, then exploding in laughter. "The hunter bested, the hunter slain by the prey, you dig? That just knocks me out."

October 25

For most middle-class whites like myself, life is a matter of chronic discontent. The problem is that there doesn't seem to be any explanation most of the time for the way we feel. There doesn't seem to be anyone to blame. We have no way of defining the source of our discontent because we have no compelling definition of what men should be to themselves and to each other.

I know why so many middle-class whites like myself identify with blacks. We say to ourselves that only blacks possess true authenticity. I know that loving George, caring about him, is part of my desire to be real. It is as if I am saying to him: "Make me real, give me the reality of hard surfaces, of steel doors and bars, prison-made shanks,* karate calluses half an inch thick. Take me

---

* Bits of metal that have been fashioned into knives.

out of my plastic world of offices and subways and apartment houses and deodorants. Make me as real as death, as fateful as murder."

What we all want from George is to be made an instrument of himself. To be made as real as death, as fateful as murder.

The one thing George wants above all else is freedom, we can't give him that. We won't help him escape.

Yet we all go on longing for this final sacrifice of ourselves, for the ultimate experience. How many times we have pushed ourselves to that point, hoping to be swept up, pushed irrevocably beyond all reason or restraint. But we always recover ourselves. Our inability to go all the way is very painful. How disillusioning it is to be still alive and protecting ourselves when so many others have died. It's almost like not being able to give yourself completely in love. Like never being able to lose yourself completely in passion.

Each of us in his own way has looked longingly into the abyss. And then recoiled with horror.

October 27
One of George's friends has been paroled from prison. There is a rumor that George plans to use him in another escape attempt. It is almost uncanny. The friend is going on trial in the Marin Courthouse on a charge of assaulting a guard. George is supposed to be brought in from the prison to testify as a character witness. It would be August 7 again and the blood would flow in the streets once more.

October 29
The judge has refused permission for George to appear at his friend's trial. Everyone seems to be relieved. It was just too soon.

"Do you know what I don't like to discuss, don't want to discuss? The details of those incidents of what went on here. See, because if it was in the wrong hands, if it got to the wrong people, it would make me appear to be a type of guy that overreacts, who isn't nice. Describing the incidents would make it look like I've allowed my environment to completely destroy my restraints."

"Uh-huh."

"But some of the incidents were so punk, so vicious. You know what I had at stake—my life."

"Uh-huh."

"A man is just inclined to defend his life to the best of his ability, and a man who comes under attack, he is going to develop the ability to anticipate."

"Yeah, uh-huh."

"And it followed logically that since I'm human, that sometimes I make a mistake in anticipating. And some trouble has resulted from those mistakes."

"That's like some of the problems here. You anticipated when there was no actual threat or you overreacted to threats."

"Both. Combining that with the fact that I'm a Maoist, Marxist, Leninist and every time I open my mouth, that's who falls out."

"Uh-huh."

"This made further trouble. Nobody gets ten years. Nobody else in this state has done ten years on one year to life. They've never been able to convict me of anything. They know little things. They tried other times. This is the first time I'm going to trial, you know. The last time, the proceedings didn't even get this far at all, not even nearly this far. But they were preparing to try me for my life about four or five different times. All right, now you know that kind of thing happens. When you look around and don't see any kind of allies, it's friend or foe, and the majority are foe. Us and them."

November 1
So many journalists have been visiting George that the prison authorities have started limiting them to one visit apiece.

November 3
Life magazine wants a photo of George holding the issue of *Life* with Angela on the cover. They are offering the inducement of a long article on the Soledad Brothers.

Today someone told me the story of Georgia Jackson and the Marin County Grand Jury.

When she was summoned to appear at the San Rafael Hall of Justice, she is supposed to have replied, "You can put me in jail. I'm not going into that place where you killed my son."

So the jury held a session at a motel outside Los Angeles. Georgia, standing at the head of the table, I am told, addressed them as follows:

"No, I'm not going to answer any of your questions. I don't like you and I don't like talking to you. You are the same people who killed my one son and locked my other son up in a cage for more than half his life. You call yourself a grand jury, but you don't know what justice is. I've watched you and . . ." She goes on and on. Implacable. Curly-haired, a little stooped, eyes slightly feverish. When she is finished, she picks up her purse and goes. The grand jury sits dumfounded. What can they possibly do with her? Cite Georgia Jackson for contempt? She is as indomitable as her son George. They all know that she stands for a higher form of justice than they could ever possibly aspire to. They realize that there is no limit to her fury or her obstinacy. They are relieved to see her go.

"Next witness. I think we can forget about that one."

Georgia was Marin and Soledad. She was her sons. "If I had known what Jonathan was going to do, I would have gone with him. My sons couldn't do anything that would make me reject them." She was blackness itself, driven beyond the point of no return like her sons.

November 5

Fay has just called. There is talk of a possible *Time* cover story on George if they can be promised some exclusive material.

November 9

Arrangements have been made for Canadian and British TV to interview George.

November 10
Mount Vernon, Illinois.

I've spent all morning tramping around graveyards. It's been raining for days, and the fields are sodden with icy water. A heavy cold wind gusts across the open spaces. The city is much bigger than I had imagined. I thought there would only be one or two graveyards at most, but there seem to be dozens. I want to call Georgia and ask her where her son is buried, but I hold back because I'm not sure about how she would react to my desire to visit Jonathan's grave.

Down Main Street—classic dichotomy—shantytown to the right, shacks tumbling into themselves, burned-out buildings, charred shells left to age, abandoned cars with gaping holes in their windshields, small patches of green stubbly lawn, a few old people in the streets, dark windows, debris everywhere. Off to one side, by the railroad track, a towering pile of crushed automobiles. All the children must be in school. George himself had hidden away in one of those shacks after his escape from Bakersfield.*

And the other side of town. It's what the other side always is— the towns you see photographed in the magazines. Sometimes it seems as if that part of town just naturally has all the sun.

I go back and forth along the streets of shantytown searching for the graveyard. I stop to ask a passer-by how I can get to the police station. When I find the station, it is empty except for one toothless hanger-on, gray stubble on his cheeks. "Where is the police chief?" I ask. "He'll be back in a minute," the old man answers.

I go out and come back. A squat man, belly hanging over his belt, is sitting at the switchboard. My long hair has been blown by the wind. I have on a summer suit, too thin for the weather. My hiking boots are sodden halfway up, the waterproofing long since worn off. Mud from graveyards is embedded in the cleats. The man speaks with a Southern accent, and I remember that I'm just a few miles away from Cairo, Illinois, in the Deep South.

"Could you tell me where Jonathan Jackson is buried, that young man who was buried here last summer?"

"You mean that nigger who was buried down at Mount Bethel by the Panthers?"

I try to be cool. I've come here to visit Jonathan and not to change the world. I just want to do that and go. I've got a plane to catch.

* Reform school.

He tells me and I leave. I walk around the block a couple of times, and then I go back. This time when I enter there are several people standing around, but the man I had spoken to isn't there. The others look at me. I ask a man who later turns out to be the chief where the deputy is who had been sitting at the switchboard.

"Why do you want to see him?" the chief asks me.

"That's all right," I reply, "just want to see him."

"He's the one who was here asking about that nigger," says one of the toothless old men in the crowd. The room is small and suddenly it seems to be packed with people. The chief puts his body between me and the others. "You'd better wait for him in that room." He motions me into a smaller room and follows me in.

"Who are you? Let's see some identification. You're from out of town. How did you get here?" Seeming to intimate that I was never going to get out. An expression of scorn as he looks over my papers. I explain that I came by car.

"Now why did you want to see the deputy?"

"I came back here to lodge a complaint against him."

"What!"

"He referred to someone, a friend whose grave I had come to visit, as a nigger. I want to make a complaint about that. I think a policeman has a duty to respect all the people he represents."

"You think what? You long-haired hippie freak. You better get out of here before you get thrown in jail yourself."

"I'm not going anywhere. I've got a perfect right to be here. I've come from New York and I'm on business."

I try to find a business card, but all I can find are other people's cards—a whole profusion of them. I jam them all back into my wallet and shove it into my pocket, imagining that if he sees the profusion of cards he will be able to charge me with impersonation.

"I don't care who you are. I told you if you don't get out of here in two minutes, you're going to be back there in a cell." Everyone is on his feet now, moving toward me expectantly.

"All right, I'm going to leave. I've got to catch a plane or I would stay."

"What do you mean, catch a plane? I thought you said you

came by car." He really wants to deal with me now. He has caught me in a discrepancy.

I try to explain. I took a plane to St. Louis, then a car to Mount Vernon. I have become an object, something he would like to squash under his feet. They would really enjoy beating me up. Obviously they have little else to do.

"All right. I'm going. I want to get out of here. You insult my humanity."

I push past the chief and walk through the next room out into the hall. I expect to be pulled back or shoved off my feet, but nothing happens. I walk deliberately to my car, stopping twice to look back to see if I am being followed. Two deputies stand by the door watching me. I find my car and circle around trying to see if I am being followed. Then I turn down Tenth Street, heading for the cemetery. A gray car seems to be following me. I slow down to let it pass, but it slows down too. I'm pretty sure they're following me. They want to catch me outside of town and beat me up. Maybe kill me. I pull over to the side of the road. The gray car passes. I get moving again.

A few hundred yards farther down, I see the Mount Bethel cemetery on the other side of the road. I pull in along the gravel road, and stop just a little bit in from where it turns. They don't have to follow me. They know where I'm going. I get out and start searching among the rows of graves, my boots sinking deeper and deeper into the cold mud. The field is desolate and exposed and the wind sweeping back and forth is getting colder and colder. I go back to my car and drag out an old sweater that I had tucked away in my suitcase. All the headstones—"IN LOVING REMEMBRANCE," "OUR DEARLY BELOVED." Old colored streamers festooned around the tombstones, cardboard pots of flowers overturned and beginning to root into the ground. Back and forth. Back and forth. Now and then, the sun breaking through the clouds. Feelings of joy and warmth. I finish traversing one section, and then go on to the next. I've heard that the grave is unmarked, and I pass a few areas where an unmarked grave might be, but I keep on, convinced that I will be able to identify the correct grave.

Finally, I finish everything except for a small plot of graves right by my car. Just in from the road are the gravestones of Georgia's mother and father, Irene Davis and George B. Davis. She died in 1956, but he didn't die until 1967, at the age of eighty-six. Right beside them is an unmarked grave that has fallen in on itself, a rectangle of turf and clay cut out from the surrounding area that has slumped into the ground. A puddle of brownish mud rippled by the wind. A piece of cellophane floating on it, an old candy wrapper. I think of cleaning the grave, but I don't think Jonathan would have wanted his grave cleaned up any more than he wanted his life prettied up. I feel as sodden as the ground. I think of putting my Soledad Brothers button on his grave. But it isn't the time for gestures. "I haven't shed a tear because I am so proud," George had said just a few days after his brother's death. So I only swallow my own tears and leave.

November 13

Mike Wallace is talking about interviewing George for nationwide TV.

November 15

The underground newspapers are constantly filled now with news of George and the other two Soledad Brothers. The *Liberated Guardian* has just brought out a special eight-page insert with photos that contains the text of some of George's letters.

Everyone on the left seems to expect something extraordinary from him. They talk about him playing a leading role in the revolution when he gets out of prison. Scores of underground journalists have made their pilgrimage to San Quentin. I know the kinds of things they say to him. I've read their pieces.

You are a great man. We need you to lead the revolution. Tell us what we should do. You are the most powerful, the strongest man we have ever met. You are like Castro, like Che. You can do it. You can do anything you want.

The more his fame and prestige grow, the smaller and smaller his cell must become. How he must hate his useless caged body sometimes.

November 18
NET has just completed a long interview with George and the other Brothers that they intend to run in a month or so.

November 20
Recently someone put me up for an award based mostly on my work on George's book. My sponsor needed support from some of my authors. I'm very touched by what George is supposed to have said about me:
"A white man who would listen—strange to me. I realize that there is a great deal to the argument of brotherhood. I dig him and his quandary. He senses mine and relates."

November 27
As George says in one of his letters, "I just breathe people in." He only has to see people once and after that they are tied to him forever. I can think of at least ten people who have fallen almost completely under his sway. George is very open about what he does. He needs people. He knows that the way to involve them is to accept them at their own estimate of themselves. It makes him almost irresistible.

November 30
George has asked Fay to buy him a pair of eyeglasses like his brother's.

December 5
A woman has been arrested in Milwaukee for attempting to hijack a plane which she intended to use as ransom for the Soledad Brothers and Angela Davis. The police had been watching her for some time. She is picked up even before she can board the plane.

December 7
George is happier this week than anyone has seen him for months. Fay gave him his new eyeglasses and he wears them all the time. "They make me look like the man-child, don't they?"

December 20

I heard a story about Georgia today. After George was sent to prison, Georgia simply stopped eating at the dinner table. She cooked and served the meals but refused to sit down and eat with the others. With her son gone, it wasn't a family dinner table. She wasn't going to pretend that it was, or that there was nothing wrong. She wasn't going to forget, she wasn't going to acquiesce. She didn't make any statement to the family. It just happened. The family accepted it because they knew there was simply no way of changing Georgia once she had made up her mind.

The other members of the family would say to her, "Try to forget, there's nothing you can do about it." All they would get in response would be a wrathful withering stare.

Just a few months after George had been accused of the murder, when Jonathan was sixteen, he suddenly realized what his mother had been doing all these years. And he asked her to sit down with them for his sake. Georgia must have known that he was right. Supposedly, she got flustered and even began to breathe harder. Everyone stirred in their chairs, one of her daughters repeated her brother's request. What a release it would have been for them all—like a sudden flow of water on a parched field. "Come on, Mother. Please, it would make us all feel so good!" They could see her face calculating and turning inward. "We need you, too, Mother. It's not the same without you." Her whole chest heaved. It was as if she were pacing back and forth in front of them. But she couldn't do it. It was just as if someone were watching her. And if that someone saw her sitting down, they would close the door on George forever. As if that person were to say, "Well, it's all right. She accepts. She finally sat down. We can get on with business." But she couldn't explain all this to them. She didn't even want to explain it to herself. And so she decided to beg the question entirely. "I'm not hungry. I don't feel like eating." She walked out of the room, and weariness fell on them all. A few minutes later they had all left the table.

December 29

A recruiting officer was shot to death in San Francisco yesterday by a young white who was immediately arrested. George is delighted. "Did you hear about it?" he asks me, glowing with pleasure. At first I don't understand what he is talking about. "You know, the pig who that guy killed." He looks at me, waiting for me to smile back at him so we can both share the joy of a pig's death. But I am too horrified to respond. George sees the event as the precursor of open warfare in the streets, as a revolutionary act, the start of the floodtide of the people's war. But all I can think about is the senseless killing and the terrible pain of the man who did the shooting.

It is not the beginning of anything, just the end of two lives.

"At one point in '67 you mention that you have a leg problem. What happened?"

"The result of a beating that the police gave me. We were testifying for a brother that they were trying to railroad on a knife beef. He was getting ready to go home. They didn't want him on the street because he was a political brother and they set him up. The cop picks a knife from a stack he has. He sits and waits because he knows that this guy got to go past him. There's coordination between the gun tower and the cop on the ground. The cop on the ground plants the knife. The guy in the gun tower is watching. He's got pictures. They all carry around pictures in their back pockets of guys who they think or they feel are a threat to their control, or guys that they feel are political, anti-institutional or something like that. It's part of their in-service training to learn who are the threats to their control. You can search any one of these officers and see the pictures there in their back pockets.

"My picture was right up in front of them all. I couldn't go anywhere. I got to the point where I stopped trying to move. It's just the same way on the streets, when you're working trying to survive, hustling. When the police get your name, when too many of them get to know you, you have to leave that area and start working another area. It's the same way here, except that there's no way to leave."

I get the sense of him being watched by hundreds of eyes. And I look up at the door and the guard is there looking in. Another guard is standing beside him. There is probably no respite for George from hostile eyes.

"We were going out to testify for this brother. They had set him up when he passed by this knife, a place where everybody has to go by. The guy in the gun tower blew his whistle. Whew! The guard who was waiting on the ground reached and grabbed this guy in a stranglehold. But that didn't prove too successful. The guard ended up on his butt. So that is two charges against the brother. Assault and the knife. And this is a beautiful type brother, if somebody reaches for him he goes into his defense-attack thing. So they have two charges on this cat now. And we were going to court. They lie, we lie—I'm not going to bite my tongue, we lied, we lied like hell trying to get him off. I get up on the stand and swore like hell I'm telling the truth. Actually I'm lying, because that's what they're doing, and this is the way I'm forced to fight. And so I have no qualms whatsoever. And I don't believe in the Bible anyway and they got my hand resting on the goddamn Bible." He laughs, as if to say, "What could be more absurd?" "But you can tell I did have some kind of reservations about lying. But I have to because it's the way they forced me to fight." Just the way they had forced him to live also. "And a cat who can't adapt, you know what happens to him. He doesn't survive." He pauses for the significance of this remark to sink in.

"So the police were mad at us, because 'these cats are using our own tactics against us. Well, you niggers have sure gotten shrewd.' You see where they got that right together. And they brought four of us back about the same time, the main four: W. L. Nolen, the one who got killed in Soledad about six months ago.* . . . another brother they called Bald . . . a brother named Willy, I forget his real name . . . a brother named Nathaniel." As George speaks their names, there is a different quality in his voice for each of them.

"What really got us bad was a white guy who was trying to help us. They had two reasons for jumping on us, for setting us up for the fight. They wanted to prove to this white guy that he shouldn't be helping blacks. And they wanted to prove to this

* One of the three blacks who were murdered in the exercise yard of Soledad's "O" wing on January 13, 1970.

white guy that blacks were really powerless, that we had no strength and no power whatsoever. That these blacks can't and won't protect him. So the way it proceeded was there were six or seven cops in there, shaking us down* in the back of the corridor. And the fight started this way. They were shaking me and the white guy down at the same time. The other guys were waiting to be shaken down . . . but what I don't know is that there are ninety of them waiting in the wings, all of them with clubs and pick handles. They had this fight set up. They're going to whup us. There are ninety cops in the wings with big heavy weighted clubs and long pick handles. You know what a pick handle is?"

I do a double take, wondering for a moment what it is that George takes me for. Then I realize in the same instant that because George has been in prison so long he probably has an unreal idea about the separation between the city and the country. And because he knows I live in the city, he probably feels I am completely cut off from all menial labor.

"All right. But it is not that simple with five of us in that small room being shook down all at once. So they started on me and this white guy. They assumed that I was the guy who they could make react faster. They're shaking the both of us and they pushed this white guy. Pushed this white guy against the wall. A lieutenant"—and George hisses the name—"pushed this guy against the wall after he'd got naked.† The lieutenant made some kind of racial remark, 'nigger lover' and blah blah blah. And I'm naked. I haven't got a thing on. This nakedness is deliberate. We're both naked, when they decide to start the fight. The lieutenant, now he's a real tough guy, thirty-five, thirty-six years old, he's been there a long time. Hairy chest, crew-cut, sleeves rolled up, righteous pig, real stereotype pig. You know, he grabs this white guy by the skin of his chest. He grabs a handful of skin on his chest and hits him in the face two or three times. But it snaps it down on me just exactly what's happening, that they're trying to provoke me. He had already punched this guy. Because this white guy, he wasn't a physical type guy. All he was trying to do was duck and dodge, keep the guy off. But now I'm thinking, I'm trying to

* Searching them.
† They are being strip-searched.

evaluate the situation. You know, he had already punched this guy. Because while this punching is going on, you know, I was trying to think of some way around this. And I'm making up my mind what I'm going to do." George mimics his moment of thoughtfulness, looking off into space for an instant.

"Well, in the process of the shakedown he says, 'Jackson, rub your hands through your hair.' And I rub my hands through my hair. 'Open your mouth. Turn your head.' I open my mouth. He looks in my ears. He says, 'Raise your testicles.' So I raise my testicles . . . and he tells me to turn around, and so I turn around. And he says, 'Bend over,' and I bend over. He says, 'Raise up your feet,' and so I raise up my feet, you know? And then he tells me to crack a smile. In other words, I am supposed to spread my behind apart." I wonder if his euphemism is for my benefit. "Dig it? Well, so I'm bent over, you see, and this is the cat who was beating up this white dude over there. I just hit this dude right in his mouth. He was over like this, anticipating, he is think- ing about me cracking a smile . . . and I gave it to him in his teeth with a back kick right in his mouth. And so the fight started, with his blood spurting everywhere. As soon as I started fighting, all the other brothers jumped in. The police came from the wings with their clubs and their pickaxes and fought it out for about forty-five minutes. It was beautiful. I loved it."

I can feel his eagerness to fight in the way the muscles of his chest and his arms have bunched up. He describes it in that tone of voice that most people reserve for the great moments of their lives, for the times when they feel they are completely fulfilled.

"We lost." He laughs to indicate that, in his opinion, he really believes they had wasted the pigs. "In the write-up (you might get a chance to read the write-up) they described it a little bit differently"—delighted by his certainty that they would have to lie to conceal what really happened. "It was all our fault and every- thing. At the time, I hit this fool with all I got with a back kick. He was out of the fight right away. Then I went after the lieutenant who was hitting this white guy. I hit him with everything, right in the throat with all I got, and he went 'Hrrugh.' " In George's mouth it becomes like a battle cry. "You dig? The times when they did get me in the head with their clubs, it wasn't hurting so bad. And I was in the best of shape, and the other four brothers were very physical. W. L. Nolen, that's why they killed him, that's why they murdered him. He really could handle himself, so they murdered him. But it was a beautiful fight, and we lost it, but we lost it at some cost to them. We sent them to the hospital. They had a little meat wagon, they had a little meat wagon . . . terrible situation.

"Look, the fight went down in an area about twice the size of this room.* How could you get ninety guys in there? They were hitting each other. Wild maniacal fiends. You just have to hate a person like that." He shakes his head, and his whole face glows. "I knew I was going to come under attack. There was no way for me to avoid it, so I just fired a shot off first. The best defense is a good attack. It didn't matter because there were ninety others, but I got two of them."

"This is when your leg got smashed up?"

"Once I went down. There were no two ways about it. Down and out. Legs just like rubber. Once I'm down, I've got a thousand pigs on me. Six or seven on each arm, some cat kneeing me in my face and I'm kicking."

It isn't just the way that George mimes the fight with his body that brings it so vividly into the room, but the way he gives off the energy of the fight, like a pulsating light.

"It's a special thing, from the ground defense-offense attacks. You can't get much higher than the groin, the kneecaps, but it hurts. The cat has got to be careful. He just can't walk up on you if you know anything about martial arts, hand-to-hand combat. There are special techniques for defenses from the ground. You've got to know them because you're going to end up there lots of times. Well, anyway, it encouraged someone to do something to my leg. That's how I got the knot on my knee. Cat took a pick handle and stood back and just started swinging at my leg to crack it at the knee. The intention was twofold. A cat with a broken kneecap, he limps for the rest of his life. He's slowed down for the rest of his life. Actually, I was in good shape when he hit me, my leg was contracted and it just made a great big old knot that just

* About five by eight feet.

stayed there for six months. But it didn't slow me down. It hasn't slowed me down." Nothing was going to slow him down.

January 15, 1971

The woman who is addressed as Joan in so many of George's letters called me today in tears. She was visiting George yesterday. In order to read some letters together they sat on the same side of the visiting table. This is some kind of technical violation of prison rules. The guards burst into the room and hauled George out. A few seconds later, as she was preparing to leave, Joan heard the sounds of scuffling in the hall outside the door which leads back into the prison. She looked out the small window in the door and saw at least twelve guards with three-foot-long clubs flailing away at George as he lay unconscious on the floor.

February 1

George tries so hard to make me believe that everything is all right and that he is still in control. But his smiles are almost all pain now. The flush of excitement over his book is past. Now he always has a feverish look in his eyes, like someone hallucinating. He doesn't want anyone to know. He doesn't even want to acknowledge it himself. So he makes an extra-special effort to appear rational.

George's words after Jonathan's death keep coming back. "I haven't shed a tear because I'm so proud. . . . Maybe when the spring comes." How could he have shed just one tear? Let one come and how could he have stopped the endless flood of tears that he had been swallowing all his life? One tear and that great massive shell that he had built all around himself would have dissolved in an endless torrent.

February 3

From the instant that I enter the visiting room I can tell that there is something special on George's mind. I can feel him waiting for the right moment to bring it up. Waiting for the right silence. At one point he stops speaking and very deliberately searches the room with slowly moving eyes. Then he gives me a look of invitation. With both his elbows stretched out on the table, he lowers his head to a point just a few inches above the surface of the table and gestures with his shoulders for me to do the same. Bent over, our faces close together, the crowns of our heads almost touch.

"You know, I could get out of here if I had the right kind of help from the outside." His voice is confidential and insinuating. "I know all the weak points." His eyes drill into my face. "There is a place over here where the work sheds are. They don't even guard it. Anybody could get some guns in there." He takes the pencil from my hands and draws a crude map. "Hide the guns, and when we were ready, we could just go get them. You know, this whole place is a tinderbox. Could go up any minute. Anything could start a riot. That's when we get the guns and break out in all the confusion." I mumble agreement as if what he is saying is just purely academic discussion.

I won't do it his way. I don't think it can work. No one can shoot their way out of here. I don't trust George's judgment. And it is still too early to tell him about my plans. I have to be sure about what I can do before I even suggest to him that I might be able to help him.

George knows I have refused to take his lead. It is just as if I had refused to take his hand. I can sense his disappointment. He turns away for an instant and takes a deep breath. We are both silent. He takes the paper on which he drew the map and curls it into a funnel and lights it with a match. Then he puts it in the ashtray. We watch as it goes up in smoke.

Later as I leave the visiting room area, a lieutenant of the guards motions me over to him. "I'm very disappointed in you. A professional man, letting him burn up paper that way. If it happens again, I'm going to have to discontinue your visits." Then he turns and walks off. I wonder if he isn't really telling me, "We are watching everything. You're not fooling us for an instant. We know everything that you do."

Every time I talk to the lawyers, I get more and more confused.
Fay is now saying how desperate things are. "One chance in twenty of winning. A possibility of getting a reversal on appeal." John always says: "We've got a winner."

I wonder what George thinks of his two lawyers, who have such disparate estimates of his fate. I wonder how much he really believes in them or in what they are doing. My guess is that he humors them the same way he humors us all. Because in the end there is just so much that we can ever understand about him or his life and there is no way for him to explain. I think he just goes along with us so far and then falls back into his sense of doom.

February 4

Someone distantly associated with the Defense Committee comes up to me on the street.

She begins almost coquettishly, with a faintly complicit smile and rolling eyes. "I just want you to tell me something," her voice soft and amorous, looking me up and down. "You are thinking of doing something to get George out, aren't you?" I look at her, trying to suggest that I might be, but also trying to tell her that I am unwilling to commit myself in words. "I just thought you might be. Something about you made it seem that you were thinking of trying something."

I take a deep breath. "That means you must have been thinking of doing something yourself."

She nods her head affirmatively. "Well," she says, "you know somebody has got to do something soon or George is going to get himself killed. Everybody knows he is trying to escape. He has to feel that people are helping on the outside or he will move precipitously and it will be all over."

We are both silent for a minute and then she continues: "I know you really love George. You have been thinking about doing something, haven't you?" Her eyes move over my face avidly.

"Of course," I answer, "I've been thinking about it, but I haven't dared to talk to anyone."

"That's what I thought." Her face expresses satisfaction. "If you really are willing to do something, we will have to get word to him very quickly. I don't know how long he can hold out." She stares straight into my eyes. "What shall we tell him? He really trusts you. He will take your word if you say you are going to do something. He will wait. Do you really think you can make a commitment?"

I think of George and how he will feel when he hears I have pledged to risk my life to get him out of jail. Nobody else ever cared about him. But I will care. I will show him that there is one white person who really cares.

"You can get word to him that I'll do it." For an instant I actually feel as if I am soaring.

"It will really mean so much to him." She has moved her body close to mine.

"You know, I think we should go somewhere and make love," she suddenly says. "I think it's the best way to get to know people, and if we are going to get involved in this together, I think it is very important that we know each other very well."

February 10

I have been trying to convince the mothers of the three Soledad Brothers to help me with the book I want to write about them and their sons. Inez is the only reluctant one.

When I told George about what I want to do, he got the idea that I needed money to finish it. His mouth opened, lips pursed, eyes suddenly glowed. I could almost see the thought forming in his mind. *Oh, now I can do something for my friend.* He proceeded to offer me half of the advance he would get on his next book. The other half would go to Huey Newton.

I keep having this feeling that everyone knows what I am thinking. It seems so obvious to me that I would have to be planning to get George out. Sometimes it seems as if people are even eavesdropping on my thoughts, as if the idea is so powerful in my head that I can't possibly contain it there.

I am certain that my phone is being tapped. There is a kind of crystalline sound whenever I pick it up like ice cubes being crushed under tremendous pressure.

February 13

I heard about a journalist today who claims that if his book on the case appears before the trial, the trial will never take place because of the things it is going to reveal. Imagining the worst and that he has uncovered some evidence of George's guilt, I call Fay immediately and arrange to have her call me back from a public phone booth. When she returns my call, her voice is weary.

"Call John and tell him. Let him handle it. I'm not very involved any more. I'm thinking of leaving the case. I've done all that I can do."

I can't believe my ears. The case is her whole life. It can't be true. It would kill George. She is the only person who can win the case.

"Oh, no! You can't mean it. There is no one who can replace you."

But with the same air of weariness she replies, "Anyone can do it now. John will be able to handle it. Besides, I'm not getting along very well with George. I'm just so tired of the whole thing." And there is nothing else to say.

I think of George and how much he depends on her. There is no way she can desert him. They are locked in the case together, just the same way he is locked in his cell. "Waving her hands like a conductor" was the way George once described her. Without Fay, there would be no sound. I know they will find a way to get back together because they need each other so much. I think of how caged George will feel without her. When I close my eyes, I can see him throwing himself against the bars of his cell, tearing away at them and bellowing with pain.

February 28

Fay has pulled out of the case. When I ask her why, she explains that George has refused to cooperate. He wouldn't wait for the outcome of the legal process. And so she has withdrawn. She suggests that he has been making demands on her which she has been forced to refuse.

March 10

George almost never stops writing about his death now. He always refers to himself now as the doomed man, the condemned man.

April 2

The Berkeley *Barb* has just interviewed George about his views on women's liberation. No one seems to be aware of the cruelty of forcing a man who has been in prison for ten years to discuss male chauvinism. So many people think George is some kind of superman who can do anything. Of course he helps to create this image of himself and he is very flattered by it. But it simply isn't true. And the final effect of this sort of distortion must be very painful for him. The reality of his life is still that he spends twenty-three and a half hours of each day in a five-by-eight cell, only getting out for visits and for a shower. The reality is that he thinks of himself already as a dying man. He has no faith in the legal process. Why should he have? He has been in prison for ten years for stealing seventy dollars.

April 5
Jonathan's son was born this week. His mother has named him Jonathan. He is supposed to look just like his father. Green eyes and blondish hair.

April 6
At a preliminary hearing in San Francisco.
John Thorne makes a motion to have the three accused men moved from San Quentin to the San Francisco County Jail. The judge refuses and announces the end of the hearing. George jumps up on a chair and leads the audience chanting "Power to the People! . . . Death to the Pigs!" Clenched fists rise in the air. The bailiffs push him away and take the copy of the Black Panther paper that his lawyer had supposedly given him. One bailiff pushes him in the ribs. "Look, don't do that again." The bailiff pushes again. "I already told you once, I'm not going to tell you again." The bailiff shoves him again in the ribs. George wheels around and knocks him unconscious with a karate blow to the temple. The other bailiffs and police converge on him with three-foot-long clubs. Seven, eight, ten of them. They spread him out on the table and beat him in full sight of the crowded court-room. His pregnant sister screams out, "They're killing my brother." Some of George's friends leap the railing separating them from the battle. The lights go out and then come on again. The judge presses a button. The San Francisco tactical squad storms in. People screaming, clubs rising and falling. Blood on the

floor of the courtroom. Finally everyone is forced outside the room except the police and the lawyers and the accused men.

April 10
George has sent revisions for the second edition of the book. Mostly about his adolescence. Target practice with his friends in the desert near Bakersfield, California. Shooting rabbits, drinking tubs of beer, stealing fruit from farmers.

"Sometimes we'd take girls who didn't mind the sun and dust. In general we lived on melons, grapes, and rabbit, girls and beer. I confess it was happy-yellow days. We slept in the car or on the ground wrapped up in surplus army blankets."*

April 20
Something George said keeps coming back to me. "How does it feel to be the most hated man in the California prisons? Wonderful. Let me tell you."

His mother knows better. "George always thought he could relate to anyone. That's what really hurt him, when he found out he couldn't." Is this why George deliberately invites so much brutality? It is as if periodically he needs all the hope and trust that build up in him to be beaten out. He can take any amount of physical punishment. It is only the disillusionment that he can't bear.

May 1
George's recent writing is all pronouncements and polemics. Hardly a trace of his humanness is left. I guess this is what he thinks people expect of him.

No one seems to realize the deep cruelty of having set him up in the role of political sage and pundit. Somewhere inside himself he must know how much he has been cut off from the real life of our time by his years in the artificial environment of prison. Yet he feels that everyone will desert him unless he lives up to their expectations. He has taken upon himself the task of providing the intellectual basis for the revolution, as if this could be done in a prison cell.

* *Soledad Brother.*

May 2

When George enters the visiting room, he has a special smile on his face. He doesn't have to say a word. The Mayday action in Washington is a fulfillment of his wildest dreams. Concentration camps in the nation's capital. Thousands of whites arrested for trying to paralyze the nation's government. "It's beginning now. The revolution is starting. All those whites getting sent to jail. They'll never forget, you know. That experience will always stick with them. Things are starting even sooner than I expected." How can I tell him the truth? That it is just another kind of demonstration against the Vietnamese war that has nothing at all to do with revolution. How can I tell him when I know that he believes that the only thing that can save him, the only thing that can give him another life, is a revolution? It feels so good just to share his joy and expectation. What harm does it really do just to dream with him a little?

May 3

I told George about my intention to help him escape. "If worse comes to worst, I have a plan that can get you out of here. I'm not going to let them get you." I wonder why he doesn't respond. The next day, I see him again, and he doesn't mention it. I feel that I have to remind him because I want him to know that he can count on me. He just nods and looks away. I feel hurt and confused. Later when I get back to New York he stops writing to me. I wonder what I could have said to him that made him angry with me. I try to recall everything I said to him on that last day. I repeat my words again to myself. This time I really hear myself. I realize that George heard me also, heard the real meaning underneath the surface of my words. It was as if I had said, "I could get you out now, but I'm not going to. I'm going to wait until I really think you need to get out. Things aren't bad enough now. Not bad enough for me to risk my life. Wait till they sentence you to the gas chamber, then I'll get you out." And I expected him to be grateful and excited. I had told him in effect: "You are dying, yes, I understand that, but you have to wait until your last breath before I can save you. Suffer for another couple of years and then I'll save you."

May 4

George told me something today that I don't think I'll ever repeat to anyone. It was just a fantasy about two people who are extremely close to him. It isn't really important in itself except for what it says about his state of mind.

He has told us all so many times in so many different ways about the damage that has been done to him in prison. Why haven't we ever really listened to him? Most of his mind is still so strong and lucid that when his spells of derangement pass it is almost as if they could never have happened.

May 5

When there is a will, there's a way. In that room which is usually reserved for the visits of condemned men, George has been making out with some of his female admirers. The room is about five by eight. Most of the space is taken up by a table and two chairs. There are doors at both ends of the room with mesh-covered windows through which guards constantly peer. But somehow George has managed to surmount these obstacles. After one of these visits, George remarked, "Next time we go all the way."

May 15

Rumors continue to the effect that the defense has no money. Everyone speculates about where it has gone and accusations fly back and forth. The most tantalizing explanation is that the money has been used for abortive escape attempts. Everyone accuses the lawyers of growing rich, but I know that it would be impossible for any of them to have taken money from the defense. They are probably just as much in the dark about it as everyone else.

May 16

Someone close to the defense has told me what he thinks John Thorne's strategy for the trial will be. John is going to bring a brick or a heavy board into the courtroom. In full view of the jury, George is going to smash it to smithereens with one karate blow. The purpose is to demonstrate that George couldn't possibly have been the one who assaulted the guard because he would have cracked the guard's head open like an eggshell. The guard would have died immediately from George's first blow. There would have been no reason to throw him over the tier. Supposedly John believes that the jury will accept this proof of George's innocence and George will walk out of the courtroom into Angela's waiting arms, a free man.

May 17
George made out his will this week. Apart from some minor bequests, he is leaving all the income from his book to Jonathan's son.

May 18
George was in great pain when I saw him today. Two days ago, he had an operation for deeply ingrown toenails and he can still hardly walk. He gave me an affidavit for John Thorne which describes what happened to him.

John Thorne had arranged for an outside doctor to perform the surgery. But at the last minute the doctor was denied entrance to the prison. George went into the operating room on a stretcher, expecting his own doctor. By the time he realized that the prison doctor was going to perform the operation, it was too late and he had no choice but to submit. Some of the guards who hated George, dressed in surgical gowns with smug smiling faces, were massed around the operating table. And after the doctor had finished the operation they had forced George to walk back to his cell through the filth of the prison. Anyone but George would have been wheeled to his cell on a stretcher. Without regard for infection, they had simply cut holes for his bandaged toes in a pair of old shoes. He was in considerable pain, but the guards refused to give him anything but aspirin.

May 20
George's toes are beginning to heal. Today he showed me that he could still perform his karate kicks, even in the small space of the condemned men's visiting room. Before I left, he showed me how he could do push-ups from a head-stand position against the wall.

George is still so young, younger than any of us. Underneath all his shells, it is as if he hasn't aged at all. Someone who knows him well described him as an eighteen-year-old boy who has been in prison for ten years.

But his back still hurts from the beating he was given on April 6 when he was attacked in the courtroom. When I left and we embraced, I could feel him wince.

He seems afraid and vulnerable and very concerned about his ability to protect himself.

May 21

In a San Francisco paper there is an announcement that Fred Bennett's body has been discovered. He had been missing for four months. Bits of his pulverized body had been found in the mountains of Santa Cruz, near a cache of dynamite and nitroglycerine. When I see George later in the day, he tells me that Bennett was in charge "of the military end of things."

I had met Fred once at Soledad House. He was elegant and gracious, like a very hip businessman. Only a few weeks later he disappeared.

I think a part of me hates George because I feel I have to risk my life for him. Part of me—I have to admit it—even wants him to die so that I won't have to save him and risk my own life. The promise I made terrifies me.

June 1

In the aftermath of Fay's departure from the case, people have become concerned over the seeming disappearance of so much of the money that was raised.

My own sense is that people talk about money but what they really mean is Fay. Without her there is no center. Quiet hopelessness has taken possession of everyone. And everyone who sees or writes George tells him different stories about what is happening and who is responsible. George is left to rage impotently in his cell.

Without Fay it must seem to George as if reality itself has disappeared—the reality of intense struggle that Fay, his mighty mouthpiece, had brought to the case, with her uncompromising need to defeat her enemies—some enemy, any enemy—with the sense of momentum she brought with her, the sense of frenzied

activity, the sense that she was always locked in mortal combat
and that she wouldn't accept defeat, the endless number of ac-
tivities that she initiated, the breathless battlefield reports—all that
is gone. With her withdrawal, it must be as if death itself has
entered his cell prematurely because everything suddenly must be
so quiet and musty.

Just a few days after they broke apart, he wrote to a friend:
"Call Fay right now and simply say 'George said he loves you
no matter what.'"

June 15

George has written me for an accounting of the money from
the book. In his letter, he complains about people lying to him.
"It's like throwing water on a drowning man."

June 17

I saw Fay today. She was staying home from the office reading
Nero Wolfe stories in her wrapper. It is as if she were convalescing
from a serious illness. Her face is soft and shiny. She reminds me
of one of the old men who have nothing left to do or say and who
sit alone on park benches in the summertime, ruminating on the
past.

June 18

George asked me today if I believed in euthanasia.

"Someone should put Georgia out of her misery. I could send
one of my hit men after her." Of course George isn't really thinking about killing his mother. I'm not even sure he has any "hit
men." Sometimes I think that when he tells me things like this, he
is just trying to tell me about what is happening to his mind. It is
like someone saying: *Please help me! Everything is getting so
twisted inside my head.* I have a feeling that with just one word of
encouragement on my part, George would tell me everything.

June 19

In the Adjustment Center today, George is unusually nervous.
At one point he looks at me as if he has finally decided to share

his most cherished secret. He raises and lowers eyelids. "I'm going to tell you something. You're probably going to think I'm mad." He draws the floor plan of a house with a doorway opening on a false hallway that is like a long thin cell. On either wall there are openings like gun ports. "We lure the pigs in here, they burst in and we just close the door automatically behind them and we're here on the other side of the wall with machine guns and we just cut them down. With something like this, there will be no more Fred Hamptons, you dig?"

His fantasy is tangible in the air around us. It is as if I am with him in his cell dreaming about his plan over and over again, reveling in it, grooving on it like daydreams of sex, re-experiencing his triumph again and again. Almost bending the walls of his cell with the intensity of his desire. Later he draws me a plan for a special tanklike truck that would be paneled with special plastic armor with concealed gun ports cut into its sides. The front of the truck would be armored like a battering ram—"With half a dozen of us inside that truck, nobody could stop us. We could go right through the gates of the prison." Listening to him, I remember my childhood, when, in my impotence, I used to dream of killing all my enemies over and over again in all the different ways I could think of. I am overcome with a feeling of déjà vu.

June 20

I have arranged to see Angela about writing a book.

Marin County Jail. Poured-concrete cells. Electrically operated doors. Closed-circuit TV cameras. Banks of monitored screens. Air conditioning. Tanned, muscular guards. Hatchet-faced matrons out of the Hollywood thirties movies. I find myself shuddering in all the different kinds of cold.

Angela's face is pale. She seems heavier and older. She wears a heavy sweater over a pale-green prison dress. She is just recovering from the flu. She smiles and we embrace. Her arms don't want to let go. They just hang on, with a kind of stubbornness that comes from deprivation of human contact, from a need of body for body that goes far beyond matters of individual identity to the primal need of people for each other.

June 21
George has asked to see Fay again. Fay's face is torn with fear as she tells me. "I'm not going alone. I'll take another lawyer with me." And she names a man who was once associated with Angela's defense.

July 2
I was visited today by someone very close to the person who originally approached me about freeing George. She doesn't want to go ahead with it any more. She's too scared.

July 15
One of the black mail boys has started calling me John Brown. Every time he passes my office he gives me a look of fantastic complicity.

July 16
Georgia, Penny and James Carr have raided the headquarters of the Soledad Brothers' Defense Committee. A white girl named Lynn was said to have been slapped in the face. After breaking some furniture, they left with all the financial accounts.

August 1
In an interview in the *New York Times* today, George claims that the only way he expects to get out of prison is by escaping.
It is almost as if he is begging to be killed.

August 2
One of the women who visits George is living with a man. George wants her to leave him. From the stitching on his dungarees, George pulls out five one-hundred-dollar bills and tries to give them to her so she can rent an apartment for herself. She refuses. He tells her that when he gets out she will have to come to him or he will send a "hit man" after her. For a long time he just stares at her.

August 5
A woman who was visiting her son last week at San Quentin caught a glimpse of George in the visiting room. She warned her

son, "I saw that look in his eyes and I said, 'Get out of the way because he's coming through.'"

August 7
The anniversary of Jonathan's death.
I know the memory of Jonathan is eating away at George. He says he still hasn't shed a tear. But there is something far worse than tears going on inside him. He is too proud to admit it to anyone.

August 9
For the first time George has written me asking for money.

August 13
A person who said he was a friend of George's called today asking for money in very heavy conspiratorial tones. No name. He is going to call back.

August 14
One of the Soledad Committee investigators called me from California. All George's visits have been cut off. Not even the investigators can get in to see him.

Death

"What is happening to me here, what has happened, what will happen, can never surprise or upset me again. My nerves have been fractured, my sensibilities outraged, for the last time. It's all a matter of course to me now. My outlook is clear and the future holds no more terrors for me. Just existing, life without joy, without real meaning does not appeal to me at all. I am very tired of waking up each morning wondering if I will be worked for nothing again today, or wondering if I will be insulted, humiliated, injured, or even done to death today."

—Soledad Brother

August 21, 1971

George is dead.

6 KILLED IN RIOT
AT SAN QUENTIN
ANGELA DAVIS PAL IS AMONG
3 CONS, 3 GUARDS SLAIN

SAN QUENTIN, CALIF., Aug. 21 (Special)—
Soledad Brother George Jackson, a convict
from the age of 15 and a writer of prison
letters that won literary acclaim, was killed
today as he tried to escape from San
Quentin Prison. Two other convicts and
three guards died with their throats slashed
in the melee that followed Jackson's attempted breakout.

Associate Warden James Park called the
attempt the work of a "revolutionary con-
spiracy."

Jackson, 29, was shot from a gun tower
as he sprinted across a prison yard with a
smuggled .38-caliber pistol in his hand.
Though he managed to let about 20 convicts
out of their cells after breaking out of his
own maximum security cell, no one got
beyond the walls.

Two white convict trusties on duty in a
mess hall had their throats cut, as did the
three guards. Their bodies were sprawled in
pools of blood beyond the bars of locked
cells in Jackson's cell-block.

LAWYER HUNTED IN RIOT
THAT KILLED QUENTIN 6

SAN QUENTIN, CALIF., Aug. 22 (Combined
Dispatches)—Authorities were hunting tonight for a lawyer who visited George Jackson just before he was gunned down during
an escape attempt from San Quentin prison.

Jackson, one of the so-called Soledad
Brothers, had a gun when he returned to his
cellblock after meeting the attorney, San
Quentin Warden Louis E. Nelson said today. He was found to have had no gun

during a thorough "skin" search before the visit.

Jackson, 29, and five others were killed when he attempted to escape immediately after reentering his maximum security cellblock.

A high-ranking source in San Quentin identified Jackson's visitor as Stephen Bingham. He was said to be a white man in his late twenties.

Mysterious Visitor

Marin County District Attorney Bruce Bales told newsmen tonight, "I am looking for Stephen Bingham. I want to talk to him in connection with the escape attempt."

First indication that the mysterious visitor was a lawyer came in a slip of the tongue from Warden Nelson today when describing for newsmen the security precautions taken with visitors.

The warden said that Jackson, after being searched, was escorted to a visitors' center where he was placed in a room with one other person.

Man From Outside

"He was seated across the table from his attorney," Nelson continued, then broke off in some embarrassment.

Officials said earlier today that Jackson forced guards to let him out of his cell by brandishing a gun smuggled to him during a visit by a man from outside the prison walls.

But they would not say officially who the visitor was or how he managed to evade detection devices to get the gun to Jackson.

Also killed in the melee that followed were two white convicts and three guards, whose throats were slashed with razor blades taped to toothbrushes. One of the guards also had been shot in the head, but it was not known by whom.

Nelson said that preliminary indications were that Jackson's attempted escape was the result of prior planning.

San Quentin's 2,300 prisoners were confined to their cells as investigators tried to piece together the events of yesterday afternoon—the bloodiest incident in the prison's 119-year history.

August 22

The newspaper and radio reports keep coming in. The incident started at three o'clock on Saturday afternoon as George was returning from a visit. While he was being searched, a guard noticed something like a pencil sticking out of George's hair. "Let me have that," the officer is supposed to have said. George reached up and pulled a gun from his hair. He forced the officer to open the cell block and release all the other prisoners from their cells. Shortly after this there was some unexplained gunfire. A guard from another tier came down to investigate. George saw him, took aim and shot, but missed. The guard ran to give the alarm. George and another inmate then ran out of the Adjustment Center. George headed in the direction of a twenty-foot wall. The other man hid in the bushes just outside the door. A tower guard spotted George with a gun in his hand, took aim and killed him with one shot.

When the captain of the guards learned of the escape attempt, he assembled a squad of guards with a machine gun and prepared for an assault on the Adjustment Center. They threw open the main door and shot a volley of machine-gun fire down the main aisle. A voice from inside called out, "We've got hostages." The guards then let off another blast of machine-gun fire. "We're coming in anyway. You'd better let the hostages go." Seconds later two hostages ran out of the cell block screaming at the guards not to shoot. Then a guard announced to the inmates that they should remove all their clothes and file out of the Adjustment Center one by one with their hands over their heads. As they came out, they were handcuffed and made to lie on their stomachs on a patch of grass. When the guards entered the Center, they found three dead guards and three other guards whose throats had been slit but who were still alive piled in George's cell. In one of the other cells they found the dead bodies of two white inmate tier tenders.

George is really dead. There is no possibility of a mistake. I thought I was so well prepared for it, but I wasn't prepared at all.

August 23
I had to go to work today. The company has decided to rush out a new edition of the book and I had to write a note about George's death. I remembered some words George once wrote about Jonathan and they revived me momentarily from my lethargy:

"He was free for a while. I guess that's more than most of us can expect."

I know George died the way he would have wanted to die. That is the only thing that makes his death bearable. That move out of the Adjustment Center into the yard must have been a step into pure magic. I see him bursting out of that door into the sunlight with a smile of joy and expectancy on his face. The battle that he had craved for so many sleepless nights had begun. He was out of his cell. He had a gun in his hand. No chains to hamper movement. His body was his own. It had been over ten years since he had been able to run. And now he was out and running free. Legs rising, bending forward. He must have known he was going to die, but everything was utterly transfigured because he had finally passed over the line and seized control of his destiny. For a few moments he was pure radiance, no fear, no dread. The ancient Greeks of Homer's time, when they went into battle, sometimes felt that a god had joined them in battle, that they were caught up and transformed by his radiance. I think that's what George must have felt—a sudden blinding flash of ecstasy as he ran out of the door and into his true self.

In the aftermath of the killings, the prison has been sealed off completely. Not even lawyers are allowed to see their clients. Tomorrow, according to the prison, they will begin to allow selected lawyers' interviews with the men who were in the Adjustment Center on the day of the killings. No provisions for doctors or reporters, however.

There is a report in the evening paper that the men from the Adjustment Center were forced to lie naked on the grass for five hours. A prisoner named Allan Mancino got a cramp in his leg. When he twitched, a guard got frightened and shot him in the leg. Mancino is reportedly in the prison hospital.

I'm leaving for California tomorrow morning on the nine o'clock plane.

August 24
San Francisco.

The press conference being given by some of the lawyers representing the men who were in the Adjustment Center with George on the twenty-first. The lawyers all tell the same story. Clients beaten repeatedly with clubs. Some unable to walk from the effect of the beatings. Cigarette burns. Eyebrows and hair shaved. Terrorization by constant threats of death. Clients afraid to come into the visiting rooms because of the beatings they receive on the way back and forth from their cells.

It seems very clear now that the authorities must have known all along that George was trying to escape. They simply let him go ahead with his plans hoping that they would be able to kill him. After all George had announced in the *New York Times* just three weeks before that he intended to escape. What could be clearer? But the authorities underestimated George, and three of their guards were killed. So who really killed those guards? Not George. Who were the real murderers? Not George!

John Clutchette and Fleeta Drumgo were brought into court today for the start of their trial. Their attorneys, Floyd Silliman and Richard Silver, attempted to have the judge issue a restraining order prohibiting the prison from permitting any further beatings of their clients. But the judge refused, claiming that he didn't have any jurisdiction. At the urging of their attorneys, John and Fleeta removed their shirts. Gasps of amazement and horror from the audience greeted the sight of their brutalized bodies.

A few minutes later, Fleeta screamed out, "Why don't you

just kill me now and get it over with? You are going to kill me anyway."

John C. gave his attorney a petition which described some of the circumstances of George's death. John claims that two shots were fired. The first struck George in the calf of his left leg. While he was lying helpless on the ground, a guard came up behind him and deliberately murdered him with a second shot in the head.

John also claims that George ran out of the A.C. not to escape but to draw fire to himself and thus prevent a massacre of the other inmates.

August 25

With George dead, John Thorne is no longer allowed in the courtroom as a lawyer. Yesterday when John Clutchette and Fleeta Drumgo took off their shirts in court to reveal the marks of their beatings from the San Quentin guards, John, who was in the spectators' section, stood up and pounded on the glass partition that has been erected to divide the courtroom from the audience and demanded a special hearing. "If you [the judge] won't grant one, then there is no justice in the land." Then, before the guards could forcibly evict him, he stormed out of the building.

Five hundred people held an all-night vigil outside the gates of San Quentin demanding that doctors and reporters be allowed into the Adjustment Center to examine the inmates.

The San Francisco *Examiner* has an article today which claims that a letter to George from Jimmy Carr, who is still in the San Francisco County Jail awaiting trial on the charges growing out of the courtroom fight on the sixth of April, was found in a pair of trousers Jimmy's wife had taken to the cleaners (relatives customarily tend to such things for prisoners in the County Jail). The letter, which supposedly had notations in George's handwriting, described elaborate plans for an escape attempt from Quentin. Details on how to short out the electrical system. Instructions on where someone should be waiting with a four-wheel-drive car. Suggestions about how to smuggle explosives and other contraband into the prison in women's vaginas. The cleaner gave the letter to the police three weeks before August 21. The police made a Xerox copy and had the tailor replace the letter in Jimmy's trousers.

Don't the police realize what they are admitting when they release such information? There can be no question about the setup now. They've admitted it themselves. They murdered George in cold blood. What else is there to know?

So many people are concerned with finding out the exact circumstances of George's death. Did he have a gun? If so, how was it gotten into the prison? The warden's assertion that the gun was smuggled into the prison hidden in an Afro wig that George was wearing is ludicrous. The San Francisco *Chronicle* has gotten hold of the same kind of gun that George was supposed to have used and attempted to conceal it under an Afro wig. A photo in yesterday's paper shows a black model wearing an Afro wig with a gun barrel sticking out about three inches from underneath it. The prison claims that George was not handcuffed on the way back and forth to the visiting room because he was known as a cooperative prisoner. But whenever I visited him, I could always hear them removing the cuffs out in the hall. And George, cooperative? There couldn't have been a more uncooperative prisoner in the history of the prison.

August 26

When I finally get Georgia on the phone, she tells me that she has already reclaimed the body from the prison. She brought the undertaker to the prison and helped him to move George's body, holding her son's head and his shoulders tightly in her arms because almost all connection between them had been blown away. At the mortuary, she examined the shattered skull, the caved-in face, the mutilations on the lower part of his body. "They shouldn't ought to have done him that way. My son was a beautiful man and he had a beautiful body." It was the second bullet-ridden, mutilated body of a son she had taken in her arms in just a little more than a year. Georgia told me that she had thought of me when she claimed the body because she had wanted me to see what had been done to George.

Someone told me today about a questionnaire that George filled out when he first entered prison ten years ago:

QUESTION: What do you want to be?
ANSWER: A writer.
QUESTION: What do you like to do most?
ANSWER: Make love in the rain.

August 27

The coroner's report claims that George was killed with a single bullet through the head.

August 28

Not even half as many people are at George's funeral as were at his brother's. At Jonathan's funeral we all shouted for revenge, and our voices when we chanted were like sledge hammers in the air.

At George's funeral it seems as if we are each alone, quiet and drawn into ourselves. And though the clenched fists go up in the air, there is no chanting. There isn't even any anger. A sense of defeat, a sense of hopelessness.

Outside the church, the crowd is irritable and tense. Pushing toward the door, shouting at the ushers who are passing out the program of the service. Everyone wants something to hold the event in their minds, to make it real and to make themselves real.

The sound of their surging and struggling carries into the church. Suddenly a stooped black woman, holding a big bag in one hand, smiling a little strangely, appears at the window on the second floor and faces the crowd in the street. She begins to speak just as if we were all together in her own living room.

"I'm glad you are all here and I want to thank you. But we can't hear inside. I wish there was more room so you could all join us, but they wouldn't give us any larger place for a revolutionary funeral. They don't like revolutionaries."

When Georgia leaves the window, the people in the crowd turn and make wondering glances at each other as if to say, "Who is that woman?" Could she really be George's mother? And we are all silent after that.

After the service I go to view George's body at the funeral home on one of the main streets in Oakland, there among the drive-ins and the parking lots and bars with their blinking neon signs.

Long lines of people, mostly blacks, young and old, circle the funeral home, slowly filing in both sides of the entrance. Almost before I know it I reach the door. For an instant I consider going back to the end of the line so I will have more time to prepare myself. But I am drawn along in spite of my hesitation through the hall and into the main room, where I see the coffin. The room is silent except for the sound of shuffling feet and the rustle of clothing. As I come closer, I see the body of a strange man dressed in a pale-blue turtleneck and a Chinese tunic with a black beret on his head, a man with a waxen face and gaunt hands folded in his lap.

I circle around the funeral home to the end of the line and again move through the street into the building through the hall and past the body. Just a stranger in a satin-lined coffin.

I arrive at the airport just in time to catch the plane to St. Louis. Georgia is surprised to see me. "I thought you missed the plane." I had told her I was coming with her because I thought after my own experience in Mount Vernon that there might be some trouble during the burial. At first I sit in the back of the plane. Then Lester gestures for me to come up and join them. I sit down with him and the undertaker. We are silent for a few minutes. Then Lester remarks, "Now I think I'm man enough to step into my son's shoes." We are silent. He adds, "Now I can start putting back on the fifteen pounds that I've lost."

When the stewardess comes, I buy the undertaker a drink. "It's always nice to travel with someone who has a sense of the proprieties."

As he sips his drink, he reminisces about some of his other burials. We fall into a stuporous half-sleep. When we land a few hours later in St. Louis, we are met by a group of Panthers from Chicago. The body is transferred to a hearse. The family is going with the body to hold a private ceremony for some relatives in East St. Louis. I stay behind and eat breakfast. Then I rent a car and drive over the bridge through East St. Louis and stop to wait for the motorcade about a third of the way to Mount Vernon along the same route I had taken before to visit Jonathan's grave.

When we enter the cemetery, a small group of people is already waiting by the open grave. The coffin is taken from the hearse by the Panthers and rested on two stays. The sun is hot, the grass is heavy and lush underfoot. I'm a little dizzy.

Photographers start to take pictures. Georgia tells them to stop. "You only told lies about him when he was alive. I don't want you taking advantage of him now that he is dead."

There is a small tent by the grave to protect the mourners from the sun. I stand just a little off to one side of it.

Photographers continue to take pictures. A scuffle breaks out and a camera is broken.

A clergyman begins to give an oration. Georgia interrupts, "I just asked you to say a few words, not to give a sermon. Why doesn't anyone ever do what you ask them to do?"

She starts to talk about George and prison and she concludes by saying, "My son was one of the greatest human beings who ever lived."

Then the Panthers lower the casket into the ground.

I go over to Georgia and put my arms around her. She turns her face to me. Dark liquid eyes. "Why did you let them kill my son, Greg?" Silence. Tears well up in my eyes. "I blame you, Greg. I blame you more than any of the others." My arms fall away from her. She moves back closer to the grave.

The workmen place two thick concrete slabs over the coffin. A truck comes up with dirt. The Panthers take the shovels and fill in the grave.

The filling-in seems interminable. The truck pulls in closer to the grave. Finally the back of the truck is raised and some of the Panthers climb in and shovel the dirt directly into the grave.

Then people start to leave. Georgia comes over to me and asks me what I am going to do. I say I don't know. "You should come back to my sister's house with us. I don't want you wandering around here where you could get hurt." So I follow her to her sister's house, where we sit and talk about the people who killed her sons.

I know what she means when she tells me that I am responsible. I am still alive. A blubbering child standing beside her son's grave. I was her son's friend, but I wasn't there when he needed me. I had started it all with the book, the process that had led to her son's death. I had helped to make him famous and that had only set him up for the kill. In her mind I was all the people who had goaded him on to that final outrageous act and then left him there to face the consequences alone. In her mind I was just the same as the white man who supposedly had given him the gun. I was all the people who helped to give him a false sense of himself and of the world, who told him he was a great leader. But, of course, he was only a prisoner, locked away in an impregnable prison within a prison. What right did we have to turn his head? What right did we have to fill his head full of all those ideas? We were there when the cameras were turning, but we weren't there for the real life that went before and after. We weren't there for the death.

August 29

After the burial, I fly back to New York. No sooner am I in the door than my daughter tells me that a letter has come for me from George.

She and her friend have already read it before I arrive. The letter begins with the words of Crazy Horse at the Battle of Little Big Horn: "The bow is taut. It's a beautiful day to die." George goes on to write about how unbearable it is for him to go on. How tortured he is by other people's expectations. How much he wants to get it over with. Not suicide, but the final action of his life. He knows that he will be criticized. But he has no choice. It has been too many years. He can't go on living up to other people's expectations of him.

He doesn't want to explain himself or seem dictatorial. He doesn't want to seem self-righteous, but he is living on a different level. And though he fights to live as Che prescribed, living isn't too very important any more. He is seized with the ungovernable impulse to humiliate those punks, to put up a total resistance. It has been too long. They have been trampling on him too long. He has to seize the threads of his life, his considered judgments, into his own hands. And explain afterward.

And then there are those words for me: "I have certainly learned to love you, man. I hope you haven't missed it. I got to know that you know."

August 31

An affidavit has been released by a member of the Marin County Grand Jury, which has responsibility for San Quentin. The juror named Rick Beban heard about the escape attempt on the radio and immediately drove out to the prison and spoke to Warden Park. This is Beban's sworn account of their conversation.

PARK: What the hell are you doing here?
BEBAN: I came to see what is going on and whether you have need of our services.
PARK: Why don't you go investigate the Communist Party?
BEBAN: What?
PARK: It is them and people like you who are causing what has happened today.
BEBAN: What do you mean?
PARK: We lost three guards—three good men. The only good thing that happened all day was that we got George Jackson. Killed him. Shot him through the head.

September 10
A report in today's paper:
On Sunday, August 22, the prisoners at Attica were marched to the mess hall for breakfast as usual, just after seven o'clock. But they did not eat. "It was the weirdest thing. They all walked in as usual, divided into two lines and walked through the serving area. But nobody picked up a tray or a spoon, and nobody took any food. They just walked through the line and went to their seats and they sat down. They looked straight ahead and nobody made a sound. You could have heard your wristwatch ticking. It was eerie. Then we noticed that almost all had some black on them— some had cloth armbands, some had black shoelaces around their arms, others had pieces of black cloth pinned on them. It scared us, because a thing like that takes a lot of organization, a lot of solidarity, and we had no idea they were so well organized."

September 15

Even though I know George is dead, I still half-expect to see him sitting in my chair when I go into my room or to find him waiting for me in my office. The sense of his presence has pervaded my life for so long now.

September 30

The *New York Times* has printed a copy of the letter Lester sent to the Parole Board over ten years ago:

March, 1961

DEAR SIR,

We love our son dearly, and we have spent more than our share of time with him, and money on him.

I hope you have had more luck in reaching him than we have. . . . He may not be released in his present state of mind. If you are able to get near him, I will be surprised. He can be reached if he sees you as a way out.

So don't let him fool you with the many faces he is capable of showing. He lived under strict house rules while under our guidance and always slipped past his mother when he wanted to break those rules.

LESTER JACKSON

October 1

I heard a story today about George from a man who had done time with him in a juvenile reformatory when he was sixteen. George escaped from the reformatory and was recaptured. The guards chained him naked to a bed and beat him steadily for two days and nights. The man who told the story explained, "That was when they started him on his way."

October 10

I was telling someone about how I didn't really know what to do with my life now that George was dead. She asked me what I thought George would have wanted. I hedged a bit, but I knew the answer instantly. "My life, what else?"

November 5

The second autopsy bears out what John Clutchette originally claimed. Two wounds were found in George's body. One in the calf of his left leg. The other entered the small of his back and traveled upward and exited through the top of his head. The path of the second bullet indicates that George was bent forward on his hands and knees when the fatal shot was fired.

November 15
Georgia is in New York demanding a UN investigation of her son's death.

November 19
Fay tells me that she represents a great many more white prisoners these days. Once they were almost all black. She has relinquished, or at least diminished, her degree of contact with individual prisoners. The whole direction of her lawyers' group has passed from individual representation to class action, from cases where the individual is most important to cases which offer the possibility for establishing far-reaching legal precedents.

Just a few days before, John Thorne told me that he has left the woman he lived with throughout the case to go off and live by himself for the first time, "to get a chance to find out who I really am."

John Thorne is in New York. I go over to his hotel on the morning of his departure. As he packs, we talk about the Soledad case. I tell him about the tape I have of George confessing the murder and of my intention to offer it to the defense attorneys for John C. and Fleeta in their murder trial which is going on now without George. He explains to me that when he took on the case, he told George that he never wanted to hear about what happened on the day the guard was killed. He didn't want to know whether George was innocent or guilty. He didn't want to be told anything that would influence his investigation or prejudice his presentation of the case.

November 28
Today I talked to Fleeta and John's attorneys about my tape of George's confession and about what he revealed about their innocence. They seem to feel that my testimony is unnecessary. With all that they have found out about the way the prosecution

has assembled its evidence—promises of parole to inmate witnesses for perjured testimony, threats of physical harm and even death for refusal to cooperate—the defense is certain they can tear the prosecution case to shreds.

December 1
There is a rumor that Bingham is dead and that his body has been washed up on the California coast.

December 5
A report is circulating that after he was killed George's body was not moved for five hours. Even though the top of his head was blown off, handcuffs were put on his lifeless wrists.

December 10
When George was returned to the Adjustment Center after his visit on August 21 and he pulled the gun on the guards, he is supposed to have announced, "The Dragon has come!"

He referred to himself in some of his letters as the Dragon, so these words are not entirely impossible. The term comes from a Kung Fu position. Dragon = the fabulous monster—the being that strikes terror in the hearts of men.

January 10, 1972
Lester has an article in this month's *Ebony*. Two sentences stand out: "Twice a month we would go to San Quentin or Soledad. George would hug and kiss all the women in tears and greet Jon and me with cold hands that made us all wonder if he were really alive."

In the waiting room watching the other prisoners' wives and children: "At times like this, I felt close to my son, even closer than when, before he went into prison, we'd driven two-thirds of the country in search of a new home."

January 15
A day and a night with Jimmy Carr, George's closest friend.
It has been only five months since George's death, and when I even mention George's name, Jimmy winces as if I were touching him with a hot iron.

But I keep talking about George and my memories of him, and finally Jimmy joins me.

"That Jack, he was a real motherfucker. That's all you could call him. Once, before he built himself up, this really big guy said he was going to make a punk out of him. So they went up to the showers to fight. And the guy was four inches taller and much bigger, but finally George whupped him. But it wasn't enough for George that he beat him. He wanted to kill him. Since he didn't have any weapon, he tried to bite through this cat's jugular vein. We had to pull them apart or George would have killed him for sure.

"When we were in Quentin together, George was a really smooth operator. He had that place sewed up tight. He used to be making thirty-five, forty dollars a day running all the pinochle tables. When he was working in the kitchen, we used to have this thing where we would sell sandwiches on the tier at night. We used to make a lot of money."

As he talks, I feel Jimmy carefully controlling his emotions and the scope of his memories. And yet, in spite of his restraint, emotions pass across his face like racing clouds.

"Once when this Mexican owed George some money, George went out with a sword to collect, and just as he was sticking it home, he slipped and fell and the sword broke. As the Mexican ran, George took the blade and threw it after him like it was a spear. And it caught the Mexican right square in the back."

He looks up at me as if he thinks I might be getting the wrong idea about George. He continues in a different vein. "George was always into helping weak guys. He would hear about some guy who was being fucked over and he would want to go over and help him. I'd always tell him that it was no use. Because if the guy was weak, he would get it anyway sooner or later. But George wouldn't listen, so I'd have to go along with him to make sure everything was okay."

Later on, Jimmy's wife comes down with their new baby girl and we go out into the garden. Jimmy takes off his shirt and we all stand there blinking for a moment in the blinding sun. He starts to work out with some weights, perspiration glistening on his shaven head. After a while, he begins to show his wife how to lift the weights. He watches, holding their squirming daughter in his huge arms. His wife struggles with the heavy metal, her body seeming almost as if it is about to crumple like paper underneath their weight.

It is only Jimmy's second day out of jail, and they are both joyful. He has been in almost continuously for seven months, charged with the assault on the police officer which took place during the hearing when George was being beaten. At the time of his arrest, Jimmy had been out on parole for a life sentence and there was a strong possibility that he would be sent back to prison for life. I think it is the sense of a certain responsibility for George's death that I see in both Jimmy's and his wife's eyes sometimes when they look at each other.

Much later when everybody is getting ready for bed, I tell Jimmy about my offer to the Soledad lawyers to testify about George's sole responsibility for the murder. Jimmy is stripped to the waist and he has a .45 jammed into his belt. As I talk, he goes around the house checking out all the windows. When I first tell him, he catches his breath and looks up with startled eyes. Then he looks away and takes another deep breath. His huge chest expands like a bellows. He looks back at me again. "Oh, that's cold. Georgia will really hate that." He can't bring himself to look at me. He turns his head away. His eyes dart around the room almost as if he had lost something very dear to him. His body and all his muscles begin to twitch almost convulsively.

I ask him what George would have thought about what I was going to do.

"That motherfucker would have just laughed himself to death."

Shuddering, he circles the room again, rechecking all the windows, his hand on the butt of his revolver, sliding the gun back and forth in his pants.

February 17

I have come out to see Angela about doing a book. It is only her second day out of jail on bail. The house where she is staying is crowded with people. Her mother, her sister and her husband, her brother and his wife and their small son, bodyguards, lawyers, various members of the Communist Party.

At one point I see Angela standing in the middle of the room and I can see that she is momentarily lost. She is suddenly distrustful of her sense of reality. After sixteen months in a small cell, she seems to be uncertain about where she really is. She is intimidated by the space all around her. I can almost see her looking for the walls of her cell that are no longer there.

Because she has been away so long, she has become unfamiliar with everything. She has to think about how to do even the simplest things, like how to drink brandy.

There is broccoli for supper and it bewilders her. She lifts a piece on her fork and regards it with amazement. "Do you eat all of this or just the branches?" But she can't eat at all because the large table and the people and the food are so overwhelming.

Later, as I am leaving, she is standing near the door with her two-year-old nephew, and he is clawing away at the air between them. She explains that the only time he has ever seen her before was when she was in jail and there had been a plate of glass between them. He is trying to find the glass. The memory of it visibly disturbs her. Trying to wipe it away, she takes the little boy's arm and shows him how to make a fist. "Can you say, 'Free Angela'?" He is silent and open-mouthed. She tries again without any more success, and then turns away with a look of bewilderment on her face to all the empty space and all the people.

February 23

One of the women who visited George in the last months told me today about how they made love. She wore a short skirt. The first time, because she is shorter than George, she stood on her tiptoes. The times after that she brought an attaché case to stand on. George stood with his back to the door, where the guards were supposed to be watching. A cigarette in his hand. Barely moving with his cock inside her. When it was over, drenched with perspiration and trembling so convulsively that he could hardly stand up.

February 28

In the winter after George's death, Inez came East to make some speeches for Angela and for her son. The first two days she stayed with me in Brooklyn. The night before she came, it snowed and the temperature dropped to about ten degrees above zero. I met Inez at the airport early in the morning and took her back to my house, where there was no heat. We both shivered from the cold. Inez had never seen snow before, nor had she ever been so cold. We went into New York that night and had dinner and went to see a play. The next day we went into Prospect Park with my daughter and my dog, chasing after each other and throwing snowballs.

Late that night when we were talking, Inez got that look that I have come to recognize as the inevitable prelude to some startling revelation. The look I had seen on Lester's face that day when he had been about to explain to me why he was like his son, the look that I had seen on George's face so many times. It was a look that said, "Maybe I shouldn't tell you this, but I have to and I just hope you can understand."

Looking out of the corner of her eye, she explained to me that one of the reasons she had decided to stay with me was that she wanted to find out if I was *for real*. She wanted to find out if I was a CIA agent or something like that. I was a mystery to her. All her experiences had told her that it was impossible for whites to be sincerely concerned about black people. And yet she could tell that I really cared about her. It didn't make any sense to her. Whites cared about blacks only so they could take advantage of them in some way. What was I going to get out of her? True, she knew I wanted to write a book which in part concerned herself and her son. But that still didn't explain my deep emotional response to her. Because she couldn't comprehend it, and she had to put it into terms that she could understand. She'd been tricked, slicked by too many people, and she wasn't going to take the chance of letting another white person put one over on her. Yet, at the same time, she really wanted to be cared about by someone who didn't have any ulterior motives.

April 3
John Clutchette and Fleeta Drumgo won their case today. Their lawyers tore the prosecution case to bits just the way they said they would. The jury took only three hours to return a verdict

of innocent. John should be out on parole soon because he was
promised a parole before they accused him of killing the guard.
Fleeta still has to face an additional murder charge growing out of
the events of August 21. But it shouldn't be too long for him either.
It is reported that two members of the grand jury which indicted
him actually resigned altogether because they were so indignant
at the way the prosecution rammed the new indictment through.

April 6
Fleeta's mother has just called from California. Jimmy Carr
was assassinated as he was leaving his house and walking toward
his car. Two men were waiting for him in the bushes with a
shotgun and a rifle. Even though he was shot six times, Jimmy
continued to walk, almost reaching his car before he fell over
dead. A .45 pistol was found butt up in the sand a few yards away
from his body.

Inez is almost hysterical. Every new murder only increases her
sense of her own son's jeopardy. She can't help thinking that
somehow Fleeta will be next.

May 1
About a week ago, I was asleep and I felt something crawling
on my cheek. I reached up to brush it away. In the morning I saw
that I had scratched myself on my cheek. I thought nothing of it,
but the next day someone asked me if I had carved a "J" in my
cheek. That night my daughter asked me the same question. I felt
a crafty look pass over my face. I looked in the mirror. There it
was. A capital "J" with a period after it. I hadn't noticed it in
the morning because it had been reversed by the mirror. The faint
impression of that "J" is still on my cheek.

A woman who used to visit George was the mother of three
children. Her oldest son had gotten roughed up and his bike had
been stolen by three young blacks. He wrote to George for advice.
George wrote back to the effect that blacks figure that since they
have been mugged and seen their parents mugged by white men,
it's all right for them to mug because turnabout is fair play. He
suggested that if it happened again, the boy should either offer

them a ride or start a conversation about China, new missiles, or something elevating. In another letter, he advised him to fight, adding that if he fought sincerely, regardless of whether he won or lost, there would be a better atmosphere for talk because a flying side thrust is often more of a peacemaker than words. I have a feeling that George's grandfather must have spoken to him exactly that way—with a gentle arm around his shoulder, tenderly explaining things that he thought George would have to know, trying not to hurt him, trying not to let him be hurt.

May 6

A former inmate of Soledad told me a story about George in the days just before the murder of the guard. All the other blacks in the prison had gone on a hunger strike to protest the murder of the three black prisoners except for George and an old man. When some of the blacks asked George why he wasn't honoring the strike, he replied, "A warrior doesn't starve himself before going into battle."

May 15

On the way to Iran to serve as an observer at a political trial, John Thorne stops off in New York.

We talk about how dangerous the trip could be. "It doesn't matter. We've all got to die sometime." And for the first time I feel really close to John. I realize that he is suffering from the kind of guilt that survivors of a disaster often have. For a long time afterward, they long for death themselves. I know how John feels because I sense it in myself also.

May 30

Lester called last night to tell me that he is going to refuse to testify at Angela's trial. He expects that the court will cite him for contempt and he will be sent to jail. "They will probably send me to jail for two weeks, but I can do that. After all, my son spent ten years in jail." I think he is really looking forward to spending time in jail because it will diminish the distance that was always between them while George was still alive. Sitting in jail will be like sitting in his dead son's room or like putting on a piece of his clothing.

May 31
Lester did refuse to testify. "I have lost two sons. I just don't want to take part in the proceedings. My mental health won't allow it." When the judge questioned him further, he explained, "Because of the death of my sons. I hope you will understand my position as a family man."

Riding home on my bicycle.
I leave the office at 7:30 for a forty-five-minute trip home to my apartment. Riding fast. Daydreaming.

I am not aware of being myself again until twelve that night when I suddenly realize that I am at home sitting up in my bed.

My daughter tells me what happened: I arrived home at about 9:15. Bloody forehead. Lump the size of an orange. I tell her I have had an accident and that she should get a doctor. "Mary, I am scared out of my wits."

Later when I regain consciousness of myself, I ask her what I was like, and she looks away from me. "Oh, Daddy, it was awful, you were acting just like a twelve-year-old black boy, talking black talk and slapping five. And I was so ashamed I didn't even want anyone to know that you were with me or that I knew you at all."

June 5
A former inmate who knew George in Soledad during the year after he was transferred from San Quentin has told me a story about him. For a long time, I've wondered whether to write about it. I think the person who told it intended to destroy George for me, or at least bring him into question. Because everything he told me about George that day had a negative cast to it. It was as if he was saying to me, "Okay, what do you think of your hero now?" George must have hurt him in some way. Or perhaps the man felt shamed by George's purity. Something about George must have made him feel shabby and uncertain about himself.

On the night of the murder this man had been in another wing of the prison. An inmate had come running in just as the prisoners were being ordered into their cells and blurted out a story about the killing. The inmate was known as Sweetpea. George's friend broke off telling me about the murder to tell me about Sweetpea.

Sweetpea, as his name might suggest, was a homosexual. Sometimes George would visit him in his cell. At one time, George had given him his typewriter. He also used to give Sweetpea food and money. The man who was telling me the story had once stood guard outside Sweetpea's cell to make sure that George and Sweetpea weren't discovered together making love. This man was disturbed because George paid Sweetpea and because George seemed to be concerned about him as a human being. I got the feeling that this man would have had more respect for George if he had been raping young boys. He believed that since George was so strong he should simply have just taken what he wanted. It was as if he felt George should have been punished or ostracized for caring about another man without brutalizing him.

In some ways, I think this is one of the most beautiful things I have ever heard about George. It is wonderful to think that he would risk jeopardizing his reputation, his image of himself, to develop what would seem to have been, at least from the description I heard of it, a tender, perhaps even loving sexual relationship with a man. The fact that George gave Sweetpea his typewriter says so much. In a way, I think that is as revolutionary as anything George ever did. He had the will power to abstain, to cut himself off. He could have made himself hard and ruthless. I think that reaching out for another man, and knowing George, he had to reach out tenderly, means that he was still protecting his innocence—his ability to love and care for and give to another human being. He wasn't allowing the prison to dehumanize him, to cut him off from loving contact with another human being, man or woman. I'm not sure that George would have thought about it that way. I think he still had some concept of machismo and so he must have been ashamed of what he did. But he wasn't so ashamed that he had to hurt or brutalize like so many of the others.

July 1
Lately I have been reading Stendhal's *The Red and the Black*, and delighting in Julien Sorel's innocent clumsy scheming and hypocrisy. As I read, I have a sense of learning a lot about George

and about myself. He must have seen a lot of himself in Julien, who put on one different self after another trying to find one that would fit or, rather, one that would seem worthy of his will to power and pre-eminence. Julien was extraordinary, and he knew it. His task was to find a self out in the world of men which would embody his exceptional self. Julien was as all men are—searching for selves that truly fit them. Julien wouldn't give up searching for the best possible self, some being that would express his superiority. Stendhal is saying that if pretense and trying to be someone else are hypocrisy, then all men are hypocrites. Stendhal also seems to be saying that the only truth is in attempting to surpass yourself and your age. Other forms of truth—religion, politics—are just things to nourish you on your way.

Twice George said things which made me realize that he was another Julien Sorel. Once he said, "Marxism was my hustle." Again, when he was telling me about Marxism, he explained that he started identifying himself as a Communist when he realized how frightened all the fat cats were by what was happening in Cuba. When he became aware of their fear of Communists, he understood that he had to become one. So, like Julien, George wasn't himself by heavenly predestination. He chose to become himself. He tried on quite a few different selves on the way. His mother had always told him he was the best. But the roles he chose, the process he put himself through, were distinctly his own. Not necessarily mine or anyone else's.

As I think about George and his hustle, I wonder what would have happened if I had chosen to be as honest with him as I have tried to be in this journal, if I had known as much before I knew him as I know now after writing it. If I had thought more about Julien Sorel, I would have realized that George would have understood, no matter where I had gone or how completely I had revealed myself. He wouldn't have changed who he was, but he would have understood and responded and found a way to encourage me. We would have been real friends, instead of a hero and a follower.

George once said three words to me which, in a way, mean more, convey more meaning, than anything else he ever said. It wasn't the words themselves, but the tone of his voice when he said them. Guttural, rasping, painful, cynical, as if to say, "We are just men and we have been through it all, we can never fool each other no matter what we do." It was something like the tone of voice that you hear on the streets of the ghetto when one street brother is talking to another. Like "Look, man, we really know each other, ain't nothing you can hide from me." I guess George forgot himself for just a minute with me. Because all of this and more was in his voice. "Now listen, cat" was all he said. Just those three words. But for me—remembering the way he said them—those three words are everything. They were said inside Soledad Prison, George in chains and shackles—a black man worried about the impression he was making in the clothes the prison had forced him to wear. Graduate of San Quentin High School (Bayside) locked up on "O" wing for twenty-three and a half hours a day. And I'm sitting beside him, a white man wearing a baggy summer suit with a floral necktie from Nepal, editor from New York, Harvard man, concerned with my own self-importance. For an instant, those three words obliterated all distinction, every single possible distinction. In the sense not just that we were brothers, but that we were each capable of everything, of anything that men can do, of all their different selves—murderer, priest, rapist, judge, homosexual, prison guard—that underneath everything we existed as all men do, completely beyond good and evil, doing only what we had to do to survive. And that under different circumstances we could have been anything, even each other.